John Coleman

Players and Playwrights I have Known

A review of the English stage from 1840 to 1880. Second Edition, Vol. 2

John Coleman

Players and Playwrights I have Known
A review of the English stage from 1840 to 1880. Second Edition, Vol. 2

ISBN/EAN: 9783337219338

Printed in Europe, USA, Canada, Australia, Japan

Cover: Foto ©ninafisch / pixelio.de

More available books at **www.hansebooks.com**

PLAYERS AND PLAYWRIGHTS
I HAVE KNOWN

A REVIEW OF THE ENGLISH STAGE FROM
1840 TO 1880

PLAYERS AND PLAYWRIGHTS

I HAVE KNOWN

A REVIEW OF THE ENGLISH STAGE FROM 1840 TO 1880

BY JOHN COLEMAN

ACTOR AND MANAGER

WITH FIFTY ILLUSTRATIONS FROM AUTHENTIC PORTRAITS

IN TWO VOLUMES

VOL. II.

SECOND EDITION

GEBBIE & CO., PHILADELPHIA

1890

PLAYERS AND PLAYWRIGHTS
I HAVE KNOWN.

BOOK I.

THE VICTORS.

CONTINUED.

CONTENTS OF VOL. II.

BOOK I.

THE VICTORS.

Continued.

INTERMEZZO.

BOOK II.

THE VANQUISHED.

LIST OF ILLUSTRATIONS.

VOLUME II.

CHARLES READE.

CHAPTER X.

CHARLES READE.

Many years ago (I forget the precise date), when
in my "teens" I was principal tragedian in Bath
and Bristol, Mr. E. T. Smith offered me an engagement to make my *début* in London, in a piece written
by Charles Reade, called "Gold." At that time I
was successful beyond my deserts ; nothing less
than Hamlet would have suited my modest aspirations ; and the offer was declined, I fear, with more
curtness than courtesy. "Gold" was subsequently
acted at Drury Lane for five or six weeks, and, it
was alleged, enabled Mr. Smith to clear upwards of
eighteen hundred pounds. The author's honorarium
amounted to twenty pounds a week and the use of a
private box. Even that sum the manager thought
too much, and after the thirtieth night he proposed
to reduce it to twelve pounds a week. Mr. Reade
declined to assent to this proposal, and he withdrew
the piece altogether. From that day to this,
"Gold" has never been acted in town, and it was
never acted in the country except at two theatres,

22—2

in both of which it was a dead failure ; yet this unfortunate play, which had disappeared altogether from the living drama, and which, in my boyish arrogance, I had disdained to act in, was not only destined to become the medium of my acquaintance with my dearest friend, but also to become a landmark in the history of dramatic literature.

Charles Reade was born in the year before Waterloo (1814), at Ipsden House, Wallingford, near Reading.

His family was of Saxon origin, and he was wont to say jocosely that he could trace its line down to the days of Hengist and Horsa.

Although the youngest, he was the biggest of four brothers. William, the eldest, was squire of Ipsden. Edward Anderson, C.B. (who died two or three years ago), was Acting Lieutenant-Governor of the North-West Provinces of India during the Mutiny. He organized the defence of Agra, rendering efficient service to Havelock by keeping him furnished with supplies.

Compton, who became a barrister, is the father of the Reverend Compton Reade.

There were two sisters, to whom Charles was devotedly attached.

Strange to say, I never once heard him mention his father. His mother, however, he loved, adored, and venerated her memory. He commenced his studies in a private school at Kettering—a quaint little town in Northamptonshire—where Edwin James was his earliest chum.

From Kettering, **Charles went to** Oxford, where he soon obtained a demyship and graduated B.A. upon reaching his twenty-first year in 1835.

He **never took** very high honours, **but he** became a **Doctor of Laws,** and ultimately obtained a fellowship, the emoluments of which he **prized so** highly as to retain them to the **day of his death.**

Before he was called **to the bar, in 1843, he** had **serious** thoughts **of going into** the Church—not **so much,** I think, because he had **a call in** that direction, but simply from the chances of preferment.

Five years later **I** really believe **that for** a time the Doctor **of Laws had some** idea of becoming a Doctor of Music. Anyhow, I have found among his **posthumous papers one** dated 1848, **and** thus endorsed :

"*How Charles Reade wrote before he was a writer.*"

This is the significant title of **an** appeal made to the Lords of the Treasury against the confiscation **of** a number of fiddles which **he** had **gathered** together during his travels **in** Italy and France. On their arrival here they were condemned **in** consequence of an alleged insufficient declaration of value.

This crude and florid composition, written before "he knew how **to write," evidently** softened the hearts **of** "My Lords," who, I believe, returned him **his** beloved Stradivariuses and Cremonas. At any rate, Sir Edmund Henderson informed me that years afterwards, when he met Reade at Oxford, his rooms at Magdalen were cumbered with violins of every description.

He strummed passably enough on the piano, accompanying himself to some old songs, which upon rare occasions he would croon out with tenderness and pathos ; but whether he acquired any manipulatory skill in playing on the fiddle I don't know. I believe, however, that his neighbours in the "quad" at this period complained bitterly that he, or certain aspiring violinists who visited his rooms, made night perpetually hideous by "rubbing the hair of the horse on the bowels of the cat."

At the time of his death, the remains of his former collection consisted of two Stradivariuses, one Guarnerius—an admirable specimen of Nicholas Lupot—and several good copies of old masters ; a Peter Guarnerius tenor, and a bass by Joseph Filius Andrea.

These were, I believe, disposed of by Puttock and Simpson, at anything but prices commensurate with their real value.

This would have been a dreadful blow to Reade, for in financial matters he was singularly clear-headed, and had quite a commercial mind.

In this respect his judgment never failed him—except when he entered the precincts of a theatre—then, indeed, he lost his head—the stage was his *ignis fatuus.*

Although he coquetted with the Church, the law, and music—as already stated—his real bent inclined towards the drama, and the drama alone.

I have often heard him dwell with boyish delight upon his first play at Drury Lane.

The very night of his arrival in town his brother Compton told him "The School for Scandal" was to be acted by the great comedians of the period.

This was the one play his mother, who rarely **or** ever went to the theatre, had seen in her youth, when Miss Farren (Lady Derby) enacted Lady Teazle.

The old lady was never weary of dilating on the grace, the beauty, and the many accomplishments of that incomparable actress, whom she likened to a damask-rose steeped **in dew at** daybreak upon a **May morning.**

Charles's anxiety to see the play was so great that he could scarcely swallow his dinner for impatience. At length the two lads rushed off to the theatre and were speedily installed in the pit.

For once the reality excelled the anticipation, and it is to be feared that performance in some measure influenced Charles Reade's future career.

At any rate, from that moment he became a confirmed playgoer—scarcely a night elapsed but he found his way to some theatre **or** other.

For fifteen or sixteen years after attaining his fellowship and being called to the bar, he oscillated betwixt Oxford, London, Edinburgh, and Paris, and once, in conjunction with his friend, young Morris, son of the Haymarket manager, he made a pedestrian tour half over Europe. During this period he wrote **for the** magazines much, studied more, and acquired his intimate acquaintance with the French theatre, although he frankly admitted that, much as he desired to do so, he never could emancipate him-

self entirely from the "fetters" of that which he
usually designated "our cumbrous, sprawling Anglo-
Saxon drama."

He had fondly hoped that the production of
"Gold" at Drury Lane would open all the theatres
to him ; but to the end of his life he alleged that he
was perpetually baffled by the caprice and stupidity
of the public and the perversity and obtuseness of
the managers. A few months before his death he
told me that he had made an appointment only a
short time previous to read a play of his in a certain
fashionable theatre. He was kept waiting for more
than an hour, and the manager did not deign to put
in an appearance, nor did he afterward condescend
to explain or apologize for this impertinence. Still
more recently, he (Reade) wrote to the management
of another fashionable theatre, offering to send a
printed copy of a new comedy for approval, and he
never even received an answer to his proposal.

At the commencement of his career the Haymarket was under the management of the late
Benjamin Webster, who had got together one of
the most powerful companies ever assembled within
the walls of that or any other theatre.

In the year 1837 the Haymarket company con-
sisted of Mr. Macready, Mr. Phelps, Tyrone Power,
William Farren, Elton, Charles Mathews, T. P.
Cooke, Dowton Buckstone, Strickland, J. Faucit
Saville, John Webster, T. J. Matthews, Fred Vining,
Daly, Hunt, Charles Selby, actor and author, Worrell,
Ross, Bishop, Collins, Haines, author of "My Poll

and My Partner Joe," etc., Bishop, Gough, Gallott, and the manager, a host in himself; Mrs. Nesbett, Miss Huddart (afterwards Mrs. Warner), Miss **Vandenhoff**, Madame Vestris, Miss Vincent (afterwards the heroine of domestic drama), Mrs. Glover, Mrs. Waylett, the celebrated vocalist, Mrs. Fitzwilliam, famous for being the original Madge Wildfire, but remembered in these later days chiefly as Nelly O'Neil and Starlight **Bess**; Mesdames Humby, W. Clifford, Tayleure; Mdlles. E. **Phillips**, E. Hormer, Wrighton, Gallott, E. Taylor, etc.

Amidst this milky-way of stars a charming young girl, known in the play-bills as Miss Alison, was one of the principal attractions, and Reade was as much impressed by her ability as by her personal charms. He frequented the theatre nightly, studied the actress's method, and composed a comedy of which he intended her to be the heroine. Obtaining an introduction from his friend young Morris, son of the proprietor of the Haymarket, he carried his play under his arm, and presented himself in Jermyn Street, where he found the pretty actress at tea, or, to be more precise, at the actors' popular "tea-dinner," with her husband and Captain Curling, who divided the expenses of the household with the Seymours. Reade impressed the little family party so favourably that they invited him to join them. During his first visit he was shy, nervous, and embarrassed. A few days later, on returning from the theatre, Mrs. Seymour found that the servant, after having helped herself to her mistress's wardrobe, had taken her departure without preparing the dinner-tea. At the very moment when **Reade** called to pay his second visit, the fair Laura was vainly endeavouring to light a fire to set the kettle boiling, and the young author volunteered to assist her. This incident he afterwards utilized and elaborately developed in the highly humorous dramatic situation between Charles and Nell Gwynne, in the last act of the " King's Rival."

The Seymours did not think much of the comedy, but they thought very highly of the author, and finding that he occupied very expensive apartments, invited him, with a view to economizing his resources, to join their modest *ménage* as a member of the family upon the same footing as Captain Curling. Hence commenced an intimacy which terminated only with the death of Mrs. Seymour long subsequently to the decease of her husband and his Pylades, Curling.

Mrs. Seymour's goodness of heart was only equalled by her generosity, but both were held firmly under control by her native shrewdness. Differing in many respects, Mr. Reade and she agreed upon one point—they would fight for farthings on a matter of right, though they would give away pounds when appealed to in the nobler spirit. At all times they had a number of pensioners, absolutely supported by their generosity ; and their hospitality was unbounded. No friend ever needed a formal invitation ; there was always a knife and fork and a cordial welcome waiting at that hospitable board.

It was in the year 1851 that Mr. Reade, then thirty-eight or thirty-nine years of age, made his first dramatic experiment.* It was an adaptation of a comedy by Scribe and Legouvé, anglicized under the name of "The Ladies' Battle," and chiefly remembered for Mrs. Stirling's admirable impersonation of the Comtesse Dautreval. After this came "Gold," with the result already stated. His next composition was a drama founded upon certain romantic incidents connected with his own history which occurred during his sojourn in Scotland. This play he sent to the late Tom Taylor, then a rising and popular dramatist, supposed to possess considerable influence with the managers of the day. Mr. Taylor himself informed me that he read the drama through one night, while swinging in his hammock at his chambers in the Temple. He was struck with the power and vigour of the diction and the exciting nature of the incidents, but thought the plot quite unsuitable for dramatic action. Under this impression he got up in the "wee small hours ayont the twelve," and wrote to Reade, urging him to convert the drama into a story, suggesting a particular mode of treatment, and concluding the letter

---

* Since the above was written, I have seen a copy of a yet earlier dramatic effort, an adaptation of Smollett's "Peregrine Pickle." It was published at Oxford. On the title-page is written, in the author's own hand, this ominous inscription : "Bosh ! Bosh !! Bosh !!! C.R."

with the famous quotation, " 'Yea, by——!' said my
Uncle Toby, 'it shall not die!'" Adopting Taylor's
suggestion, Reade ultimately converted the drama
into the delightful story of "Christie Johnstone."
He, however, always alleged that he still felt that
his first idea was the correct one, and in cor-
roboration of the opinion he quoted the fact that
"Christie Johnstone" had been adapted and acted
in America, with remarkable success, thousands of
times.

Previous to the production of this work in narrative form, he wrote "Peg Woffington." Taylor
thought the subject admirably adapted for dramatic
treatment, and he proposed to Reade that they
should collaborate in the transmogrification of the
story into the comedy of "Masks and Faces,"
which was produced at the Haymarket Theatre, and
in which Mrs. Stirling and Ben Webster distinguished themselves so highly as the large-hearted
Peg and the poor starving author Triplet.

It has been alleged that the garret scene in this
play was suggested by Kotzebue's "Armer Dichter,"
a condensed version of which had already been popu-
larized here through the medium of Morris Barnett's
Monsieur Jacques; but there is about as much resemblance between the two pieces as exists between
the rivers in Macedon and Monmouth. There is a
garret and a starving musician in the one piece, and
there is a garret and a starving playwright in the
other. Here the likeness ends. The incident,
however, of cutting a hole in poor Triplet's picture,

and thrusting **Peg Woffington's face** through it, is a distinct crib from the older play of Kotzebue's, **the** name of which **I forget,** but which was adapted **to our own** stage **by Dibdin under** the title of **" The Old** Commodore ; or, **The Birthday,"** Munden distinguishing himself **in the** Commodore and Jack Bannister as **an old** Jack **Tar.** The picture incident, by-the-bye, Bayle Bernard **availed** himself of in **" The** Mummy" long prior **to** the production **of " Masks** and Faces," and it **has been acted in** I don't know how many *ballets d'action* before and since.

Alas ! **there is nothing new under** the sun.

Reade told me **that the** present last act of this play **was** originally intended **for** the **first,** and **that** when **it was transposed** to **the** position it **now** occupies, **he wrote a new** first **act,** which **he submitted to Taylor** for his approval.

The latter returned **it** with **a** laconic note stating that **it** was not worth the decimal part of **a** dump, that, in **fact,** there were only six lines worth retaining, and that they wanted rewriting.

The Charles Reade **of** that epoch was not the Charles Reade of later days.

At this period of his career as a dramatist, evidently he believed that "humility is the first step on the ladder of wisdom," inasmuch as he wrote back to his collaborator : " You say there are only six lines worth retaining. **I can** find only three. These I've preserved, and the others I've put on the fire !"

Although this work brought great kudos, it brought little coin to the authors, who, under happier

auspices, repurchased their rights, **and were ulti-**
mately enabled to realize a considerable sum from
royalties accruing from the performance of the play
at the Prince of Wales's, the Haymarket, and else-
where.

"Christie Johnstone" immediately followed **the**
publication of " Peg Woffington," and Charles Reade
made his first mark as a novelist.

In her youth **Mrs.** Seymour had enjoyed the
advantage **of** being on terms **of friendly** intimacy
with **all** the distinguished actors **of her time, including**
Macready and Charles **Kean. Many a time and**
oft, when people **used to complain of** Macready's
temper, have I heard **her exclaim,** " Ah, you didn't
know him ! He was a darling, **and** the truest,
noblest gentleman **in the world !"** Charles Kean,
she also declared, was a most lovable, charming fellow
(and so he was). **She** told me once, with perfect
naïveté, that when he was engaged at **Drury Lane,**
under Bunn's management, at Charles's request she
devoted the whole morning preceding his *début* **to**
preparing **laurel-wreaths,** garlands of flowers, etc.,
in anticipation of the coming triumph. Kean came,
and took some **away for** his friends : the remainder
Mrs. Seymour disposed of among her friends, **but**
"they were all right at night." These little expedients **to** pepper up popularity were, **it** seems, in
vogue before the days of Patti and Nilsson, Rossi,
Salvini, and many others on our own stage. Owing
to Mrs. Seymour's influence with Kean, Reade and

Taylor's now almost-forgotten play of "The First Printer" was produced, with questionable success, at the Princess's. This was soon followed by "The Courier of Lyons," in one respect a truly remarkable piece of stage-craft. Most of Reade's dramas are distinguished by prolixity and redundancy ; but here, in adapting another man's work, he produced a masterpiece of construction. Except Palgrave Simpson's adaptation of Edmund Yates's novel " Black Sheep," which is a model of dramatization, there is nothing on the modern stage which, for terseness, simplicity, and strength, can compare with Charles Reade's arrangement of the third and fourth acts of "The Courier of Lyons." Although a mere expression of individual opinion, this may at least be accepted as an impartial one, since I myself had previously adapted the play, and had acted it repeatedly, but upon seeing Reade's version I put my own into the fire. Excellent as his manipulation of this work was, " The Courier of Lyons " did not at that time do much to advance Mr. Reade's reputation.

The fact was that at that period we were licensed to pillage our neighbours with impunity, and the managers in central London conscientiously availed themselves of the privilege.

Here is a remarkable corollary on the condition of the London stage of that epoch.

On Easter Monday, April 12, 1852, in the provinces and in the suburbs, English plays were being acted everywhere.

At Sadler's Wells, Phelps produced the Reverend John White's play, "John Saville of Haystead," for which the author received £400 in a lump sum—more than Charles Reade earned for all his dramatic work in ten years.

At the Surrey, Creswick was acting "King John;" at the Marylebone, Mr. George Bolton produced "The Tempest;" at the City of London, Charles Pitt was acting Gerald Griffin's noble play of "Gisippus;" James William Wallack was acting "Shakespere" at the Queen's (since Prince of Wales's); while in the far-off east, Henry Betty, the actor's benefactor, was enacting "Lear."

In central London the English drama made no sign, save at the Olympic (then under Mr. William Farren's management), where Mrs. Walter Lacy was acting Portia, while Henry Farren tried his 'prentice hand on Shylock.

Now let us see what the fashionable theatres were doing. At Drury Lane, the Poet Bunn produced (with reduced prices) "Robert the Devil," and "Une Fête Napolitaine;" but the theatre was closed despite the reduced prices, three nights afterwards, in consequence, it was alleged, of a dispute between Bunn and Sims Reeves. At the Princess's, Kean produced, first time, "The Corsican Brothers;" at the Haymarket, "White Magic" was acted; at the St. James's, there was a French company (Regnier, Lafont, and others); at the two opera-houses (Her Majesty's and Covent Garden), "L'Italiana in Algeri" and "Guglielmo Tell."

J. W. WALLACK AS JAQUES.

" Les Dames de la Halle " had made a great hit in Paris, and our managers, being privileged to " prig," immediately proceeded to appropriate the French author's property.

No less a personage than George H. Lewes went through the plundering process for the Lyceum, where his adaptation, " A Chain of Events," was produced on the aforesaid Easter Monday, in eight long acts, occupying the entire evening in representation.

A very splendid production it was. The cast included Charles Mathews, Basil Baker, Frank Mathews, Belton, Rosiere, Madame Vestris, Julia St. George, and Laura Keene.

One effect, the sinking ship, with all hands aboard, has not since been excelled ; it is doubtful if it has been even equalled.

At the Adelphi, Webster himself did the " picking and stealing." Here also the piece was admirably cast ; besides Celeste and Woolgar, Ellen Chaplin and Kathleen Fitzwilliam, there were Wright, Sam Emery, A. Smith, and that accomplished actress Mrs. Keeley.

Now, Reade had also appropriated (" convey, the wise it call ") " Les Dames de la Halle," and he applied to Copeland, the manager of Punch's Playhouse (the Strand) to produce it. That gentleman was too astute to enter the lists with the Lyceum and the Adelphi ; he, however, produced a piece of Reade's (another Frenchman), called " A Village Tale," which was a failure, and on the very first

night a notice was put up for the theatre to close
in a fortnight.

Then commenced the first of the numerous
theatrical speculations in which Reade was perpetually worsted.   He took the theatre on "his own
hook," and on the 26th of April produced his adaptation of "Les Dames de la Halle," under the title of
"The Lost Husband," with Mrs. Seymour in the
part played by Mrs. Keeley at the Adelphi, and by
Madame Vestris at the Lyceum.   To attempt to
compete with the magnificent productions of the
Lyceum and the Adelphi was simply absurd.   The
result was exactly what Copeland had anticipated, a
total failure, and Reade's first theatrical speculation
terminated in a fortnight's fiasco, involving considerable loss.

He, however, always maintained that "out of the
nettle, danger, he had plucked the rose, safety," and
on the strength of this month's appearance at the
Strand he obtained several provincial engagements
for Mrs. Seymour.

Finding the London theatres closed as usual against
him, and determined not to be kept out, he, in conjunction with Mrs. Seymour, went into management
at the St. James's on his own account, where he
commenced his campaign with " The King's Rival,"
a strong but clumsy play, remembered principally
for Mrs. Seymour's inimitable performance of Nell
Gwynne, and beyond that, for the noblest eulogy on
the Lord Protector (the great Oliver) the English
language (no disrespect to Carlyle) has yet produced.

The play is rarely acted, and is almost unknown to the present generation. I avail myself, therefore, of the license of occasion to describe the situation in which this magnificent philippic occurs :

At one of the deepest periods of shame in our island story—at a period when the Dutch Admiral, Van Tromp, and his gallant sailors have swept the chops of the Channel with a broom at their mast-heads, when their victorious fleet lies anchored and unmolested in the Medway, the French King's pensioner, the airy, charming gentleman yclept—God save the mark!—" The Merry Monarch," and his merry satellites, are making night wanton at an orgie in Spring Gardens.

At this very moment the thunder of the Dutchman's artillery is heard in the Palace of Whitehall ; it is heard in the people's palace—the Commons' House at Westminster ; it is heard here in Spring Gardens ; it drowns the bacchanal's song, the roar of the reveller, the ribald laughter of pimps, panders and harlots !

Silence falls like a pall on all around. At this ill-omened moment one parasite more shameless than the rest calls upon the half-drunken Richmond to drink " to the King !"

With eyes aflame and heart afire, the indignant nobleman springs to his feet and, trumpet-tongued, exclaims :

" No, gentlemen ; no ! Those guns have sobered me ; they ring the knell of England's honour in my ears ! Yes, I will give you a health—the health that

should be drunk to that ignominious music! Fill
your glasses high, ladies and gentles of the court,
for I drink to the memory of a man, by birth a yeo-
man, and by soul an emperor. Raise your glasses
high, dwarfs, for I drink to a giant. Whilst he lived
no Dutchman swept our English seas. No Castle-
maines dishonoured the high places, and insulted
the matrons of the land. Vice and folly trembled at
his eye, and all good things lay safe beneath his
mighty shadow. He died, and then dogs took
courage, and tore the great man's body from the
tomb—from hallowed ground—but no power can
tear him from his immortal sepulchre in England's
heart. Honour and reverence to those dishonoured
bones that were the Protector; aye! the Protector of
every honest man and chaste woman in the land;
and the scourge of cowardly soldiers, of unchristian
prelates, of cut-purse nobles, and lascivious
kings!"

Talk about blank verse!

No nobler poetry has been written since the
spacious times of great Elizabeth than these soul-
stirring lines.

Another noteworthy event of this management
was the production of Captain Spicer's scholarly and
admirable adaptation of the "Alcestis."

The experiment, I fear, involved a serious loss, to
relieve which Mrs. Seymour went once more into
the country, supported by a company the most
notable members of which were the Robertson
family, including the future dramatist, who, all uncon-

scious of his coming greatness, fulfilled the humble, but onerous duties of prompter!

The tour, at this period of the year—the dog days —was, of course, predestined to failure, and Reade returned to town a poorer, but not a wiser man.

His next dramatic effort was a collaboration with Mr. Tom Taylor in the composition of "Two Loves and a Life,"—a noble play, but never attractive to the extent of its merits, either in town or country. As literary work, there can be no doubt it is far in advance of any drama of the same class in this century. There is nothing more touching or more beautiful in the whole range of dramatic literature than the story of Juanita in the second act; yet, such is the perversity of public taste, this play was only acted in one or two important country theatres, and has never been revived in London since its first production at the Adelphi. I had such faith in it that during the first year I went into management I expended three or four hundred pounds upon its production, with most direful results. The manager, as well as the author, is unfortunate who is "before his time."

Up to this period Reade had devoted his literary work almost entirely to the theatre. What the amount of his losses in his numerous speculations was I cannot even guess, but I can calculate his gains almost to a shilling.

He received for "Gold," which was acted six weeks, at £20 a week, £120; for "Masks and Faces," a moiety of £150, £75; for "Two Loves and a Life," a moiety of £100, £50; for " The Courier of Lyons," £100 ; and for his other pieces, nothing, save the reputation of being a flighty and indifferent dramatist with a " bee in his bonnet."

In fact, for ten years' work he received a steady, splendid average of £35 per annum !

It was at this crisis in his career that the sound, practical common-sense of Mrs. Seymour came to the rescue, and she incessantly urged him to quit the precarious pursuit of the drama, in which he was so often defeated, and to devote his great powers and his undivided attention to narrative literature.   He was now forty years of age, and as yet had done nothing to satisfy his ambition ; but he knew his own strength, and felt convinced that everything, the world itself, comes round to him who knows how to wait, and who lives long enough.   It was at this time he said to his brother Compton, " I am like Goldsmith and others : I shall blossom late." And he kept his word.

Four years later, he awoke one morning to find himself famous.   " It is Never Too Late to Mend " had been published, and at one bound he had leaped into the foremost rank of living authors.   Then followed in regular succession all the works which constitute the claim of Charles Reade to be remembered as one of the greatest writers of fiction of this century.

Up to forty-three years of age his life had appeared almost a wasted one.   Before he had reached fifty he had acquired fame and fortune.   Yet amidst

his continually-increasing successes as a novelist he
perpetually hungered for the glamour of the **foot-**
lights and the applause of the audience, and was
never happy out of the theatre. With this feeling
ever dominant, circumstances now occurred which
were peculiarly aggravating. " It is Never Too Late
to Mend" caught the public eye and heart, rushed
through several editions, and became the rage of the
hour. Its great and continually-increasing popularity
attracted the attention of the minor theatre dramatists.
Various unauthorized dramatizations of the novel
were produced in **town** and country, which crowded
the theatres nightly and replenished the managerial
coffers, while not a cent **ever** found **its** way to the
pocket of the original author. It must be confessed
that to a less irascible man this would have been
annoying enough, but **it** incensed Charles Reade
almost to madness. He had given his best work to
the theatre, had been repeatedly baffled, defeated,
had lost time and money—and yet, **on** the very first
occasion when he had "struck **oil**," **a** horde of
pirates and plunderers rushed **in** to rob him with
impunity, and made heaps of money by the nefarious
transaction. Justly angered at this anomalous state
of affairs, he commenced the prolonged litigation
which ultimately settled the question of dramatic
copyright as it now stands.

The judges had decided, in the first instance, that
the author had no exclusive right to the dramatization
of his own novel. Often baffled, but never beaten,
Mr. Reade returned again and again to the charge.

At last it occurred to him that " It is Never Too Late to Mend" was (except the prison episode) founded upon his own dead and buried drama of " Gold." Now, the law which permitted the pirates to steal his novel surely would not allow them to pilfer his play. Acting on this happy inspiration, he changed his front, and based his claim for compensation on the infringement of his rights in the drama of " Gold." The result was that he gained a signal triumph, and the final verdict laid down the law, " that if an author will take the trouble to dramatize, however crudely, his novel, prior to its publication, his rights are absolute."*

At this period I read the book—fortunately I had not seen any of the spurious plays on the subject— and I was immediately struck with the dramatic capabilities of the story. Without delay, I ran up to town, presented myself at Bolton Row, Mayfair, and introduced myself to Mr. Reade. Thus, after all these years, the obsolete drama of " Gold," at which I had turned up my nose in my youth, brought me into immediate communication with the author of " It is Never Too Late to Mend," and led to an intimacy of twenty years' duration.

---

* While these pages are passing through the press, the specious decision of Mr. Justice Stirling *in re* the piratical dramatization of Mrs. Burnett's story, " Little Lord Fauntleroy," has left the matter more confused and more confounded than ever.

Is it too much to expect that the collective wisdom of English authors shall draft a short Bill, clearly defining and making absolute the author's right in his own property, and that some sympathetic M.P. will undertake to pilot it through the House during some interval of the Irish Question next Session ?

On arriving at **Bolton Row, I** was shown into **a** large room littered **with** books, manuscripts, **and** newspapers of every description, from the *Times* and the *New York Herald* down to the *Police News.* Before me stood a **stately and** imposing man of fifty **or** fifty-one, over six feet high, with **a** massive chest, herculean limbs, **and a** bearded leonine face, showing **traces of a** manly beauty which ripened into majesty **as he grew** older. He had large bovine eyes, which **could at times** become exceedingly **fierce,** a fine head, quite **bald on** the top, but covered **at the** sides with soft brown hair, a head strangely disproportioned **to the** bulk **of** the body; **in** fact, I never could understand how **so** large **a** brain could be confined in **so** small **a skull.** On the desk before him lay a huge sheet **of** drab paper, **on** which he had been writing: it was about the **size of** two sheets of ordinary foolscap; in his hand one **of** Gillott's double-barrelled pens. **(Before I left** the room, he told me **he** sent Gillott **his books,** and Gillott sent him his pens.)

His voice, though very pleasant, **was** very penetrating. **He** was rather deaf, but **I** don't think quite so deaf as he pretended **to be.** This deafness gave him an advantage in conversation: it afforded him time to take stock of the situation, and either to seek refuge in silence, or to request his interlocutor to propound his proposal afresh. **At first he** was very cold, but at last, carried away by the ardour **of** my admiration for his work, he thawed, and in half an hour he was eager, excited, delighted, and delightful.

When I said that I wanted to dramatize his book,
he told me he had dramatized it already ; that he
had sent printed copies to every manager in London,
and they had not had the decency even to acknow-
ledge his letters on the subject.   He had lost all hope
and heart about it, he said, but if I liked I might take
the play and read it, and form my own opinion as to
its chances of success.   I read it that night, and breakfasted with him the next morning, when we arranged
to produce it forthwith at my theatre in Leeds.

Mr. Reade's frank egoism is so well known, and
it was so *naïve* and so amusing withal, that I cannot
refrain from chronicling my first impressions of it.
After breakfast, he asked me to read him George
Fielding's farewell to the farm.   There was a lady
present, and the tears rose in her eyes at the touching
lines about "church-bells and home."   Seeing this,
Reade rose, and paced the room in violent agitation,
muttering to himself, " Beautiful—beautiful !—music
—music !—music, isn't it ?"   He then turned to me
abruptly, and desired me to give Tom Robinson's
curse in the prison scene.   I gave it, to the best of my
ability.   When I had done, he became quite wild
with excitement, and exclaimed, "Sublime ! sublime !
My only fear is, if you let him have it like that
they'll be sorry for that beast of a Hawes.   Now,
seriously, on your honour, sir, do you think that
Lear's curse is ' in it ' with this ?"

When we laughed at his almost boyish exuberance,
he was not at all offended, but laughed as heartily
as we did, while he continued :

"No, no, it isn't exactly that; but I can't help kicking when those d——d asses, the critics, try to hang dead men's bones round living men's necks !'

That night there was a cosy little dinner - party improvised in Bolton Row in honour of "the young man from the country," who had had the temerity "to beard the lion in his den"—so Reade always described the process of my introducing myself to him. The only persons present besides myself were Mr. and Mrs. Dion Boucicault, Dr. Dickson, Mr. Reade, and Mrs. Seymour. This charming woman had long passed her *première jeunesse* when I became acquainted with her. She was still beautiful, but in the heyday of her youth she must have been supremely lovely ; and Mr. Reade always maintained that at her zenith she was the most delightful and ebullient comedy actress he had ever seen. I can well believe it. The first time I ever saw her was on the stage of my own theatre, at Sheffield, with the Haymarket company. On that occasion she acted Mrs. Charles Torrens in the comedy of " The Serious Family." I can see her now as she appeared then, just in the full, ripe prime of womanhood—a trifle below the middle height, a fair complexion, oval face, frank, open brow, large, bright hazel eyes with long, dark lashes, a profusion of light-brown, glossy, curly hair, a pure, yet delicate, aquiline nose, an exquisitely-cut mouth, with dazzling teeth, a slender waist and a magnificent bust, a bright, ringing laugh, a crisp, clear, sympathetic

voice, which at times was " soft, gentle, and low—an
excellent thing in woman."   In her Quaker dress of
lavender silk she was piquantly charming ; but when
she appeared in ball-room costume, which revealed
her majestic neck and shoulders, she was dazzlingly
beautiful.   I almost think I can hear her now, as
she exclaimed, " I have been deceived, betrayed,
insulted ! Take me from this house, Charles, or I
shall stifle."

Years afterward, when our friendship had ripened
into intimacy, Mrs. Seymour informed me that she
was the daughter of an impecunious physician, who
hailed from somewhere in Somersetshire. From
her earliest childhood, she was the Little Dorrit of
the family, and had to be bread-winner for her sister
and herself. As early as fifteen years of age Miss
Alison made her *début* as Juliet, at the Victoria
Theatre, then under the management of Abbot and
Egerton, and subsequently she transferred her
services to Braham, the singer, under whose management she appeared at the St. James's Theatre and at
the Coliseum in Regent's Park.   Thence she went
to the York Circuit, and subsequently to the Theatre
Royal, Dublin.   On her return to town, the necessities of her family urged her to a marriage with
Mr. Seymour, a man much older than herself, and
reported to be in affluent circumstances. It appeared
that this rumour had no foundation in fact.   Hence,
soon after her marriage, accompanied by her husband,
she went to America, vainly hoping, by the exercise
of her profession, to obtain the fortune which her

unfortunate **matrimonial** alliance had certainly **not** brought her. **The** American tour was a disappointment, and the newly-married couple returned **to** England. At or about this time I **am** under the impression that **she acted** Desdemona and parts of **a** similar character with Macready. Ultimately she **was a** member of the Haymarket company, where, **as** already stated, Reade **first** became acquainted **with** her.

It was a genuine and **unexpected** pleasure **to me** when I recognised in this genial and graceful lady the presiding genius of the little house **in** Mayfair. What a delightful evening **that was** on which I first made her acquaintance!

When **Mr. Reade** chose, he could be austere **as a** stoic, dumb as an oyster ; **but** when he unbent, he was a boy, and could talk **like a** woman. **On this** occasion he was as frolicsome as **the** one, and **as** garrulous **as the** other.

Boucicault was, **and is,** a delightful *raconteur ;* the ladies, too, contributed their quota, and **Dr.** Dickson was inimitable. Availing himself every now and then **of** a pause **in** the **witty** warfare between the **two** authors, he would let out some quaint, pawky saying which convulsed us with laughter. I had just been reading " Hard Cash," and Dr. Dickson's manner struck me so much that I couldn't help hazarding the remark, " Pray pardon me, but you remind me wonderfully **of** Dr. Sampson." At this there was **a** roar. Dr. Dickson was Dr. Sampson himself, and his honest face flushed with gratified vanity, as indeed did the author's, at my involuntary compliment to the fidelity of the likeness.

" Ah, you villain," said Dickson, " see how brutally you have caricatured me, since this boy is enabled to spot me the·moment he sees me. I'll bring an action for libel against you, Charlie ; I will, now, 'pon my soul I will."

After dinner, Boucicault sang us " The Wearing of the Green " (this was before the production of " Arrah na Pogue ") with such fervour that it set every drop of Irish blood in my body boiling, and made me for the time being as big a rebel as my grandfather was before me, and he was pitch-capped twice, and hung up to a lamp-post once, once taken out to be shot, yet was at the last moment saved through the intervention of the Duchess of Leinster, and lived to tell the story nearly half a century after '98. But I forget ; these are not " Tales of My Grandfather," but recollections of Charles Reade.

With that night commenced an intimate friendship between him and myself, which existed to the day of his death. In the relations in which we were placed there was sometimes a little friction, but that was of the slightest and most temporary character, and no more than might naturally be expected from two men of equally impetuous temperaments and different opinions. We scarcely had, however, the slightest difference on the subject of the management of the stage—over which, in every instance, I exercised complete control, arranging and inventing the entire stage-business of most of his important pieces exactly as they **now** exist.

Perhaps **it was as well** that the reins were in my hands, for occasionally **Mr.** Reade's stage directions were most eccentric. In my copy of "Gold," the following manuscript note occurs :

"The actor will **here turn** his back to the foot-lights, and, by the artificial means so well known on the stage, will remove every particle of colour from his face, so that when he turns round to the audience he will be **as pale as** the 'trembling coward' who drew Priam's curtain in the dead of night to tell him half his Troy was burnt."

Note for George Fielding's farewell to the farm in " **It** is Never Too Late to Mend " :

" If the actor is equal to his business, this speech cannot fail. He must throw his whole heart and soul **into it.** If, by the time it is finished, his fellows on the stage, and the audience in front of it **are** not dissolved in tears, the speech will have **been** improperly spoken, and he is a duffer."

" **It** is Never Too Late to Mend " was produced for the first time at Leeds. We had new scenery and appointments, and a cast of characters which has not since been excelled. It elicited considerable enthusiasm during a run of four or five weeks, although it was never played a single week to its current expenses. Fortunately, I was able to bear the brunt, and, as I believed in the piece, I too resolved, like Uncle Toby, that it should not die. I arranged, therefore, a tour of all the principal towns, commencing at the Theatre Royal, Manchester. The sequel justified my confidence : from that moment the success of the piece was assured, and wherever we went the theatre was crowded nightly.

My friend the late George Vining at that time was manager of the Princess's Theatre, and he came down to York and Manchester to see the play, eventually arranging for its production in town. Both he and Reade paid me the compliment to ask me to play my original part, but I had not refused repeated offers to act in town to *débuter* at the Princess's in a convict's dress and a scratch wig after all.

Reade riled considerably at what he called "the insensate egoism" of the "apex actor," for so he, or Mr. Burnand, or both, christened me. Leo's anger was, however, of short duration ; while as for George Vining, he was soon reconciled to Tom Robinson, which proved to be one of his most successful parts.

The first night of this play at the Princess's was made memorable by a deplorable scene, not wholly unprovoked by a revolting piece of realism, introduced, against my advice, in the prison-scene. A perfect riot ensued, and a by no means undistinguished journalist so far forgot himself as to jump up in the stalls and harangue the audience, protesting against the conduct and character of the drama. This gentleman had reason to regret the part he took

DION BOUCICAULT.

in this transaction ; **for,** finding afterward **that** he sought under **a** pseudonym to justify his conduct on that occasion, Reade scarified and pilloried **him** in an article **which, for** scathing invective, equalled **any-** thing which **ever** came from that terrible double- barrelled **pen.**

Annoying as it was to the **author and** actors at **the** moment, this shameful scene served to attract atten- tion, and indeed was a sensational advertisement.

It was alleged at this period **by an eminent** critic that **" It is** Never **Too Late to Mend "** was founded **upon a** French drama.

Now the truth **is** that, after **"** Gold **" was** produced at Drury Lane, Reade went to **Paris for the avowed** object of getting the play translated **and** produced in **a** French theatre. On **his arrival, to** his astonish- ment and vexation, he found **a drama (also** suggested by the gold fever in Australia) had **already** been produced, and was then running under the title of **"** Les Chercheurs d'Or."

" Gold " seemed doomed **to death—but he** still believed in the subject—and **resolving** that so much good work, and so many admirably drawn characters, **should** not **be** thrown away, **he** resolved to utilize them in a narrative form.

Shortly after his return from France, happening to be in Durham, he was shown over **the** Castle. This almost accidental visit directed his attention more particularly to the atrocities of **the** model prison in **B——,** which **were** then largely exciting

the public mind. Immediately obtaining the blue-
books, the horrors therein recited set his blood on
fire, and with that ever-active sympathy with the
suffering and the oppressed, that intense hatred of
the wrong-doer, which to the last moment of his life
were his most dominant feelings, he girded up his
loins to do battle.

A mere pamphlet would not achieve the object in
view—blood, brains, life, must be put into the dry
bones. Tom Robinson was already in existence,
and Reade made the wretched convict his *cheval de
bataille.* Hence the episode of the Model Prison
was incorporated with the original story of "Gold,"
and "It's Never Too Late to Mend" leaped from
the author's brain in the first instance, to set all
English hearts aflame with generous indignation;
and in the next, to inaugurate a Parliamentary
Commission, which tolled the death-knell of the
accursed system.

Although thirty years and more have elapsed since
the great author pilloried the monster at B——,
and pointed out the horrors of the great secret and
silent system, still much remains to be done, not
only for the amelioration of the condition of the
wretched criminal, but for the protection of the poor
but honest debtor. We move slowly in England, and
perchance in thirty years more we shall have learned
to treat our prisoners like human beings—"fed with
the same food, hurt with the same weapons, subject
to the same diseases, healed by the same means,
warmed and cooled by the same summer and winter."

Yet thirty, sixty, or a hundred years hence surely Charles Reade's name will go down to posterity as the first man who, since the days of Howard and Fry, had the courage to attack this iniquitous system in its very stronghold.

As to the alleged plagiarism, it must be admitted (although the fact has escaped the cognizance of the critics) that the inimitable " Jacky " was suggested by a long-forgotten drama called " Botany Bay." What then ? " Hamlet" was founded upon Kyd's blood-and-thunder drama ; " Othello," on a novel of Cynthio's, etc.

" It is Never Too Late to Mend" is English to the backbone.   The men are sons of the soil ; Susan Merton is as sweet an English maiden as ever came out of Berkshire ; the lines are idyllically English. There is not a pastoral scene in the story, either in England or Australia, in which the spectator does not " see green meadows and hear the bleating of sheep," while the crude savage of " Botany Bay " is transformed by the hand of genius into the wonderful creation of " Jacky."

All authors are more or less plagiarists ; but *il y a fagots et fagots.*   Since Homer's time, men have parodied his incidents and paraphrased his sentiments.   Molière alleged that he "took his own where he found it."   But "the thief of all thieves was the Warwickshire thief," who stole right and left from everybody ; but then he "found things lead and left them gold."   Reade's complaint was that his plunderers found his work gold and left it lead.

24— 2

'Tis quite true that he utilized Macquet's "Le Pauvre de Paris" in "Hard Cash;" 'tis also true that he adapted his novel of "White Lies," and his drama of "The Double Marriage," from the same author's "Le Château Grantier;" it is equally true that he founded "Drink" upon Zola's "L'Assommoir;" but in each and every one of these instances he recognised the justice of the French authors' claim by obtaining their consent and paying them a liberal commission for the right to utilize their works.

With reference to real plagiarisms I have discovered quite recently a remarkable coincidence between a story of Reade's, entitled "The Picture," and another story, called "What the Papers Revealed," by an anonymous writer, in the twentieth volume of *St. James's Magazine*, page 8. Both tales are distinctly derived from the same French source; in fact, Reade made his a tale of the Terror; the other adapter has laid his *donnée* in England; but it is to be observed neither writer alludes directly or indirectly to the original source of his inspiration.

There is also in an early volume of *Household Words* a story from which "Single Heart and Double Face" is unquestionably derived. It is, however, possible that Reade may have been the author of both stories.

While staying with me in Leeds, an eminent iron manufacturer told us a story of a strike in which the ringleader justified his conduct by continually saying, "I'm a man, not a mouse!"

Reade immediately annexed the phrase, and introduced it in "Put Yourself in His Place," and also in his play of "Dora." In Scene I of the latter, Farmer Allan says, "After all, I am a man, and not a mouse." In Act II. Dora rings the changes on the phrase, e.g., "As for me, I am *not* a man, you know; I am a mouse—a poor little mouse that lives in a lion's den!" And later, "You see, sir, I am not *quite* a mouse!"

Apropos of Dora, it is not generally known that the phrase, "The Grand Old Man" (since conferred by the voice of a nation on an Old man Grander still!), was originally applied by this peerless maiden to Farmer Allan (see page 38 of "Dora").

I may here remark, with reference to his dramatization of the late Mr. Anthony Trollope's "Ralph the Heir," which was resented by that gentleman as a grievance, that Reade assured me—first, that from their intimate friendship he did not think it necessary to ask Trollope's permission to dramatize the work—indeed, had he deemed it requisite, he could not communicate with him during his absence in Australia; next, that Trollope never signified an intention of dramatizing or reserving the right to dramatize any of his works; and last, that he (Reade) compiled the comedy for their mutual benefit and emolument. Undoubtedly, Mr. Trollope had a "right to do what he liked with his own," although one can scarcely understand the feeling which prompted him to resent as a wrong what most men would have considered a compliment, emanating from such a source. I am under the impression that although Reade persistently

pressed Trollope to receive half the royalties accruing from the representation of this comedy, he with
equal persistency refused to accept the proposal.
The latter assured me that after this they frequently
took part in a game of whist at the Garrick without
exchanging one word with each other. To his
sensitive mind this estrangement was a great grief—
a grief which was afterward enhanced by Trollope's
posthumous attack in his autobiography on his old
friend.*

To return, however, to " It is Never Too Late to
Mend." The play was a great commercial success,
and crowded the theatre nightly until the termination
of the season. From that time to this its attraction
has been perennial. It has been revived at the
Princess's, it has been acted at Drury Lane and
the Adelphi and at all the minor theatres with considerable success, and at this moment there are two
or three companies touring the country with it in
various directions.

After its production at the Princess's, the late
Benjamin Webster reproached me bitterly for not
having recommended the play to him, utterly ob-
livious of the fact that it had passed through his
own hands and he had never taken the trouble to
read it, although he knew Charles Reade to be the

---

* Since the above was written, I have learnt on the best authority
that Reade and Trollope 'made friends' in '81, and indeed corre-
sponded after the latter had paid Reade a visit for the purpose of
ascertaining how he managed to obtain such large sums from American
publishers for his advance-sheets, while he (Trollope) could get nothing,
or next to it.

author. I have dwelt at length upon the circumstances relative to the production of this play, for the encouragement of young authors. Here was a work of world-wide popularity, by a great man, which went begging from stage-door to stage-door, and no manager would look at it, yet after its production in the provinces it became a great metropolitan success, and is so to this day.

The triumph so long delayed, but at length achieved, filled Reade with a fever of delight, and contributed greatly to the intimacy which existed so long between us. For many years he always found a home whenever he pleased in my house, and whenever I came to town I found a home in his.

During my frequent visits to Albert Gate I had ample opportunities for observing his systematic mode of going to work. He scoffed at the idea of burning "the midnight oil." Maintaining that a man of letters had no right to lead the life of a recluse, he worked in the early part of the day, the rest he devoted to society. Literature was the business of his life, society its relaxation.

At the period of our early intimacy he got up at eight, skimmed the papers, and breakfasted at nine. In those days he had a healthy, almost a voracious, appetite, and usually made a substantial meal which set him up for the day. Fish, flesh, eggs, potatoes, fruit—nothing came amiss to him. From breakfast-time he never tasted anything till dinner, at seven, or, when he went to the theatre, at six. From ten

till one or two he stuck to the desk.   Two chapters
he considered a fair average day's work.   I have
often sat with him for hours together without our
exchanging one word.   Sometimes, indeed, he would
jump up, and say, " My muse 'labours,' but the jade
won't be ' delivered.'   Come into the garden, John,
and let's have a jaw."   After a few minutes' talk, he
would return to his work with redoubled ardour.

One day in every week was devoted to his agendas
and scrap-books.   Magazines and papers of every
description from all parts of the world were piled
round him in shoals.   Armed with a long pair of
scissors, sharp and glittering as a razor, he would
glance over a whole sheet, spot out a salient article
or   paragraph — a   picturesque   illustration   from
Harper's, Frank Leslie's Pictorial, the *Graphic*, the
Illustrated London News, the *London Journal*, down
to the *Police News*—snip went the scissors, slash
went the article as it dropped into the paper-basket.
During these operations he would sometimes pause
to let out an exclamation of astonishment or disgust,
or a Gargantuan roar of laughter, or occasionally he
would read a more than usually interesting paragraph aloud, and comment on it.   When the slashing
was completed and the room was littered over in
every corner, the maid was called in to clear away
the *débris*.   Then came the revision.   Paragraphs
and illustrations were sifted, selected, approved, or
rejected.   Those that were approved were there and
then pasted into scrap-books and duly indexed; long
articles were stowed away into one or other of his

numerous agendas, so methodically that he knew
where to lay his hand upon them at a moment's
notice. It was by this process that he prepared
those wonderful storehouses of information which
his friend Edwin Arnold thus describes : " The
enormous note-books which he compiled in the
course of his various publications, with their elaborate system of reference and confirmation and their
almost encyclopædic variety and range, will rank
hereafter among the greatest curiosities of literature, and be a perennial monument of his artistic
fidelity."

To complete his record, and have a means of
referring at any moment to a reliable authority for
verification of dates, etc., he always filed *Lloyd's
Weekly News*, which he called his " epitome of
current events."

I well remember the pride with which his brother
William, " the Squire," turned up one day with an
annual volume of *Lloyd's*, which he had carefully
indexed from the first page to the last.

Upon inquiring how he had managed to hit off
the idiosyncrasies of Dr. Dickson so accurately, he
(Reade) replied : " Come into my workshop, and I'll
show you how it is done."

We went into his study, where he picked out of a
hundred huge sheets of drab mill-board, one headed
" Dickybirdiana " (" Dicky " was a pet name for
Dickson). The sheet was divided into sectional
columns, like a newspaper, and every column was
filled with manuscript, containing anecdotes, traits of

character, peculiarities of pronunciation, and a perfect analysis of Dr. Dickson. It was thus that Reade laboured from first to last in the construction of character and in the building up of his works.

So thorough was he even at the beginning of his career, that in order to acquire an accurate knowledge of the details requisite for the story of " Christie Johnstone," he lived amongst the fisherfolk for some time, and he absolutely entered into the herring fishery business, as a commercial speculation, providing the requisite capital, and going out with these good people night after night on their fishing expeditions.

Amongst his unpublished papers he has left one, written at that period, endorsed thus :

"AUTO-CRITICISM ON ' CHRISTIE JOHNSTONE.'

" Curious, and really not bad.

" The author of ' Christie Johnstone' is full of details ; but they are barren details. He deals in those minutiæ which are valuable according to the hand that mixes them ; but he has not the art of mixing his materials. Hence the compound, with some exceptions, is dry and lumpy. . . . Mr. Reade has good thoughts which he could clothe with logic ; but he cannot dress them in the garb Fiction requires.

" He should associate himself with one of our authoresses ; we have several whose abilities are his counterpart. He has plenty to tell us, and cannot tell it ; they have nothing to say, and say it to per-

fection. The pair would produce a novel considerably above the average—something we should read
with pleasure, *and lay aside with delight.*"

In another unpublished paper he falls foul of the
author of a bumptious and atrabilious article published in *Fraser* in 1858, called " Poets and Players."
The writer (anticipating Mr. Burnand by more than
a quarter of a century !) starts with the assumption
that Shakespere's are not good acting plays for our
days ; that they are two hundred years too late ;
that they may do very well for the closet ; that the
actors of the time (including Macready, Kean,
Phelps, etc.) were incapable of comprehending the
bard, or of acting him so as to interest the public, etc.

It is perfectly delightful to see the ease with
which this Fraserian blockhead is shut up by Reade.
He commences by pointing out that besides being a
poet, Shakespere was a player and a manager ;
that the criticasters who pretend to an intimate and
perfect knowledge of the unacted and unactable plays
of the great master, absolutely know nothing whatever
of him except through the medium of the familiar
acting plays, and the inspired utterances of the very
players whom they constantly endeavour to depreciate.

In confirmation of this statement, Reade affirms
that if ninety-nine out of a hundred of these learned
pundits were asked who was the author of the lines,
" Off with his head ! so much for Buckingham !"
and " Richard's himself again !" they would unhesi-
tatingly reply, " Why, Shakespere, of course !"

After a glowing eulogy upon Macready's Macbeth—which he (Reade) alleges throws more light upon the subject in three short hours than all the tedious twaddle critics and commentators have written in three centuries—he demolishes the assertion that "Shakespere's plays were made for the closet" by showing that the poems, the sonnets— "Venus and Adonis," "Lucrece," etc., which were really intended for the closet—were published in the poet's life-time, while the plays, which were intended for the stage, were jealously kept in manuscript, and were only to be seen or heard through the medium of their chosen interpreters, the players, till the playwright's death.

The position Reade assumes towards the players in this article reminds one not a little of Johnson's attitude to Garrick. Ursa major would bully "little" Davy himself, but woe betide any outsider who attempted to lay profane hands on the great little man while Bruin was to the fore!

Amongst other features of Reade's workshop there used to be one or two books full of remarkable letters from eminent or eccentric people, which he would occasionally invite me to read.

The letters themselves—except in rare instances —I am not at liberty to quote, but his endorsements are such curiosities of literature that I have ventured to quote a few of them.

On a letter from Boucicault about "It is Never Too Late to Mend" he wrote: "B—— advises me to cut out the Jew and Jacky. Aha, old fox! they will outlive thee and me."

One from Wilkie Collins is endorsed : " An artist of the pen ; there are terribly few amongst us."

Another from George H. Lewes states : " An article by you that wouldn't be worth printing would be a curiosity in its way ; it must be so infernally wrong. Are we never to see you on Sunday between five and six ? We are always in, and generally get some good talkers to come."

Martin Tupper : " A man unreasonably pitched into ; he is not the only man who has made an easy hit with a single book. Examples : ' Dame Europa's School,' ' Tom Brown's School-Days,' ' Rab and his Friends,' ' Self-Help,' ' Jane Eyre.' None of these writers could write two remarkable books if they wrote for ever."

Kate Terry : " The meekest, tenderest, and most intelligent actress of her day. Young in years, but old in expression, and fuller of talent than an egg is of meat."

Ellen Terry : " An enigma. Her eyes are pale ; her hair fair and long ; her complexion delicate. Her expression *kills* any pretty face you ever see beside her. A pattern of fawn-like grace. She possesses to perfection what Voltaire calls ' le grand art de plaire.' "

Sothern : " A dry humorist. I believe he professes to mesmerize, and is an imitator of the Davenport Brothers. He can get his hands out of any knot I can tie. His Dundreary is true comedy, not farce. He is as grave as a judge over it, and in that excellent quality a successor to Liston."

Ada Menken : " A clever woman with beautiful eyes, very dark blue. A bad actress, but made a hit by playing Mazeppa in tights. A quadrogamist. Her last husband was, I believe, John Heenan ; I saw him fight Tom Sayers.* Goodish heart ; loose conduct. Requiescat in pace !"

Ben Webster : " An admirable actor when he happens to have studied the words."

If any special information were needed upon a particular subject, Reade had recourse to one or two humble followers whose success in literature had not been commensurate with their industry and ambition : these gentlemen were employed to hunt up authorities, make excerpts, etc., at the British Museum ; and thus it was that his fiction always appeared like fact.

In preparing his material for the press he was equally precise. He would rush off his copy, in his great sprawling hand, on huge sheets of drab-coloured paper—which he alleged rested and cooled his eyes —then carefully revise. This done, he would frequently read aloud to us chapter after chapter, and discuss incidents, treatment, etc. It was seldom that he did not avail himself of some suggestion, and frequently some happy thought would occur in the course of conversation. After the next revision the chapters were handed over to his copyist, who wrote

* So did I, and a very fine fight it was.

a hand like copper-plate. Then came the final revise. If this did not deface the manuscript too much,
it was sent to the printer. If, however, the manuscript was illegible, then a second copy was made,
although he had not been always so particular.
Punch once declared that a perplexed compositor
threw himself off Waterloo Bridge in a fit of despair,
occasioned by the illegibility of Reade's manuscript.
He took this to heart so much, that he thenceforward
made legibility his first consideration.

The copyist who worked for him for years died some
three years ago under very distressing circumstances.
Poor S—— had been a prompter in his time. His
was the old, old story : there had been a faithless
wife, a deserted home, a motherless child who died.
The man lost himself, took to drink, became a slave
to it, and was a pitiable object to behold. This infirmity was the one of all others which Reade most
loathed, yet he always bore with poor S——, and
did all he could to protect him from himself. If the
unfortunate creature ever got a lump sum of money
into his hands, he melted it immediately in drink :
hence it was always doled out to him by instalments.
Latterly it became absolutely necessary to have the
work done in the house. When I last saw him, he
came to draw some money : he took it without a
word, and passed out like a man in a dream. A
fortnight afterward I read in the papers that he had
been found dead, seated in a dilapidated chair, in a
dismantled garret—one of those horrible places described in George Sims's awful book — a place

festooned with cobwebs and reeking with filth. An empty gin-bottle was by his side ; the pipe, which had fallen from his hand, lay smashed to pieces on the ground ; a few shillings were still left in his pocket.   At the post-mortem examination the stomach was found to be entirely empty.   It was stated that he had lived for years in this wretched den, where he had never been known to receive a visitor, nor had any human being ever crossed his threshold from the time he took possession of it till they found him sitting dead in the broken chair.

The routine at Albert Gate was pretty regular. From two to four was devoted to receiving company.   People of every description came—frequently Americans, who would come with or without introductions (he was very partial to America and Americans)—"swells," brother-authors, actors, and actresses, especially the latter.   Some of them had never acted, but they only needed the opportunity to "set the Thames on fire ;" others had acted, but had been "crushed" by managers, and were out of engagements.   Hither, too, came disappointed poets, playwrights, escaped lunatics, broken-down sailors, ticket-of-leave men, etc.   To most of these he would give a patient hearing, and not unfrequently consolation, advice, and assistance.

After his reception, he usually devoted a couple of hours to calling on his friends, generally winding up in Covent Garden, from whence he returned to dinner laden with fruit and flowers

MISS J. L. DE LUNDREARY.

whenever **they were in season.** Lunch, as before intimated, he **never** took. "**It is an insult to** one's breakfast," **he** alleged, "**and** an outrage on one's dinner." The *menu,* unless **upon** state occasions, commenced with fish : **soup** he detested. His taste in **fish was** peculiar : he preferred herring (which, when fresh from the sea, he maintained **was** the most delicate and delicious fish that **ever came** to table) **to** turbot, sole to salmon. The **next course** consisted of mutton **(beef he** abominated) **or** white meats, followed by **game,** pastry, **and** fruit, **washed** down by sparkling wine, **of which he was a** connoisseur. During all our acquaintance, **I never** saw him **taste a glass of beer ;** and he loathed the very smell **of** tobacco. **Spirits he** rarely **or ever tasted.** Once, however, when **he was staying with us in the country,** my landlord, who was a famous wine-merchant, **made** us a present of a case of **wonderful** white **Santa Cruz** rum. It was very old, and, made **into** punch, **it was a** most insidious beverage. **On** one occasion, when **we** came home cold and weary from a long night-rehearsal, **I** broached a bottle, and tempted Reade into tasting **it ; he** took to **it** very kindly ; indeed, during the remainder of his visit he invariably looked **out** for a nightcap of this pleasant tipple. Next time I came to town I brought with me **a** dozen bottles, and he used to say nightly, with **a** grin, "Produce the poisoned bowl. You are continually leading me into temptation. **If I fall** into **evil it** will be your fault."

Our pleasantest times **were** when **we** were dining

alone, because then I could induce him to talk without *arrière-pensée*, and—ye gods!—how he could talk when in the mood! He preferred to talk about his plays rather than his books. I preferred to talk about his books, especially about his masterpiece, "The Cloister and the Hearth." The labour and research involved in this remarkable work were enormous, yet it was nearly strangled at its birth, and even at its maturity never had half the vogue of "Hard Cash," "It is Never Too Late to Mend," "Foul Play," or "Put Yourself in His Place." Originally brought out under the title of "A Good Fight," in a certain periodical, its publication was suspended in consequence of the editor's tampering with the "copy," an indignity which the author resented by breaking off further relations, and the story was left unfinished. Ultimately, however, it saw the light in a complete form under its present well-known title. The unfortunate editor was shortly afterward immured in a lunatic asylum, whereupon Reade made one of his characteristic remarks. "Poor fellow!" he said, "poor fellow! I'm sorry for him. Of course I'm bound to be sorry as a Christian, but what else could be expected from a fellah who presumed to tamper with my copy?"

In discussing the merits of his works (he was by no means averse to discussion on this or any other subject, except politics and the Athanasian Creed), I always maintained the supremacy of "The Cloister and the Hearth". over all his other books; but in this case, as in the drama, his barometer was failure

or success. After "Griffith Gaunt," he declared
that he would never go out of his own age again.
"I write for the public," he said, "and the public
don't care about the dead : they are more interested
in the living, and in the great tragi-comedy of
humanity that is around and about them, and en-
virons them in every street, at every crossing, in
every hole and corner. An aristocratic divorce suit,
the last great social scandal, a sensational suicide
from Waterloo Bridge, a woman murdered in Seven
Dials, or a baby found strangled in a bonnet-box at
Piccadilly Circus, interests them much more than
Kate Gaunt's piety or Gerard's journey to Rome.
For one reader who has read ' The Cloister and the
Hearth,' a thousand have read ' It is Never Too
Late to Mend.' The paying public prefers a live
ass to a dead lion. *Similia similibus:* why should
the ass not have his thistles ? Besides, tthisles are
good, wholesome diet for those who have a stomach
for them. No, no ! No more doublet and hose for
me : henceforth I stick to trousers. Now, after
that, if you please, pass the wine and change the
subject."

Of all his contemporaries he yielded the palm
to Dickens, and to him alone. Him he always
acknowledged as his master.

Next for variety and scope came Bulwer.

Carlyle, he said, was a Johnsonian pedant, bearish,
boorish, and bumptious, egotistical, and atrabilious.
His Teutonic English was barbarous and cacophonous ; yet, notwithstanding, every line he wrote

was permeated with vigour and sincerity, and his "Cromwell" is a memorial of two great men—the hero and the author.

Macaulay always posed himself,

> "As who should say, 'I am Sir Oracle,
> And when I ope my lips let no dog bark!'"

but with this intellectual arrogance he combined a grand rhythmical style, a marvellous learning, and a miraculous memory.

Disraeli was "the most airy and vivacious of literary coxcombs, the most dexterous and dazzling of political harlequins, the most audacious of adventurers, the most lovable of men (when you got on his weak side), and, altogether, the most unique and remarkable personage of the age."

Thackeray he designated "an elegant and accomplished writer." "Esmond," he added, "is worthy of Addison at his best; but some of 'The Yellow-Plush Papers' would be a disgrace to Grub Street, and the miserable personal attacks on Bulwer, who has written the best play, the best comedy, and the best novel of the age, are unworthy of a gentleman and a man of letters.

"Trollope wrote a good deal that was interesting, and a good deal that was—not interesting.

"For literary ingenuity in building up a plot and investing it with mystery, give me dear old Wilkie Collins against the world.

"George Eliot's *métier* appears to me to consist principally in describing with marvellous accuracy the habits, manners, and customs of animalcula as they are seen under the microscope.

"Ouida has emerged from dirt to decency—and even dignity—and there is nothing in literature more touching and beautiful than the tale of 'Two Little Wooden Shoes.'*

"Miss Braddon is as quiet, as modest, and unassuming as she is accomplished. Her fertility of invention is boundless, her industry phenomenal, her style sound and vigorous, and she has rare dramatic instincts.

"Rice is a capital fellow, and one of the best constructors of a story going.

"Besant is an artist in words; he has fecundity, fertility, invention, pathos, humour, power : except that he is occasionally too discursive, he has all the qualities of a great author, and he is not yet at his zenith—the greatest is behind.

"Payn's books have beguiled me of many a weary hour. For accuracy of detail, ingenuity of construction, and sustained interest, he treads hard upon the heels of Wilkie Collins, while he has a quaint grace of manner and an occasional epigrammatic sprightliness all his own.

---

* I remember one afternoon he commenced to read "Ariadne." Apparently he was trying to interest himself in the first chapter. By-and-by I heard him mutter, "It was an Ariadne, it was a beautiful Ariadne ! it was a divine Ariadne ! It was Ariadne the invincible ! Ariadne, the all-subduing ! Ariadne, the omnipotent ! Yes, no one could doubt that it was Ariadne !" As he shied the book to the other end of the room, to the imminent peril of the sheets of plate-glass with which it was lined, he impatiently exclaimed : " Of course it was Ariadne ! Who the deuce could doubt it after being told who it was a dozen times running, except he was as great an idiot as the author !"

"Oscar Wilde—ah! that airy young gentleman is a *poseur*, there's no mistake about that; but he's much cleverer than people think. A fellow doesn't take a high degree at Oxford for nothing; besides, he has written some noble lines. Then he knows a good deal about art, and nearly everything about painting. I saw him one morning at the Academy spot with unerring accuracy every picture worth looking at. It's true, there were not a great many; but such as they were he spotted them.

"Hardy and Blackmore? Big men, sir, big— almost as big as they are made nowadays. Those two divine girls—'Bathsheba' and 'Lorna Doone'— I'm in love with 'em both, and I like the two men— I mean the labourer and the big fellow, John, John —I forget his name. When I read 'Lorna Doone,' I can see Exmoor, smell the bracken, hear the rush of the roaring river.

"Victor Hugo? Ah, now you speak of a demi-god!

> "'Why, man, he doth bestride the narrow world
> Like a Colossus, and we petty men
> Walk under his huge legs and peep about!'

He is the one supreme genius of the epoch, but geniuses, unfortunately, have the nightmare like other people.

"Georges Sand should have been a man, for she was a most manly woman.

"Glorious old Alexandre Dumas has never been properly appreciated; he is the prince of dramatists.

"Walter Scott was one of the world's benefactors."

Reade execrated poetasters, but adored poets; although he maintained that there was no nobler vehicle to give expression to thought than nervous, simple prose—that prose which he himself cultivated to so true a pitch of art.

"Tennyson," he alleged, "is more pretty than potent." When "The Cup" was produced at the Lyceum, he said, "It might have proved an interesting spectacle if the words had been left out!"

"Browning is a man of genius, but he gives me too much trouble to understand.

"Yes, your friend Buchanan is a poet, but I like his prose best; it is most poetic prose. Balder, I admit, is beautiful, but 'The Shadow of the Sword' is poetry itself.

"Edwin Arnold has sparks of the divine afflatus, and holds his own amongst the best.

"Swinburne has a heart of gold, a muse of fire—a little too fiery, perhaps; but I was young once myself, and I, too, love the great god Pan!"

He always harked back to Byron, Shelley, and Scott; the last, however, was his greatest favourite, and he would recite by heart, with fervour, long passages, almost cantos, of "Marmion" and "The Lady of the Lake."

He sometimes complained bitterly of what he called "the Shakesperean craze," stoutly maintaining that the people who talked most of the bard

knew least about him. In a more genial mood he
frankly admitted the supremacy of the "celestial
thief" to all men who came before or after him. If
I could only set him going about "Othello"—the
one perfect play through all the ages—he would
discourse "thunder and lightning."

Music was his special delight, but his taste was as
exacting as it was cultivated. Italian opera, he
always maintained, was both in form and method an
emasculated and degraded school of art. Wagner
was a giant a hundred years in advance of his age,
and his theory was sublime ; but, alas ! after all, he
lacked melody.

It was very trying to one's temper to sit beside
Reade in a theatre, especially if we happened to
be in the stalls. He would writhe under a bad performance, and not hesitate to express his opinion
openly and freely about it.

"High art" in music he didn't believe in.
"What!" he would exclaim ; "call that braying
with brass and torturing of catgut music ! Ah, give
me music with melody."

Painting and sculpture were either his delight or
his abomination ; a great work he reverenced—nay,
adored ; small things tortured him.

His appreciation of the "younger of the sister
arts" was but too frequently affected by the public
estimate ; hence the idol of to-day was the idiot of
to-morrow, or *vice versâ*. A lady would be a
"goddess" in one part, "a soulless lump of clay,"
in the other. An actor was to-day eulogized

as a genius, to-morrow he was stigmatized as a
" duffer."

A few years ago we went together to see a comedy
acted at a West-End theatre. At the end of the
fourth act Reade rushed out in disgust. Next day he
was rampant about "this idiotic exhibition." He
was especially furious in his diatribes against a
gentleman who formerly had been his *beau-idéal* of
all that was gallant and chivalrous. I took exception
to this wholesale slaughtering, and reminded him of
his former eulogies upon the man whom he now
" slated " so unmercifully.

" I know, I know !" he exclaimed ; " I was ass
enough to admit he was an actor during a temporary
aberration, but then I hadn't seen the beast in ——.
Call that epicene creature, with the parrot's nose
and the peacock's voice, that feather-bed tied in the
middle, supported in a perpendicular position by
two bolsters, masses of wool and wadding, that he
calls legs—call that Punch-like thing the genial,
jovial, manly ——? No, no !

‘These things must not be thought
After these ways : so, it will make us mad.'

I don't think he was quite just to the present
generation of actors, and I should only scatter heart-
burnings were I to quote his opinions, which indeed
varied from day to day, from hour to hour. He was
himself too apt, in connection with this subject,
to " wreathe dead men's bones about living men's
necks."

The two great artists whom he incessantly cited

as being " the choice and master spirits of the age "
were Macready and Farren the elder.   In his estimation, no living actors were fit to be named in the
same century with them.   After them came Mrs.
Glover, who was comedy incarnate.   Mrs. Kean,
however, was only a " matronly and respectable
actress ;" Mrs. Warner, " a passable" Lady Macbeth.   Charles Kean was a " magnificent stage-
manager, but a mediocre actor."   Phelps was "a
great comedian, but a bad tragedian ;" Charles
Mathews, *un petit maître ;* Sothern, " an intellectual
absurdity."   " Bucky " was " funny," Keeley was
"sleepy," Compton was "funereal," Webster was
"artistically spasmodic and perpetually imperfect ;"
and so on to the end.

Among our neighbours he admitted that Rachel
and Lemaitre were geniuses ; but he could not
endure Fechter.   One night, during the latter's
management of the Lyceum, we went to see " The
Master of Ravenswood."   During the contract-
scene, Edgar became very angry with Lucy, and, in
approaching her, gesticulated so violently that for
a moment it seemed as if he were about to strike
her.   Reade growled, " He'll hit her in a minute, I
know he will !   Ah, it's always the way with those
Frenchmen where women are concerned—when they
are not sneaks, they are bullies."

The teacup-and-saucer comedy, with the semi-
chambermaid heroine and the *petit crevé* hero thereof,
he despised utterly.   " Give me," he would exclaim,
" a man—one of Queen Elizabeth's men ; a woman

—none of your skin-and-bone abominations, but a real live woman ; let them have heads on their shoulders, hearts in their bodies, limbs they know how to use, above all limbs, and plenty of them, and 'hair of what colour it shall please heaven;' voices that I can hear, voices that fire me like a trumpet, or melt me like a flute. Those godlike instruments make more music for me than all the fiddles that ever squeaked since the time that Nero fiddled when Rome was afire."

Among his brother-dramatists he yielded Boucicault the first place. "Like Shakespere and Molière," he said, "the beggar steals everything he can lay his hands on ; but he does it so deftly, so cleverly, that I can't help condoning the theft. He picks up a pebble by the shore, and polishes it into a jewel. Occasionally, too, he writes divine lines, and knows more about the grammar of the stage than all the rest of them put together."

Planché was "the modern Aristophanes. His every line glitters with Attic salt, classic grace, culture, and refinement."

Wills was "a splendid poet, but only a passable playwright.

" Herman Merivale's fantasy, ' The White Pilgrim,' is the most poetic play of the period ; but it reads better than it acts—a fatal fault. When he has mastered the art of construction, and learned the use of the pruning-knife, this poet ought to become a big playwright.

"Albery has written one play so good, that I can't understand why he has not written others better.

"Burnand, if 'imitation be the sincerest flattery,' is the greatest flatterer in the world. A mimetic phenomenon. A literary free-lance, who can write without scruple on any subject, and on any side, with equal facility.

"Palgrave Simpson : Dear old Pal's lines are written in water, but his plots are engraved in steel.

"Victorien Sardou : The dramatic genius of the age, and a prince of stage-managers.

"Dumas *fils :* A vinegar-blooded iconoclast— shrewd, clever, audacious, introspective, and mathematically logical.

"Scribe : The cleverest constructor of plots that ever scribbled."

Henry Byron's fertility and fecundity excited the elder dramatist's astonishment more than his admiration. I maintained that Byron wrote admirable lines in abundance. Reade admitted that, but alleged that he could not construct a plot. Of "Our Boys" he remarked : "It is an amusing farce, but the only human character in it (old Middlewick) is Lord Duberly, in coat and trousers, transmogrified into a Cockney chandler."

He was scarcely just to Tom Robertson, alleging that he had palmed off Benedick and Augier's work (" School and Home ") for original composition. Notwithstanding, he was constrained to admit that Robertson had fine moments, especially in the second acts of "Ours " and "Caste." He

maintained, however, that his men were mani-
kins, his women (except the comic ones) clothes-
props ; that his method was small, his comedies
charades. Occasionally I took up the cudgels on
the opposite side, but the argument always ended
when we arrived at the last act of "Caste." That
unfortunate baby of George D'Alroy's always stuck in
the throat of the author of " The Double Marriage."
" Zounds !" he roared, "the brutes yelled at my
poor bairn, but I believe the idiots would have
encored that horse-marine caricature of Rawdon
Crawley if he had given the little beast the pap-
bottle *coram populo.*"

Up to the production of " 'Twixt Axe and Crown,"
he had invariably maintained that Tom Taylor was
one of the strongest and straightest playwrights we
have ; " but," said he, " one must draw the line at
Shakespere and milk-and-water."

Critics he detested, and alleged that their attempted
jurisdiction was a simple impertinence to men of
letters. He was never weary of dilating upon "the
insolence, the ignorance, and the intolerable stupidity
of the gentlemen who arrogate to themselves the
right to form and guide public opinion."

" My great disadvantage among these gentry,"
said he, " is because I write the English language,
which they don't understand, and because I belong
to the 'not inconsiderable class of men who have
not the advantage of being dead !' While Dickens
and Bulwer and Thackeray were alive, these gad-
flies stung and irritated them. Living, they were

very small potatoes ; dead, they are giants.   **There's**
one comfort : when I 'move over to the majority' I
shall take my proper place, and leave these **noble**
youths to the congenial occupation of making mud
pies wherewith to bespatter the coming **race** of
authors."

Caricaturists of noble ideas, especially caricaturists
of his own works, and society journalists, he designated "the scavengers of literature ;" and yet, with
characteristic inconsistency, he suffered **himself to**
be exhibited " At home " **in one of the very journals**
he so persistently decried.

If there **was one** thing about which he prided
himself—even more than **his** plays—it **was his pic-**
tures.   Here is a **list of** the most remarkable in his
collection :

1. **"** The Graces," by Etty (a masterpiece).

2. **" Roland** Graeme and **Catherine Seyton,"** by
John Faed.

3. " Fire in Theatre" (during the pantomime ; a
clown rushing through **the flames with a child in his**
arms), by Laslett Potts.   •

4. " Rydal Water," **by Carrick.**   (This picture
was much praised by Ruskin when it was exhibited.)

5. **" The** Crusader's Return," by Pickersgill.

6. " Andromeda," by Etty.

7. " A Madonna," by Sant.

8. " Portrait of the Chevalier **d'Eon,"** by Reynolds.
(This last is now in the possession of General
Meredith Read, of New **York.)**

The gentleman who does or who did the " Celebrities at Home" in the *World* called upon Reade, saw all these pictures (except " The Graces," which was then at Magdalen), and a dozen others equally valuable, then calmly chronicled his host's want of appreciation for painting, as evidenced by the absence of any pictures of note in his house.

When we were without company, we sometimes played a game of whist : he took dummy, and always beat us.

Apropos of cards—one evening, strolling down Piccadilly, we turned into the Egyptian Hall to see Maskelyne and Cook's entertainment. The room was very full, but the officials, who knew me, brought us two chairs in front. Reade became very much interested in a remarkable mechanical figure which played at cards and won every game. After observing it for some time, he was convinced that he had discovered the trick of it. I had little difficulty in persuading him to mount the platform and try his skill against Psycho. To his astonishment, he was beaten easily, almost ignominiously.

" Well," he said, as we came away, " that's extraordinary ! I never found a man who could lick me game and game ; yet I've been knocked out of time three games running by a beastly automaton.

"'Sblood ! there is something in this more than natural—if philosophy could find it out."

Like women and dogs and the lower animals, he was instinctively pronounced in his likes and dislikes, so much so that his conduct was occasionally most embarrassing to other people ; indeed, at times he was an *enfant terrible* of gigantic growth.

Upon one occasion while he was staying with us, ignorant that she was a pet aversion of his, I asked him to take a certain distinguished actress in to dinner. He gave me a vicious glare, and then marched off with the lady ; but all through dinner he retired upon the impregnable citadel of his deafness, and spake no word, good, bad, or indifferent.

When our guests had departed, he opened fire with, "What did you mean by planting on to me that Gorgon with the head of a seal and the voice of a horse ?"

Au contraire, he could be the most amiable of men, the most genial of gentlemen. When in the mood no one played Amphitryon with a more courtly grace or a more cordial welcome.

Of many pleasant evenings at Albert Gate, I remember one or two with more than usual pleasure, especially one where we had merely a *partie carrée* — our hostess, Reade, myself, and Edwin James, the once eminent barrister, then recently returned from America. The brilliant career of this unfortunate gentleman, and the melancholy termination which compelled him to fly the country, will be fresh in most men's minds. On his return, after an absence of some years, he was left in the cold by all his old friends and associates ; but Reade stood manfully by him. I was particularly interested in the record of this blighted life. The

name of Bonaparte had always been hateful to me
since the *coup d'état*, and I had a vivid recollection
of James's magnificent defence of Dr. Bernard. Nor
was this all : I was cognizant of many generous acts
done by Mr. James in his days of prosperity. One
which occurred within my own knowledge had
always impressed me strongly. One day he found
on the brink of the Serpentine a beautiful young
girl who had been driven from her home by the
barbarity of a brutal step-mother. The wretched
child contemplated suicide. Her demeanour attracted his attention. He spoke to her, induced
her to confide to him her unhappy story, found her
an asylum, fed, clothed, educated her, and enabled
her to go on the stage, where she achieved a distinguished position. To this day that lady reveres
the memory of her benefactor.

Reade and James had been schoolfellows together
at Kettering. Master Edwin had always been the
"bad boy," and he recounted with great glee how
he had induced Charles to play truant with him to
go to Northampton to see a prize-fight, and how
they both caught "toko" when they went back. It
was pleasant to hear "the veterans act their young
encounters o'er again." It was said that Dickens
built his strident legal bully (for whom poor Sidney
Carlton plays lion's provider), in "A Tale of Two
Cities," on Edwin James, and that the great novelist
prided himself on the fidelity of the portrait. I at
least detected no single trait of resemblance between
the learned serjeant and the genial gentleman whose

acquaintance I was delighted to make on the **occasion** of this pleasant **meeting.**

The success of "It is Never Too Late to Mend" being an established fact, Reade's work **was** now in demand, and **Mr.** Alfred Wigan selected "The Double Marriage" (taken **from** "Le Château Grantier" of Macquet) to inaugurate the opening of the new Queen's Theatre—that unfortunate building, destined **to** prove hereafter so disastrous to Reade, so ruinous **to me.** Here, indeed, appeared **a** magnificent opportunity. A new, elegant, and commodious theatre, **in an** eligible situation, **a** fashionable management, with abundant capital **at** its back ; never **was there a better chance for** author to distinguish himself. The play, too, is "an excellent play, **well digested in the scenes, and set down** with **as much modesty as cunning."** Magnificent scenery, costumes, and appointments, **a** powerful **and** admirable company, **were provided. Anticipa-**tion and expectation were on tiptoe. **A** few breezes had occurred at rehearsal, **but** they were **mere** summer-storms, and had been smoothed over. All **was** in good order : **the author was** sanguine, **the** actors hopeful, the management confident of success. An eager **and** excited audience crammed the theatre from floor to dome **on the opening night.**

The play began **well ; the audience were pleased. As act** succeeded **act, they became more and more** interested. **At last** came the **great** situation **of the fourth** act, which it was confidently anticipated would take the house by storm. And it did, but not in the way the author intended.

Josephine, the heroine of " The Double Marriage," has given birth to a child under circumstances which, though ultimately explained satisfactorily, appear at the moment most compromising. The child is discovered ; the unfortunate mother's honour, happiness, her very life, are at stake. In this supreme moment, her sister, a young girl, the incarnation of truth, purity, and innocence, comes forward in the presence of her affianced husband and her mother, the haughty Comtesse Grandpré, and, to save Josephine from shame, brands herself with infamy. Taking the child in her arms, the innocent girl declares that it is hers.

I can conceive no dramatic situation in existence stronger than this. Miss Ellen Terry had returned to the stage ; to her well-grounded skill was entrusted this striking incident. Circumstances had invested her first appearance with unusual interest. She was equal to the occasion : her form dilated, her eyes sparkled with fire, her voice trembled, as she exclaimed, in tones of passionate emotion, " *I* am its mother !"

At this moment, Reade told me, there burst forth a roar of derision which shook the building, and a howl of savage laughter arose which he should never forget if he lived to the age of Old Parr. The curtain fell amid yells, and the piece was doomed there and then : indeed, it was only kept in the bill until something could be prepared to take its place.

The presence of that unfortunate baby "cooked" " The Double Marriage ;" and yet at or about that very time another theatre was being crowded nightly with audiences, which not only tolerated the wonderful D'Alroy baby in the last act of " Caste," but "gushed" at it. The critics who saw genius in the one piece could detect nothing but the essence of absurdity in the other. The adage that one man may steal a horse and ride off on its back, unmolested, to glory, while if the other looks over the hedge he is dragged to durance vile, was never more appositely illustrated than on this occasion.

Here was another facer for my poor friend : at the very moment when he felt assured that he had got firm held of the dramatic public, hey-presto ! the phantom vanished, and he had to begin all over again.

Immediately preceding the production of " It is Never Too Late to Mend," " The Colleen Bawn " had achieved a great success. Boucicault and Reade were on terms of friendly intimacy. It naturally occurred to them that the names of the authors of " The Colleen Bawn " and of " It is Never Too Late to Mend " were names to conjure by. They would write a novel first, dramatize it after, and sweep both England and America with it. The novel was projected, and I believe the publishers paid for it the largest sum ever given up to that period in this country in advance for a work of fiction.

In its narrative form " Foul Play " was highly successful. Then came the question of the dramatization, and it was soon found that when "two men ride on horseback, one must ride behind." Both authors objected to take a back seat, and they rode off in different directions. Boucicault took his version to the Holborn Theatre, where it failed most signally. Reade brought his adaptation to me. It was a powerful but sprawling play; strength, however, it had in abundance, and all that was necessary was to lick it into shape: when it was first put into my hands, the second act was in seven scenes. I put them all into one, suggested the whole of the business of "The Crossing the Line," in the third act, and transposed and arranged the island act until it assumed its present form. The drama was produced the first season of my new theatre at Leeds, with immediate and pronounced success, and I am emboldened to say was one of the best-acted and best-mounted plays that has been produced in this generation.

Reade was always jealous of his "words," and woe betide the unhappy wight who dared to tamper with them. It required great diplomacy to induce him to accept my cutting and slashing and reconstruction before we commenced rehearsals; but when we got on the stage, not another word would he allow to be excised. At the end of the fourth act he had allotted me a speech of twenty tedious, explanatory lines to speak after the heroine had quitted the stage, and I was left alone on Godsend Island. It was in vain that I pointed out that the speech was an anticlimax, that the explanation could

be deferred to the next act, etc. : " My composition,
my boy ; my composition," he exclaimed ; " besides, it
is the articulation " (a favourite word of his) " of the
act." I might as well have whistled against thunder
as argue with him while he was in the imperative
mood : so I said no more about it, but took my
own course. I arranged privately with the prompter
to " ring down " at the proper climax of the scene,
and the result was as I had anticipated—the act-
drop fell amidst a perfect tempest of applause. We
had achieved a genuine *coup de théâtre*, and the audience rose at us ; nor would they suffer the play to
proceed till the author himself bowed his acknow-
ledgments, when they cheered him again and again.
Then he came round, panting with excitement, tears
of joy running down his cheeks, and he absolutely
hugged me with delight, as he exclaimed, " Oh !
you traitor—you villain—you young vagabond !—
you were right, after all !—it's beautiful—beautiful !"

This is only one instance out of a hundred I could
cite to prove that, despite his elaborate theories
about art, my friend was in reality only guided by
actual practical results. I have frequently known
him take grave exception to an actor's conception of
a part at rehearsal, but if the offender struck fire at
night, the end justified the means, even if his views
were diametrically opposed to those of the author.
If from some adverse circumstance—a bad house, an
east wind, an unsympathetic audience—the play did
not elicit the usual modicum of applause, then the
actors were stigmatized as " duffers "—" duffers, sir,

who have defiled my composition, mixed ditch-water
with my champagne, murdered **my work.**" The
next night perhaps there was a good house, perhaps
the wind was not in the east, perhaps a thousand
things : at any rate, if the play was received enthusi-
astically, then all was condoned and forgiven. The
popular applause was music to him ; he would
ensconce himself in his box, turn his back **to** the
stage, and as the audience laughed **or cried** he
laughed and cried with them, and their tears or
cheers **were always** his barometers **of the** actor's
ability. I have often heard him say that he thought
the great orator or the great actor, quaffing the full
wine of applause crushed in one moment into a
golden cup and drained from the public heart, **was**
the most enviable of human beings.

No man, except himself, ever combined in **one**
and the same person such an extraordinary mass of
contradictions as Charles Reade. If anyone assailed
him he dipped **his pen** in vitriol, and poured the
vials of his wrath upon his luckless adversary. On
these occasions nothing could restrain the headstrong
rush of his impetuosity, nothing check the torrent
of his effusive objurgations. Yet, on the other
hand, if called upon to advise a friend under similar
circumstances, he not infrequently exercised quite a
judicial function, and was the very incarnation of
mildness.

A remarkable illustration of this occurred while
we were at X——. The night before our opening,

a certain pressman had announced over his pipe and
his pot his intention of "slating" us.   This orna-
ment to journalism turned up at night very drunk,
and absolutely unable to get into the theatre without
assistance.   He slept quietly and composedly through
the greater portion of the performance.   All the
same, the next day we got the promised "slating."

Perhaps no man has been more fulsomely flattered
or more villainously abused than I have been, consequently I have learned to take "fortune's buffets
and rewards with equal thanks;" but this onslaught,
knowing its origin, was more than I could stomach,
so I rushed at pen, ink, and paper, and wrote a
letter that was, I fear, more distinguished by vigour
of vituperation than anything else.   When I had
finished this precious epistle, I took it to Reade.
He read it carefully, and said very quietly:

"Yes, a good letter—very good.   Couldn't you
make it a little hotter?"

"I'll try," said I, and in the innocence of my
heart I took it away, and, after half an hour spent
in polishing it up, and embellishing it with every
epithet of scorn and contempt in my vocabulary,
I returned in triumph.

"Not hot enough by half, my boy," said he.
"Put it by for a week, then read it; put it by for
another week, and then—put it in your scrap-book,
or, better still, put it in the fire.   Stop! I'll save
you the trouble."   And he put it in the fire there
and then, saying, "Now it is as hot as it can be
made."   So there was an end of that letter.

Now for the obverse of the picture. Upon a certain occasion we had gone to pass Sunday at my house in York, and on our way to Manchester, after my wont, I bought all the papers and magazines I could lay my hands upon at the railway-station. Among them was a copy of a satirical journal called the *Mask*. Upon opening it, I found a loathsome caricature of Reade and Boucicault on the first page, and, farther on, a violent personal attack on both authors, accusing them of having stolen " Foul Play " bodily from a French drama (by an author whose name I have forgotten) called " La Porte-feuille Rouge." Side by side with the Boucicault and Reade composition was printed the text of the French author. As I looked up I saw Reade in the opposite corner of the carriage, with eyes apparently closed. In certain moods he had a facility for feigning sleep, just like a cat waiting to spring upon an unfortunate mouse. Holding my breath, I furtively tried to slip the *Mask* under the seat. At this moment, to my astonishment, he opened his eyes wide, and said, " John, when you've done with that yellow magazine, hand it over this way."

I handed him the *Cornhill* and tried to hide the other behind me.

" Not this !" he said : " the other *yellow* thing !"

There was no help for it, so I gave it him. He cast a disdainful glance at the caricature, and shrugged his shoulders in silence ; but when he had finished reading the *acte d'accusation*, he flushed up to the eyes, exclaiming, " It is a lie, an infamous calumny! I never even heard the name of the infernal piece."

I don't think he had; but if his *collaborateur* had not, I am very much mistaken. Anyhow, he had hit on the same idea, the same incidents, and something very like the same words as the Frenchman, only unfortunately the Frenchman had hit upon them first. The "undying one" was too old a bird, and too accustomed to poach upon other people's preserves, to be trepanned into correspondence on the subject. Reade, despite his good advice to me, rushed at his assailants like a bull at a piece of red rag, and vented his rage in a rabid and remarkable paper, published under the title of "The Sham Sample Swindle." It is easier, however, to pelt one's adversaries with hard words than to refute a charge of plagiarism, and in this instance it must be admitted the "pseudonymunculæ" had the best of it.

After "Foul Play" had been acted five or six weeks at Leeds, we took it to Manchester, and subsequently to all the great provincial theatres, where it invariably attracted crowded houses. Notwithstanding its success in the country, the doors of all the London theatres were closed against us, in consequence of the failure of Boucicault's previous adaptation. It was therefore arranged between Reade and myself that I should go to America to produce this and other plays. It was essential for me to set sail on a particular day, so as to anticipate the action of certain Transatlantic pirates who had stolen a copy of our play. My baggage was in Liverpool, my berth secured, when an accident prevented my sailing. I had to attach my signature to the lease of one of my theatres. Fortunately for me, the document was not ready ; inasmuch as upon the production of the piece in New York a curious exchange of civilities took place. I forget the exact circumstances, save that I know revolvers were introduced and used pretty freely, and two or three people were killed and others wounded. On the whole, I did not regret my absence on that interesting occasion.

Abandoning altogether the projected tour to America, I suggested to Reade the subject of the Sheffield outrages for a story, and a drama with a part in it which I thought especially adapted to my method and resources. He accepted the suggestion, and we went over to Sheffield together, where I introduced him to Mr. Lang, the courageous journalist ("Holdfast"), through whose initiative, and the indomitable pluck of the late Mr. Roebuck, the Parliamentary Commission was obtained by means of which the perpetrators of the atrocities were unearthed. Before leaving the town, we interviewed the miscreant, afterward introduced into the story as Grotait, and went to his public-house to make certain sketches ; we also visited the scenes of the various outrages, so as to provide ourselves with local colouring for the future drama. On its production in the *Cornhill*, the novel created a great sensation ; but the drama ?

Our intention was to play the piece for a week in Leeds, at the end of the summer season, as a sort of public rehearsal, then to take the Adelphi and produce it there. The difficulty was that it involved as much expense to "get up" the play for a week as for a month or two; but that could be got over by bringing it to Leeds again after its run in town. Although the drama was as yet unwritten, we arranged about the scenery, and my people went to work with a will, and a very elaborate production it was.

My own company being then on tour with "Foul Play," I had to engage people from all parts of the kingdom.

Reade promised to be ready with the manuscript and parts for the first rehearsal, which was to take place a week previous to the date arranged for the production of the play. When he arrived from town, I found, to my dismay, that he had only completed the first act. He assured me, however, that he had it all in his head, and that he could get it out as quickly as he could write it down. We commenced our rehearsals, and he stayed at home to work at the remainder of the play. Alas! the next day he was taken seriously ill with a violent attack of neuralgia and toothache, which prostrated him during the greater portion of the week. It was not until the following Monday (the day on which the play actually ought to have been produced) that we got even the second act!

I was so dissatisfied with the state of affairs, and

with the construction of the play, that, foreseeing nothing but failure, despite the great expense already incurred, I was disposed to abandon the idea of doing the piece altogether; but he appealed to me so strongly on the subject that my better judgment gave way, and I yielded to his wishes.

The position was most disheartening and distressing. It was now Wednesday, the third act was a bitter bad one, and there was neither time nor opportunity to revise or alter; under no circumstances could the existence of the piece be prolonged beyond Saturday, inasmuch as on Monday the Italian opera-company opened; after them came Schneider and company with the "Grande Duchesse;" after her, Charles Mathews, Phelps, Sothern, and the dog-days. Altogether, it was a bad look-out. Driven to desperation, I announced the piece for Friday. The company were quite perfect in the first three acts, and by half-past eleven on Thursday night our rehearsals were as complete as I could make them.

We then set the scenes for the fourth act. At twelve o'clock Reade, pale and exhausted, came with the last act. I had prepared some refreshment for the company, and requested them to wait in the green-room while I ran through this act with him. I then called everybody on the stage, and, holding the manuscript, I read through every part, and arranged the business of every situation three times consecutively. This occupied us until two o'clock in the morning. Dismissing the rehearsal, I then called the last

act for two o'clock in the following afternoon. I
copied my own part there and then. The prompter
and copyist, whom I had taken the precaution to
send home hours before, so that they had been at
rest all the evening, now took the manuscript, and
sat up all night to copy the other parts. At nine
o'clock in the morning every lady and gentleman
was furnished with his or her part. And now
occurred a circumstance without parallel or precedent in my experience. Notwithstanding the
fatigues and anxieties of the preceding night, and
the lateness of the hour at which they quitted the
theatre, to the honour of the company be it stated
that everyone was letter perfect in the text at the
two o'clock rehearsal, and that night "Put Yourself
in His Place" was produced textually perfect, and
without one hitch from the rise to the fall of the
curtain!

My worst anticipations were, however, realized.
Through the uncertainty of the announcements,
there was a very bad house. The first act struck
fire; the church-scene, in the second act, electrified
the audience. In the third act, the interest drooped;
in the fourth act it died out altogether, like the
expiring gleam of a farthing rushlight. On Saturday the house was no better, and the verdict of the
preceding night was not reversed. The play was a
direful failure, and involved me in a loss of between
five and six hundred pounds on the two representa-
tions, as well as depriving me of a cherished illusion,
as I had hoped to distinguish myself as the hero.

There was an abundance of splendid material in the
work, finely-drawn characters, vigorous lines, exciting
incidents ; but it was put together so hastily and so
crudely that it was utterly impossible for it to succeed.

I suggested an entire reconstruction of the drama,
but at that period Reade would not hear of it.
Finding that he remained obdurate, I decided to
have nothing further to do with the piece, which
was fortunate for me, inasmuch as its production at
the Adelphi, shortly afterward, involved a very considerable loss.

I am happy to say, however, that my secession
from this speculation in no way interfered with our
friendly relations ; and, indeed, Mr. Reade scarcely
ever produced a piece afterward about which he did
not do me the honour to consult me.

The publication of " The Wandering Heir " in a
Christmas number of the *Graphic* yielded him a large
sum, and evoked a very hot controversy with the
late Mr. Mortimer Collins and his accomplished wife
as to an alleged charge of plagiarism from Swift in
various parts of the story. There was some very
hard hitting on both sides in reference to this matter.
When his honesty was called in question, Reade's
sensibility was deeply wounded and his indignation
was unbounded ; yet I have reason to know that he
afterward deeply regretted some of the strong things
he emitted on this occasion. His was " a most
manly wit," and was pained to " hurt a woman."

It was with the money earned by the publication

of the story that he rushed headlong into management, to produce a drama founded on it. As usual,
the London theatres were closed against him, and,
being occupied with my engagements in various
parts of the country, I could no longer assist him as
I used to do. He therefore took the Amphitheatre
in Liverpool, where the risk and responsibility were
great, and the profit little, if any.

At his request I came over to Liverpool from the
Isle of Man to see the production of " The Wandering Heir." Mr. Tom Taylor and his family had
been staying in Douglas for the season, and, as they
were returning on the Monday, they asked us to
stay and accompany them. During the voyage I
more than once regretted that we did not take their
advice, for when they came over the sea was like a
mill-dam, while we had a most awful passage : a
ship, with all hands aboard, went down before our
very eyes, and we reached Liverpool more dead
than alive. Nevertheless we managed to crawl to
the theatre that night somehow, and, oh, how kind
and hospitable Reade was ! He gave up his own
rooms to us, and welcomed us with all his old win-
ning grace and ever-genial hospitality.

I pause here to remark that Mrs. John Wood's
impersonation of Philippa was a delightful performance. Of course this admirable actress was, if
anything, too much the woman, and a very fine
woman she was, and is, for that matter ; but she was
a trifle too plump, too ebullient, and too knowing to
realize typically the girlish Philippa. Yet what

JOSEPH JEFFERSON AS RIP VAN WINKLE.

splendid art it was! what depths of tenderness lay
under the superstructure of archness! what sublime
assurance asserted itself at the tip of her saucy nose!
what wealth of fun lay lurking in the corners of her
eyes, and ready " to play Bo-peep and burst out in
spite of her!" It was worth being sea-sick from
Douglas to Liverpool only to hear her say, " Parson,
please buy me a pair of breeches and make a boy
of me !"

After the run of "The Wandering Heir" in
Liverpool, Mr. Reade organized a company to take
it on tour. He commenced operations in Notting-
ham, where he invited me to come and stay with
him for a few days ; and a very jolly time we had of
it out of the theatre. In it, he was still doomed
to be unfortunate, for the houses were wretched.
Subsequently, he brought the piece and his company
to Leeds ; here again he was disappointed, so was I.
Anyhow, it was of no use crying over spilt milk, so I
proposed that we should go over to the Theatre
House in York for two or three weeks.

Dear old York is a charming city at all times, but
in the summer it is delightful. This holiday is one
of the pleasantest recollections of my life : we both
cast care to the winds, and gave ourselves up to
idleness and enjoyment. In the few brief holidays
of my busy life, like a truant school-boy, I have
always felt that I had broken bounds, and that if I
were found out I should be chained and secured,
perhaps beaten, before I was driven back to my
books ; and I believe this was what Reade felt at

that time. Certainly, he was the biggest boy in the house, always a jest on his tongue, always a laugh on his lips. Day by day we explored the antiquities of the city and the neighbourhood. Then there were driving, boating, and swimming. In those days he stripped like Hercules, and easily knocked me out of time in swimming, though in walking I certainly had the best of it. At night we returned, hungry as hunters; and so, with good company, good fare, quaint stories, honest mirth, and song, the joyous hours sped fast, till the bell of the old minster reminded us that it was time to go to rest, if we meant to get up at a reasonable hour on the morrow. The days passed all too quickly. He had to return to take charge of his company, and I had to go somewhere to act—I forget where now.

The night before we left York, a strange and remarkable coincidence occurred. As we strolled along in the moonlight, by the river's bank, he told us a terrible story of a man who had married a servant of his. There was a child born of the union, a little boy of four or five. The poor woman had left the child with her mother. The husband, a morose and drunken ruffian, who when he was not drunk was mad, quarrelled with his wife, and in a fit of drunken frenzy took the child away. Some weeks after, the poor little fellow was found strangled in a cellar in St. Giles's. Suspicion, of course, attached to the father, but he had disappeared; no trace of him could be found. The poor mother left Reade's service, drooped, and died. At this stage of the

story we had approached the bridge. Just under
the archway a strange object was gently floating up
and down in the water, under the moonbeams. It
was the dead face of *the* man, the very *man* he had
been talking about.

The next day we left York.

Up to the very last Reade regarded this little
holiday as a green spot in his life. Only a few
months before his death, after a fit of despondency,
he brightened up and exclaimed, "Ah, John! if we
could only recall the days and nights at York, at
Lion House*—the wit, the dalliance, the health, the
strength, the appetite, the happy hours! Ah me!
ah me! the days that are no more!"

The tour of "The Wandering Heir" still continued
to be unsatisfactory. The want of attraction in the
piece Reade charged to the stupidity of the public.
He became quite obstinate on the subject, and, to
prove the provincial public wrong, he took the
Queen's Theatre, then in the market, and brought
out the unfortunate play there. It commenced admirably, but got so dreadfully out of latitude at the
end that just as it was in sight of port—smash, it
came to pieces. The result, as usual, was a considerable loss. Soon after this he telegraphed me to
dine with him at the Garrick, to discuss an important proposal, which turned out to be that I
should join him in management at Astley's, where
he proposed to produce "It is Never Too Late to

* My house at Leeds.

Mend," with Miss Ellen Terry, Mr. Calhaem, and
other distinguished artists ; but I not only declined to
participate in the speculation, but tried to dissuade him
from it. It was in vain that I recalled to his recollection the Boucicaultian fiasco at the Theatre Royal,
Westminster. " He would have a shy," he said,
" if he lost his hat." I suggested that he would lose
his head first. Anyhow, he lost his money.

For some time after this he stuck to novel-writing,
but always buzzed about the theatres, as a moth
buzzes around the flame of a candle, and but too
frequently, like the poor insect, he singed his wings.

It was about this period that I entered upon my own
ill-starred speculation at the Queen's Theatre. Then
he was once more in his element; scarce a day or
night passed that he was not at the stage-door, or
my house, advising, suggesting, and taking as much
interest in the fortunes of Henry V. as if he were
to be the hero of Agincourt, instead of myself.
Months of hard work began to tell on me. A few
weeks before the production took place, he said to
me, " You seem tired and overworked. I want you
to be as fresh as paint when you come out. Let us
run down to Oxford for a week, and I'll undertake
to freshen you up."

So to Oxford we went. He did the honours of the
glorious old city, showed us all the lions, the stately
colleges, the beautiful gardens, the statues, the libraries
—the Bodleian especially, where he assisted me in
hunting up certain authorities I wanted. On Sunday
he donned his cap and gown and escorted us to his

collegiate church. It seemed strange to hear everybody call him "doctor," though not at all strange that everyone he met seemed to know him and to love him. The glimpse of Oxford life afforded by this brief visit has left quite a pictorial imprint on my mind, a memory which no time can efface, but which others have described so well—notably, my friend Herman Merivale—that I dare not attempt it. I asked the "doctor" where the theatre was. He flushed with indignation as he made answer :

" In the old times plays were acted in the colleges by the great players of the Elizabethan age and later periods before kings and queens, chancellors, vice-chancellors, deans, proctors, and the like ; yet now, here, where every stone in the street knows my foot-fall, where, please God, my name will be remembered when I am dead—now, while I am living, there is not a place where one of my plays can be acted ; for the theatre—the theatre, my dear boy, I should be ashamed to show it to you—would disgrace a decent show at a country fair." While listening to this indignant denunciation, I little dreamt that in time to come I should even for a single night be condemned to act in the miserable shed which, to the discredit of the municipality, the authorities of the university, and the nineteenth century, is still designated the " Theatre Royal, Oxford."*

When the curtain fell on " Henry V." on the night

* Since the above lines were written this scandalous anomaly has been removed, and Oxford has been provided with an elegant and commodious theatre.

of my *début* in town, Charles Reade was the first
man to come round to my room to congratulate me,
and the last to leave it. Had I been his son, he
could not have taken greater pride in me or have
manifested more tender sympathy. The next morning at ten o'clock he was at my house. A
certain journal had distinguished itself by the viru-
lence and mendacity of an onslaught on me and my
production. I had seen it before his arrival. He
burst out, "You've seen it; of course you have.
Some damned good-natured friend would be sure to
let you know. Don't heed it, my dear boy; don't
heed it. Look how they served me. Remember
how that wooden-headed bully and blockhead in the
Edinburgh and the donkeys in the *Saturday* let me
have it. Bah! what does an idiot like that know about
art or acting? What was it Dryden said to Nat Lee?

> "'They praise while they accuse
> The too much vigour of your youthful muse;
> For how should every sign-post dauber know
> The worth of Titian or of Angelo?'

"There, there! not a word about it; don't even
think of it. We shall expect you to dinner to-night,
seven sharp. Ta, ta." And away he went, leaving
me all the better for his sympathy.

When, later on, I went to star in the country, he
produced "Foul Play," transformed into "The
Scuttled Ship," at the Olympic, and a comedy taken
from a piece of Sardou's, of which, though I saw it
acted in Paris and Rouen (much better acted at
Rouen than in Paris!), I cannot recall the name. I

believe both plays achieved a *succès d'estime*, but that
was all.

A story was soon after this **published in** America,
called "That Lass o' Lowrie's." It was written by
a lady, Mrs. Hodgson Burnett, evidently an English-
woman, for it was a very faithful picture of Lancashire life. Mr. **Joseph Hatton and** the late **Mr.**
Mathison dramatized the book and produced it for a
short time at one of the West-End **theatres.** Mr.
Reade saw it, and **was struck, not** with the drama
(although that, I have been assured, was a very good
one), but **with** Miss **Rose Leclerq, who** made **a** great
mark as the **heroine;** and he intimated that after a
certain **time had elapsed** he **should** dramatize the
subject himself. Here ensued **another** wordy **war-**
fare; Hatton and Mathison **grumbled,** but with the
aid of a slight subsidy **from** Reade **an amicable**
understanding was arrived at with them. **Mrs.**
Burnett, however, was not **so** easily appeased; **and**
it must be admitted she had the **best of** the argument. When Reade urged **that** every play he
had done had been pirated **in** America, the irate
authoress retorted that **she had** never pirated his
plays, and therefore he had no right to pirate her
story. In vain he offered **to** divide any emolument
which might accrue with her. The lady remained
obdurate, he remained obstinate; and once more he
had recourse to the Amphitheatre at Liverpool for
the production of "Joan"—so he called his new play
—and again the ill-luck which persistently attended
his every attempt at management followed him.

At this very time I happened to be fulfilling a fortnight's engagement at the Theatre Royal, Manchester. To my astonishment and delight, Mr. Reade turned up at my rooms the morning of my arrival (his lodgings were but a stone's-throw from ours). While we remained in Manchester we were inseparable. "Joan" was being acted at the Queen's Theatre there, by his company. He admitted frankly that it was a commercial failure; he could not understand the reason why, but there was the fact staring him in the face nightly in the shape of empty benches.

We were so fortunate as to "strike oil" in my play of "Valjean," taken from " Les Misérables," which, when last in Paris, I had obtained Victor Hugo's permission to dramatize. Guided, as usual, by practical results, Reade turned his back upon his own play and came to see ours nightly. After he had been once or twice, he began, after his old fashion, to take stock of the audience and to interpret the play through their smiles and tears and their applause. Evidently this popular barometer satisfied him, for that night at supper he proposed to me to come to town and open the unfortunate Queen's with "Valjean," at Christmas. He would provide a magnificent *mise en scène*, revise the play, and attach his name to it as joint author. He was eager for the fray, and wanted to go into it at once. Unfortunately, I had made other engagements, and was thus compelled to forego a chance which might have retrieved his losses and my own.

At the end of my engagement in Manchester I

had to go to Scotland, but, at his request, we prolonged our stay in order to see "Joan." After the
play he took us home to supper, and then frankly
asked me what I thought of the piece. I told him
that I thought he had never written nobler lines or
more graphic sketches of character, but that the
barbarous and cacophonous dialect, the gloom, the
squalor, the everlasting minor key which pervaded
the entire drama, would prevent its ever becoming
a popular success. In the fulness of time he himself reluctantly arrived at the same conclusion.

As we went away into the winter's night—or
rather morning, for it was two o'clock when we
started for the North—he took a huge silk muffler
from his own neck and tied it round mine. We
never paid so dearly for seeing a play, for the very
marrow in our bones seemed frozen when we got to
Glasgow the next day.

The failure of "Joan" had almost disgusted him
with the theatre, and he had actually retired from
active participation in the fight, when it occurred to the
new management of the Princess's that "It is Never
Too Late to Mend" had not been acted in town for
years, that it had been a great success at that theatre
before, and might be so again. Arrangements were
therefore made for its production : there was only one
difficulty, the part of Jacky. Adequate representatives could be found for all the other parts. Indeed,
Messrs. Henry Loraine, George Vining, Sinclair,
Vernon, and Henry Neville had already played my
part, and Mr. Charles Warner was now anxious to

play it; but there was but one Jacky, and his name
was Calhaem.   Upon the first production of the
drama, Mr. Calhaem wished to play Crawley (the
part originally intended for Robson), but, fortunately,
he yielded to my persuasion and played Jacky—an
impersonation marked by genius of the highest order.
"The race is not always to the swift nor the battle to
the strong," and this admirable and versatile actor has
unfortunately been debarred other opportunities for
distinction.   This unique and extraordinary creation
is, however, quite worthy of being remembered with
the Dundreary of Sothern, the Rip Van Winkle of
Jefferson, and the Digby Grant of Irving.

Strange to say, at the time of the proposed revival
of "It is Never Too Late to Mend," Mr. Calhaem
was again under an engagement to me in the country.
I could ill afford to lose him; but when Reade and
the manager both appealed to me, I could not say
"Nay." So Jacky once more assisted to pilot "It is
Never Too Late to Mend" into the haven of success.

At or about this time I came across Zola's extraordinary book, "L'Assommoir."   It struck me that
some of the incidents might be utilized in a drama
of English life.   I prepared a scenario—got a friend
to assist me—the play was completed and ready for
representation. When I came up to town shortly
afterward, I found that Reade had gone to Paris
to see the play then acting at the Ambigu, and
to confer with Zola on the subject of transferring it
to the English stage.   I wrote to Reade, telling him
what I had done in reference to the same subject,

and asking whether my piece would trespass on his *donnée*. He wrote me in return, reminding me how often he had been baffled and defeated in the theatre, assuring me that he was in sight of port at last, and imploring me in the name of our old friendship not to cross him in the ambition of his life. I could not withstand this appeal, and my unfortunate piece disappeared into the wastepaper-basket.

A few months afterward, " Drink " was produced, and I was delighted to find him once more a successful dramatist ; he was happy, triumphant.

In the midst of his happiness, at the height of his triumph, the blow fell which left him a desolate, broken man. I was abroad at the time, but there is a letter lying before me now in which, after recording the continued success of the new play, he refers to the struggles of his youth, the vicissitudes of his manhood, his repeated failures, his perpetual disappointments in the theatre ; "and now," he continues, " now that I have attained the summit of my ambition, now that I am rich and prosperous, now——"

There is an inscription on a tomb in Willesden churchyard which will best tell the remainder of the sad story. I quote this memorable epitaph in full :

'Here lies the great heart of Laura Seymour, a brilliant artist, a humble Christian, a charitable woman, a loving daughter, sister, and friend, who lived for others from her childhood. Tenderly pitiful to all God's creatures, even to some that are frequently destroyed or neglected, she wiped away the tears from many faces, helping the poor with her savings, and the sorrowful with her earnest pity. When the eye saw her it blessed her, for her face was sunshine, her voice was melody, and her heart was sympathy. Truth could say more, and Sorrow pines to enlarge upon her virtues, but this would ill accord with her humility, who justly disclaimed them all, and relied only on

the merits of her Redeemer. After months of acute suffering, bowing
with gentle resignation, and with sorrow for those who were to lose
her, not for herself, she was released from her burden, and fell asleep
in Jesus, September 27, 1879, aged 59 years. " Blessed are the merciful,
for they shall obtain mercy" (Matt. v. 7). This grave was made for
her and for himself by Charles Reade, whose wise counsellor, loyal
ally, and bosom friend she was for twenty-four years, and who mourns
her all his days.'

Twelve months or more passed before we met
again. He was greatly changed, and lived more in
recalling the past and preparing for the future than
in the present ; but we found many topics of common
interest, and he loved to talk of old times.

I persuaded him with difficulty to accompany me
once or twice to the theatre. We went to Drury
Lane to see the Meiningen people, who appeared
to interest him.

When I next quitted London I understood from
him that he was engaged upon some Biblical studies,
and that he did not intend to write for the theatre
again.

Apropos of Biblical studies: at this very time
he related with great gusto a story about the
late Sheridan Knowles. In his declining years,
especially when he was ill, the veteran poet, who
was a fine, noble-hearted, but hot-headed and eccentric Irishman, became exceedingly pious ; as soon
as he got better he changed his views, illustrating in
fine form the adage :

> "The devil was ill, and the devil a monk would be ;
> The devil got well, and the devil a monk was he."

During his fits of piety he regarded, or affected to
regard, the play-house as the bottomless pit of

abomination ; but, though he scorned the sin, he did
not scorn the wages of it. I don't mean "death,"
but the fees arising from the representation of his
plays. He was "death" on to them, certainly !
And, ill or well, pious or otherwise, woe betide
the luckless manager who ventured to do one of
Knowles' plays without paying him for it !*

One morning, ever so many years ago, in Reade's
earliest juvenalia, the two authors met at the door of
Mr. Benjamin Webster's house in Brompton. At
that period Reade was more famous for his facts
than for anything else, and it was well known how
hard he worked in getting up his data. Knowles
was coming out savagely pious because Webster had
declined to accept a play of his. Reade was going
in with a pile of manuscript under his arm, hoping
to succeed in inducing the manager to cast his eye
over a comedy. In his usual effusive fashion Knowles
roared out, "How are you, my boy ? God bless my
sowl, how are you, and how have you been this age
past ? You're the very man I wanted to see ! It's
no use trying to see him," indicating Webster : " the

---

* Apropos, while these lines are actually passing through the press,
I read that, at her recent death, the poet's widow (formerly the beautiful Miss Elphinstone the actress) bequeathed £1,000 each to the
Pastors' College in connection with the Metropolitan Tabernacle, the
Midnight Meeting Movement (Red Lion Square), and the Stockwell
Orphanage for Boys (Clapham Road) ; £100 to the minister, deacons,
and elders of Ardberg Baptist Chapel (Rothsay, Isle of Bute), for
general purposes. Evidently the Tabernacle does not disdain to sub-
sidize the temple of Satan, nor did the late lamented withdraw the
plays from the stage, inasmuch as she has bequeathed £300, and all
the manuscripts and writings and the interest arising from the acting
of the dramas of James Sheridan Knowles, to Mary Knowles Rice.

owld thief had the impudence to tell me just now
that tragedy's a dhrug in the market, and that he's
got enough comedies to keep the Haymarket going
for the next century! How lucky is this matin'!
I've got a splendid pot-boiler—a commission to write
a polemical pamphlet to pitch into the Papists! I'm
all right except for the facts. I don't know anything
about them. Unfortunately, that's my wake point,
but it's your sthrong one; so if you'll do the facts
I'll do the fighting, and we'll divide the plunder
between us."

Whether that pamphlet ever saw the light or not
I am unable to say; I only know that Reade left
the poet to do the " facts " as well as the " fighting."

To my astonishment, some few months after I
left town, I received the following letter :

'Blomfield Villas,
'Oct. 16, 1882.

" DEAR JOHN,

" I was in hopes you would have reported
progress from the Channel Isle [Jersey] ere this.
. . . Will you now kindly draw on your memory
and send me a list of good old short pieces—say
forty-five minutes—merry, but interesting, and not
all practical jokes and nonsense? I want one for
the Adelphi, which I lease from November 18th, for
three months, to bring out our new drama, ' Love
and Money.' Low comedian, young man, two or
three ladies if necessary.

" Yours always,
" READE."

I was rather glad to hear that he was in harness once more, knowing as I did that loneliness and want of occupation would prey upon his mind.

He told me afterward that he had gradually drifted into this speculation against his inclination. The American right of the drama " Love and Money " * had been disposed of for two thousand pounds to an enterprising manager in the States, upon condition that it was to be brought out first at the Adelphi Theatre. The money was paid in advance. All at once a difficulty occurred. The management of the Adelphi declined to accept the play. If it was not produced there, the American purchase-money would be forfeited. The authors were on the horns of a dilemma. In the end they decided to take the theatre and produce the drama themselves.

To give a fillip to the business, the drama of " Dora," founded upon Tennyson's poem of that name, was revived. I ought to have referred to this play in the chronological order of its production, but women and actors are not good at dates. I have tried to keep pretty straight in this particular, but I fear I have not succeeded. I remember, however, as though it were yesterday, that seventeen or eighteen years ago Reade took me and a couple of friends down to Richmond and gave us a dinner at the Star and Garter, previous to which he read us " Dora," and very much delighted we were. As we drove back in the cool of the evening, he proposed

---

* Written by him in collaboration with the then rising dramatist, Mr. Henry Pettitt.

that I should play "Farmer Allen," the "stern parient." At that time I had got the poetic drama on the brain, and I replied, with more candour than consideration, "that as yet I had not arrived at the 'King Lears,' and that when I did go into that line of business I'd rather go to the original than to an agricultural specimen of the article." He growled out his favourite platitude about "the insensate egoism of the actor," and subsided into a sulky silence.

Afterward, by the light of more mature experience, I read this play, and, "albeit unused to the melting mood," I must candidly admit it beguiled me of a tear or two. What a charming work it is! I am convinced that even now, properly placed in a small theatre, it would run for an entire season. It was, however, as unfortunate on its revival as on its first production at the Adelphi in 1867, when Reade wrote a pamphlet in which he vivisected the unfortunate painter, whom he alleged had damned the play. Once I ventured to take up the cudgels on behalf of his victim, stating, moreover, that he was dead.

"So is my piece, sir, and he killed it," roared Reade. "Murdered it; for it was nothing less than murder!

> "'Murder most foul, as in the best it is,
>   But this most foul, strange and unnatural.'

I've no patience to think of it!—the flesh and blood and bones and brains of two great men—a great poet and a great dramatist—murdered by a wretched scene-painter!"

MR. KNOWLES AS MASTER WALTER.

" But," I replied, " he was not a wretched scene-painter; on the contrary, he was a very admirable one. He was good enough for Charles Fechter; and when I opened my new theatre he painted all the scenery, and he didn't kill ' Hamlet.'"

" Because he couldn't ; but he would have done so if he could ! But there, there ! you never saw the scene ; you never saw the sun. There never was such a sun in the heavens, or on the earth, or in the waters under the earth ! It was a beastly sun—a sun which went to bed drunk and got up groggy in the morning, looking like a blazing copper warming-pan !"

Having since enjoyed the luxury myself of paying a thousand pounds for the damning of a piece through the eccentricities of a drunken carpenter and the vagaries of an erratic moon, which wiggle-waggled up and down incessantly all through my most interest-ing scene, I can sympathize now better than I did then with my friend's anger with the " duffers behind," and his scorn for the idiots in front, who concentrated their attention on sun, moon, stars, and cornfield—upon anything and everything except actors and author.

In this remarkable pamphlet, which is now scarce and out of print, Reade proceeds to say, " The act-drop rose on the cornfield. We all know how the poet has painted it, and his picture was in the scene-painter's hands as a guide. But that gentleman preferred his own ideas of corn. He gave us the flowery mound and two wheat-sheaves, but his stage-

cloth represented a turnpike road, with three rows
of cut stubble (property), and his cornfield was a
shapeless mass, streaked with fiery red and yellow
ochre.

" 'Dora, my girl,' said Farmer Allen, 'come to
have a look at the whut.' Once informed that the
splashes of blood and ochre on that cloth were
"whut," every Cockney who had voyaged into the
bowels of the land as far as Richmond began to
snigger. 'Opens a farmer's heart, it does,' says
Allen, 'to look at a sixty-acre field of whut like
that.' Howls of laughter from floor to gallery, and
the piece fell."

On the revival of "Dora" in 1882, nothing was
left to accident with regard to the scenery. It was
of the most elaborate, realistic, and perfect character.
Miss Sophie Eyre acted the title-rôle, and Mr.
Charles Warner, who did not appear in the *pièce de
résistance*, acted the patriarchal farmer, and, I believe,
both distinguished themselves highly. The play was
admirably cast in other respects, but it was unfortunately placed. It commenced the evening's performance at seven o'clock, so that in fact it was
half over before there was anyone in the house to
see it, and Reade ruefully informed me that so far
from its production helping the receipts, they continued to dwindle down and down, until both pieces
were finally withdrawn. Thus his latest theatrical
speculation, and the very last performance of one of
his most cherished works, was destined to end in a
cruel disappointment.

The last time I met him in a theatre was at Drury Lane, the first night of " Freedom," in August, 1883. He had just returned from the Continent. He seemed feeble and tired, and left before the play was over. I brought him out and put him into a cab. He wished me to go home with him to Shepherd's Bush, whither he had migrated in order to be near his brother Compton and his family, but, unfortunately, I had a lady with me whom I had to pilot to the wilds of Clapham—a circumstance I have regretted ever since, for he seemed to feel rather hurt by my refusal. I think that this was his last appearance in a theatre.

It was in the natural fitness of things it should be so. It was in that theatre that he saw " The School for Scandal" when he came to London a boy; it was in that theatre that " Gold " was produced; it was there that I had last met him when the Meiningen troop were acting. It was there he saw his first play in London ; it was there he saw his last one.

During my frequent visits to Shepherd's Bush his health fluctuated, but I thought he was more hypochondriacal than really or seriously ill. The sequel showed how much I was mistaken ; and yet he wrote and worked pretty much as usual. Indeed, at this very time he informed me he had completed a novel, which he revised and left ready for publication. When the weather was favourable he would occasionally take an hour or two's drive, or pick himself up for a game at lawn-tennis ; but he soon

became fatigued, and after dinner, in the very midst
of conversation, he would drop off into a stupor of
sleep for an hour or two.   Years ago, when we were
travelling together, whenever I had to act at night
it was my custom immediately after dinner to
adjourn to the nearest sofa for my siesta, a pleasant
but pernicious habit acquired from long companion-
ship with the late Charles Mathews, who had always
found it indispensable to take forty winks before
going to the theatre.   At these times Reade used to
chaff me about my indolence.   I replied, " Ah, it's
all. very well ; but you haven't had a dozen letters
to write after a long rehearsal, and you haven't to
air yourself before the public for four or five hours
to-night ; but *I* have."   Now it was changed : it was
his turn to sleep, mine to watch and wait.   When
he awoke he would soon pull himself together, and
say, " Ah, John, it's your turn to chaff now."

His eyesight, which had always been weak, now
got worse and worse.   Even when a dozen candles
were alight (he never used gas) he would exclaim
querulously, " Dear me ! how dark it grows !"   All
these symptoms of decaying nature alarmed me,
though I did not think the end was so near.

The last night I was at Blomfield Terrace, previous
to his leaving England, he read me a remarkable
paper (recently published in the *Leisure Hour*) on
the Book of Jonah.   The subject was handled in his
most masterly manner, but in the full flow of his
impetuous eloquence we stumbled upon one of his
characteristic blotches.   It was to this effect :

" Having now arrived at this conclusion, we must go the whole hog or none."

I made a *moue*.

He stopped, and said, "You don't like the hog, I see."

" I don't," I replied. " Do you ?"

"Well, it's a strong figure of speech, and it's understanded of the people ; but you are right, John —yes, you are right ; it's scarcely scriptural : so out it goes."

It seems appropriate to recall that on that occasion we discussed, as we had done many a time and oft before, the everlasting problems of life, death, time, and eternity. Years ago he was pronouncedly agnostic in his views ; now he hoped with a child's humility. When I was leaving, after some hours' earnest conversation, he said, " Well, when all is said and done, when Tyndal and Huxley have demonstrated to their own satisfaction that protoplasm is the beginning, when Darwin has shown that the great gorilla is the middle, and Mill has proved that annihilation is the end, there yet remains this fact which they can't get over—there can be nothing more wonderful in our going hence than our coming here ! Therefore perpend, my son, here are two quotations, both by great authors, Charles Reade and Alexander Pope. The first is this (two lines from your pet part, John) :

" ' There are on earth but two things which never die : Love, which decays not, and Faith, which binds the soul to heaven.'

The last is—

" ' Hope humbly then, on trembling pinions soar ;
    Wait the great teacher, Death, and God adore.'

Now, 'mark, learn, and inwardly digest' those two choice morsels : meanwhile, remember Albert Gate at four to-morrow."

On the morrow I was at the old home at Albert Gate, according to appointment. It had not been occupied for some time, and he had just arranged to let it. On my arrival I was shown into his disused study, the one so graphically described by him in " A Terrible Temptation." He had not yet come, but was expected momentarily. I had not been there for five years. How dreary and dismantled it looked ! The withered leaves which had fallen from the trees in the garden had been blown under the door-sill into the room, the fire was nearly out, the gloom of the gray wintry afternoon was settling down steadily from the gloaming into the murk. How changed it all seemed since the old happy times !

Presently he came in. Strange to say, he had not looked so bright and cheerful for ever so long. Age became him—his white beard and silky white hair looked quite handsome ; his eyes were sparkling, his cheeks a little flushed. His dress, too, was singularly becoming. He wore a large sealskin coat, sealskin gloves, and his usual sombrero. Round his neck was a large soft muffler of white silk.

To the last his interest in the theatre had remained unabated, and it was his intention on his return to go into management once more.

His play of " Griffith Gaunt " had never been acted in town, and its success when produced in the country by the late Mrs. G. V. Brooke (Avonia Jones) had been but doubtful. It was a pet subject of his ; but he was dissatisfied with the construction of the drama, and he asked me to take it in hand and see what I could do to remodel and put it into shape. I entered into his views *con amore*, revised the whole work, rewrote the fourth act, and altered the last one, very much to his satisfaction. He was quite sanguine as to its chances of success, and entered into an arrangement with me to manage a theatre for him on his return from Cannes. Alas ! *L'homme propose et Dieu dispose.*

When we parted, he seemed elate and confident. Of the two, I was the more sad and disheartened at his going away, although I little dreamt he was going to his death. I wished him God-speed, re-newed health and strength, then he went one way and I another.

I had promised that I would settle some business for him at the Adelphi Theatre that evening ; but as yet I had been unable to see the Fisheries Exhibi-tion, and it was to close that night. Obviously it was a case of now or never; so to the Fisheries I went from Albert Gate. As marvellous a sight as the exhibition itself was the vast concourse of people which moved about in one continued stream through every avenue of the building, except in the weird and wonderful Chinese annex, which I had ex-clusively to myself and the electric light, save for one huge Chinaman, who looked as dead as Con-fucius and as stiff and wooden as the figure-head of the great junk. I had lost myself in another land, in another century, when all at once it occurred to me that the commission I had undertaken lay not in Pekin but in the Strand, and if I didn't look alive I should be too late to fulfil it. I had to take Paddington on my way back to town by train. Lucky for me it was that I alighted there, as it enabled me to escape by the skin of my teeth being mixed up with the dynamite explosion which took place five minutes afterwards.

Having executed my commission, I duly advised him thereof. Not hearing from him, I wrote again, and received the following letter in reply:

"Hôtel Splendide, Cannes,
"December 4, 1883.

"My DEAR COLEMAN,

"I certainly must have missed your letter somehow, and now write to thank you for your zeal and ability on my behalf.

"I shall be happy to receive communications from you with regard to any matter of public or private interest, so please note my address.

"My own condition is a sad one. Either I have a cancer in the stomach or bowels, or else a complete loss of digestion. So far as animal food is concerned, I have been obliged to resign it entirely, excepting in the form of soup, and soup is to me, as you know of old, little better than hot water. I am making arrangements to have a cow milked twice a day into my pitcher, and, if two quarts of milk and twelve raw eggs *per diem* will keep an old man alive, I may live another year.

" This is a delightful place if you keep in the sun, which is quite as warm as the sun of May in England, but it only warms the air where it strikes it. I find it winter in the shady streets, and everywhere after sunset ; but there is a great difference between the temperature of this place and Paris, for here are avenues of palm-trees flourishing, not in boxes, but in the bare soil, not very lofty, but with grand and beautiful stems ; there are also aloes in bloom, and orange-orchards weighed down with the golden fruit ; there are also less pleasant indications of a warm climate : the flies are a perfect pest during meals, and at night I am eaten up with mosquitoes.

" Now, what are you doing ? Please tell me. I have never been well enough to work on ' Griffith Gaunt,' but I have got your manuscript by me, and fully appreciate your excellent suggestions. . . .

" The charge for a letter to me is now only two and a half pence, and in my solitude and affliction a little gossip from my old friend will be doubly welcome. Write me, as soon as possible, a good long letter. Attack a sheet of foolscap—don't be afraid of it—and, above all, believe me

" Now and always yours,

" CHARLES READE."

In compliance with his request, I gave him a full and particular account of all that was going on in town, at the theatres, etc., and endeavoured to laugh him out of his sad presentiments, quoting the ex-

amples of Lyndhurst, Disraeli, Gladstone, Monte-
fiore, etc. After this I wrote three or four times;
but the above is the last letter I ever received from
him. Knowing how erratic he was in his correspondence, his prolonged silence, though it pained
me, gave me no cause for alarm, especially as I had
read his letter on the Belt case, published in the
Daily Telegraph immediately after the Lord Chief
Justice had formulated his extraordinary dictum as
to the value of opinion *versus* fact. In this, Reade's
last published utterance, I was delighted to find all
his old intellectual vigour and all his irresistible
logic, all his remarkable power of grouping facts and
balancing the weight of evidence for and against, all
his judicial faculty of deciding fairly and impartially
upon the merits of any case in which he was not
himself personally interested. To my thinking, he
had never struck out straighter from the shoulder,
never written anything better or stronger: I concluded therefore that he was regaining health and
strength, and I looked forward to his returning, like
a giant refreshed, to commence our campaign next
season.

Beyond the information contained in the above
letter, I had no knowledge of his doings on the
Riviera, until a few months ago I chanced by mere
accident to meet at the club a popular journalist,
who happened to be staying with his wife at Cannes
about the beginning of March, 1884.

This gentleman informed me that one day, while

basking in the sunshine in the garden of the hotel, he sought to beguile the time by reading " It is Never Too Late to Mend," in one of the popular editions, with a sensational illustration on the cover.

Immersed in the story, he had not noticed a tall elderly gentleman swathed in rugs, who sat near him in a huge wicker arm-chair.

Looking up, their eyes met.

The stranger smiled, as he said in a soft, gentle voice, "Would you mind reading an old man a chapter of that remarkable-looking book, sir?"

This request was complied with, evidently to the delight of the listener. To the reader's amazement he learnt that his interlocutor was no other than the author of the book.

The day was bright, sunny, and cheerful, so was Reade.

Upon calling the following day, my friend found Reade lying prostrate on the floor of the room. His head was propped up by pillows, and he literally gasped for breath. For a fortnight or more he suffered tortures from rapid changes of temperature —to-day well, to-morrow ill; but well or ill, a martyr to nostalgia.

He grumbled incessantly at the service of the hotel, complaining that he could get nothing to eat, and that he could not have his fire lighted at night— at least, not without a fight for it; and the delicate condition of his lungs rendered a fire in his bedroom not only necessary, but absolutely indispensable. He would piteously inquire of his visitor, " Have

you any English tea? This 'rot' isn't fit to drink!
Can your excellent good wife make me an omelette?
I think I could eat one after those dainty little fingers."

This lady and another feminine visitor ministered
to his wants as well as they could, frequently getting
up in the middle of the night to mend his fire or
make him a cup of tea.

During these wakeful nights he was very feeble
and depressed, and continually troubled with a
terrible cough.

When his fair nurses tried to cheer him up, he
was wont to shake his head and smile sadly while he
replied, " It's very good of you to say so, but I feel—
I know I'm booked for kingdom come! The doctors
have begun to inject morphia, and the beggars never
do that until a fellah's at the back of God-speed."

In these despondent moods he was repeatedly
heard to mutter to himself, "I hope I shall get
home to die; I should not like to shuffle off my
mortal coil in this beastly hole!"

Before my friend's duties called him back to
England, he had the satisfaction of knowing that
Mr. Reade's relatives had arrived to take charge of
him.

On Thursday, April 3, I was startled by the news
that he had returned to England dangerously ill. I
went down to Shepherd's Bush at once, and begged
to see him; but the doctors had given imperative
instructions that no one was to be admitted except
those who were in immediate attendance upon him.
I was informed that he had been alone (save for his

secretary) through the winter, and, finding himself
death-stricken, he had summoned his relations to
take him home. They found him almost *in articulo
mortis*. When they arrived at Calais the Channel
was dreadfully rough. In his best days he was a
martyr to *mal de mer*, and had a horror of the sea;
it was this alone which had prevented him from
accepting numerous invitations to visit America,
where he was more popular even than in his own
country, and where a royal welcome awaited him any
time these twenty years.

For nearly a week his departure was delayed by
the weather. At last came a lull, of which his
friends took advantage. When they commenced
to move him, the motion of the carriage caused him
intolerable pain; but his nieces walked on either
side holding his hands, and so they soothed him
until at last he consented to be carried on board.
Strange to say, he suffered very little during the
voyage; but the railway journey home shook him
terribly. When he got to Shepherd's Bush he had
just strength to articulate, "I have come home to
die."

His words were prophetic. When they had
carried him to his chamber it was only too apparent
that he would never quit it alive.

It was the second time within two months that
the shadow of death had fallen on that roof. Only
a few weeks previous, the head of the house—"the
Squire," as they called him down at Ipsden—Henry,
the son of Charles Reade's eldest brother, a stout,

hearty man of forty, had been stricken down with a mortal malady, and died in that very room.

It is idle now to think of what might have been, but it is my firm conviction that if, years ago, before functional derangement had set in, Mr. Reade had consented to be guided by medical advice and to take physic (which he always detested), above all, to submit to proper dietetic treatment, he would have been alive now. It is quite certain that the eminent physicians who attended him during his last illness found that he had been entirely mistaken as to the nature of his disease. There was no indication of cancer in the stomach; but for years he had been suffering from induration of the liver and emphysema of the lungs, combined with functional derangement and impaired digestion.

From the moment of his return it was seen to be impossible for him to recover, but all that loving care and kindness could do was done to alleviate his sufferings.

On Sunday, April 7, I took my last leave of my poor friend. His nearest and dearest were around him. He was quite unconscious, and but the shadow of his former self. I asked him if he knew me, but he made no answer. I thought he pressed my hand gently as I kissed his; but in such moments as these our nerves are so shaken that we never really know what actually does take place. I only know I felt myself in the presence of death, and that I realized the fact, from which there was no escaping, that all hope was past, and that those who loved him best could only pray that the end might come soon—the sooner the better.

The favourable bulletins which appeared for the next few days did not deceive me, and I was not surprised when the news of his release came on Friday.

They told me afterwards that toward the end he wandered slightly, sometimes spoke in French to imaginary servants who were helping him aboard the boat at Calais ; that he called for money to give them ; and then at last

" Life lulled itself to sleep, and sleep slept unto death."

I propose now to speak, not of the brilliant dramatist, the great writer, but of the dear friend, the large - hearted, hot - headed, impetuous, generous, loving, and lovable man—the man who was brave as a lion and gentle as a lamb, the man who was "the truest friend and noblest foe" I have ever met. It is not to be supposed that during all these years and the many transactions that occurred between us we did not have our points of departure : we were both too human to be infallible.

Others will doubtless dwell upon his weaknesses, his faults, his follies. I do not care to note the spots on the sun : it is enough for me that he irradiates the earth and lifts my soul to heaven.

Were I to tell of the thousand generous and benevolent actions done by Charles Reade in silence and in secrecy, I should require a volume. A few instances, however, will suffice.

Of course everyone knows that on the occasion of the famous trial in which the late Hepworth Dixon was concerned, Reade sent him, unasked, a cheque for a thousand guineas: that Dixon did not accept the offer does not diminish Reade's generosity.

Four years ago he asked me to go down to see a play of his at an East-End theatre. I did, and reported favourably upon a gentleman who played a principal part. The next day he received a complimentary letter and a "little cheque" from Mr. Reade.

A few months later a poor actor in great straits wrote imploring help in the name of the dead. He received by return of post a bank-note, merely inscribed "A Voice from Willesden Churchyard."

The wife of a literary man, then dying, and since dead, wrote to Reade, asking the loan of a few pounds. She received for answer, "Madam,—I never *lend* money, except on good security; but please hand the enclosed to your husband." The husband opened the letter and found a cheque for thirty pounds, with a hasty scrawl: "Dear X.,—A dear dead friend of yours and mine has left a little fund at my disposal. If she were alive I know she would send you the enclosed; I am, therefore, only carrying out her wishes. I send it upon one condition—that you get down to Margate immediately and save your life for the sake of your wife, who is an excellent woman."

A poor lady, whom we had both known well in the heyday of her youth and beauty, the widow of a

HERMAN VEZIN.

mutual friend, a distinguished actor and manager,
"had married again in haste and repented at leisure."
This haughty and imperious beauty was struck down
with a mortal malady. She wrote one line: "Dear
Charles Reade,—I am ill, dying, in want." He was
in her miserable garret as soon as the first hansom
could take him there. Two hours afterward he had
removed her to decent apartments and placed her
under the charge of a Sister of Mercy and one of
the most eminent physicians in London. It was too
late to save, but not too late to soothe her last
moments and to surround her with everything
which generous care could provide.

One instance concerns myself. At a critical period
of my life I had lost my whole fortune in a disastrous
enterprise which left me high and dry without a
shilling. I had dined at Albert Gate the night
before. Next morning, he burst into my room and
planked a bag of sovereigns on the table, quite
sufficient to enable me to tide over my immediate
necessities, exclaiming abruptly, "I saw you seemed
rather *gêné* last night: there, that's something to
buy postage-stamps with; and if you want any more,
there's plenty left where that came from." And he
was gone before I had time to reply. I could mul-
tiply these illustrations of the generosity of that
large heart *ad infinitum*, but methinks I have said
enough.

On Tuesday, April 15, all that was mortal of
Charles Reade was buried in Willesden Churchyard.

The funeral rites were as unostentatious as his life had been. There were only ten chief mourners— kinsmen and old friends — among whom I was privileged to take a place. Wilkie Collins was peremptorily ordered by his physician to refrain from attending; but he wrote a most touching letter, bewailing the loss of his oldest friend—a friend of forty years' standing. Mr. Edwin Arnold, who had a few days previously testified so eloquently in the columns of the *Daily Telegraph* to the sterling worth, the nobility of character, and the genius of Charles Reade, was also debarred from joining us.

The art of reading the " Order for the Burial of the Dead " with propriety is an accomplishment which appears to be rarely or never included among the acquirements of the average clergyman ; but on this occasion the inspired words were read so nobly that they gained an added beauty from their touching and tender utterance by the Vicar of Willesden, who is, I believe, an old friend of Mr. Reade's.

The morning had been cold and gray, but the moment we left the church the sun shone forth bright and glorious on the masses of flowers which were heaped upon the coffin, on the lid of which was the following inscription :

"CHARLES READE,
Dramatist, Novelist, and Journalist.
Born June 8, 1814.   .
Died April 11, 1884."

"Dramatist" first—always **first**! At his own request the words were thus placed. The ruling passion was **strong** in death, **and to** the **last he re-**mained faithful **to** his first **and** early love—the Drama.

When they laid **him** in **the** grave, as far **as my** eyes could see through the mist which rose **before** them, there were present two hundred people, more or less, **among whom I could** distinguish of **men** of letters only **two—Robert** Buchanan and George Augustus **Sala ;** of actors **only** three—Messrs. Calhaem, Billington, **and Davenport.** I noted also **two** tender-hearted **women** who came from **a** distance **to strew** flowers over the grave **of** their friend.

They do "manage **some** things better in **France,"** at least they **do nowadays, for it is too far back to travel to** the "maimed rites" **of the obsequies of** Molière, poor Adrienne le **Couvreur, and her friend** Voltaire. Assuredly had Charles **Reade been** a Frenchman, all Paris **would** have **been in** mourning, and the people **in** their thousands would have followed to his **last** resting-place the man who from the first moment that **he** took pen in hand used it **in** behalf of the weak, the helpless, and the oppressed.

After all, what signifies the absence **of a few** score authors **or** actors, **or** a few thousand spectators? Their absence **or** their presence troubles him not now. He sleeps none the less soundly beside his "wise counsellor, loyal ally, and bosom friend."

On his tomb these words are inscribed :

'Here Lie

By the Side of his Beloved Friend the Mortal Remains of

CHARLES READE,

Dramatist, Novelist, and Journalist.

His last Words to Mankind are on this Stone.

'I hope for a resurrection, not from any power in nature, but from the will of the Lord God Omnipotent, who made nature and me. He created man out of nothing ; which nature could not. He can restore man from the dust, which nature cannot. And I hope for holiness and happiness in a future life, not for anything I have said or done in this body, but from the merits and mediation of Jesus Christ. He has promised His intercession to all who seek it, and He will not break His word : that intercession, once granted, cannot be rejected ; for He is God, and His merits infinite ; a man's sins are but human and finite. "Him that cometh to Me, I will in no wise cast out." "If any man sin, we have an advocate with the Father, Jesus Christ the Righteous, and He is the propitiation for our sins."'

"Though he is dead, his name will live for evermore."

Yes! So long as England remains a nation, so long as the stars and stripes float over the great country which he loved next to his island home, so long as the language of Shakespere and of Milton is spoken in any quarter of the habitable globe, so long will the name of Charles Reade be

'Familiar in men's mouths as household words !'

CHAPTER XI.

A MAN of middle height, with lithe, sinewy figure, a massive brow, covered with a thatch of iron-gray hair, rugged features, a celestially defiant nose, a pugilistic jaw, bristling with a crisp beard of gray, and eyes which glittered like steel, an immovable eyeglass, with stony and relentless gaze, which fixed me like the bull's-eye of a policeman's lantern. How it remained perpetually *screwed* in its place appeared an inscrutable mystery. I arrived at the conclusion that the owner thereof must have slept with it, and was perplexed and astonished when, upon our going to bathe together, years later, in the creek at Douglas, he actually took it out preparatory to taking a header.

It was at a dinner, given at the Langham by a feminine literary celebrity, that I first encountered this impressive and somewhat aggressive personality. We sat exactly opposite. He glared, and I glared, but neither knew the other. I asked the men who sat next me who this mysterious stranger was, but none of them knew.

The following night was a memorable *première* at the Olympic. Sitting in the front row of the stalls, I caught sight of my eccentric *vis-à-vis* of the previous night, snugly ensconced in a private box.

The play was a success, and at the fall of the curtain the author was called for. The author was the man with the bull's-eye, and the man with the bull's-eye was Tom Taylor, barrister-at-law, poet and playwright, publicist and journalist, art critic, chief of the Board of Health, and I know not what else.

The multitudinous labours of Mr. Taylor as a journalist and art critic attest his proficiency and industry; but it is by his dramas he is now chiefly remembered. Here, indeed, his fecundity and versatility were marvellous.

He wrote upwards of a hundred more or less successful plays, many of which still hold the stage.

Some were adapted from various sources, native and foreign. Many were entirely original, although it must be admitted that his most successful works were not of native growth.

In no case was he a servile translator; indeed, every play which he manipulated underwent a thorough process of transmutation.

Nowadays when a playwright obtains not unfrequently £5,000 or £6,000 for a successful play, it appears almost incredible to realize that this accomplished dramatist received only £150 for "The Ticket-of-Leave Man"—a drama which crowded

the theatre for twelve months consecutively on its
first production, and which has since made the fortunes of managers in both hemispheres.

After a lapse of a quarter of a century this play
remains as attractive as ever. Last summer it was
conspicuously successful, upon its revival at the
Olympic, and at this present writing it is again
crowding that theatre nightly.

After this production, Mr. Taylor raised his tariff
of prices ; but even at the maximum he was content
to take £100 an act for original work, and £50 an
act for an adaptation.

He sold "The Unequal Match," "The Overland Route," and I don't know how many other
pieces, to Knowles, of Manchester, to enable him
(Taylor) to complete the purchase of his delightful
retreat at Lavender Sweep ; and at one period
" Clancarty " could actually have been purchased for
£300.

In 1871 a very ingenious writer maintained, in
the course of an animated discussion in the *Athenæum*,
that most of Taylor's successful plays were plagiarisms or adaptations from other sources. With
admirable taste and temper, Taylor retorted, ad
mitting that one-tenth of his plays were adaptations
but that the remaining nine-tenths were original.

That correspondence forms "a very pretty quarrel
as it stands," and it remains on record to speak for
itself.

Byron, it is said, stated to Moore that Sheridan
had written "the best comedy, 'School for Scandal'"

(though, methinks, I have heard the originality of that immortal work severely called in question!) ; " the best operetta, 'The Duenna ;' and that he had made the best speech—the impeachment of Warren Hastings—that had ever been uttered by a states-man :" so I maintain that Taylor wrote the best domestic drama, "The Ticket-of-Leave Man" (although founded on a French original) ; the best romantic play, " Clancarty ;" the best drawing-room drama (though based on a French story), " Still Waters Run Deep ;" and the best comedy dramas, " The Unequal Match" and " The Overland Route," of the epoch in which he lived.

After that night at the Olympic we met some-times in society, and continually at the theatres ; but having never been introduced, we still glared at each other, as well-bred English folk usually do under similar circumstances. At length he came down to Leeds to review the pictures at the Art Exhibition for the *Times*, and Charles Reade, who was staying with me, introduced us to each other.

During a subsequent visit to town Mr. Taylor did me the honour to express a desire to a mutual friend (then private secretary to the great Mar-quis) that we should meet and have a friendly jaw about certain matters in which we were both interested.

H. invited us to dine with him, and a very de-lightful evening we had, the three of us.

The master was disposed to be rather bumptious

and dictatorial, but there was so much *bonhomie* about him—above all, there was so much brains— that younger men might well instinctively yield him precedence.

Yes! it was a delightful evening, and the commencement of a delightful acquaintance.

Taylor was a sort of tutelary divinity of undiscovered geniuses. He had been the professional father of the Terry family.

Recently he had discovered the Rousbys in the Channel Islands, and he was full of them.

Wybert Rousby was the Kean of the provinces, a sprightly, clever little fellow, bright and sharp as a needle—at least, he was when I first met him in Hull in my *première jeunesse*, and years after when he acted at Norwich in my pieces.

His wife was an interesting young Irish girl in her noviciate.

Taylor was struck with her beauty, and with Rousby's ability, and he got them an engagement with Mr. Labouchere at the Queen's Theatre.

Herman Vezin had translated one of Madame Pfieffer's German plays, which he gave to Taylor to adapt for Mrs. Vezin and himself (Herman).

A misunderstanding occurred. The actor alleged that the author had not carried out his instructions. The author's back got up ; there was a row and a rupture, with the result that he retained the piece which Vezin had originally suggested, and the translation which he had actually provided, which was rather rough on Herman. I think so now, and thought so then, and didn't scruple to say so to Taylor's teeth—very fine teeth they were, by the way.

Anyhow, when the rupture was at its height, he invited a select circle of friends, amongst whom I was included, to hear the play read at his house at Lavender Sweep.

He astonished everybody by turning up for the occasion in a suit of black velvet knickerbockers and silk continuations, with shoes and diamond buckles to match.

Combined with a turn-down collar (a large one), this get-up gave him quite a Shakesperean appearance.

He was an admirable reader, and for my part, I thought the reading better than the play ; so did Reade and Oxenford.

Apropos of that play, long after its production, one day at Lavender Sweep, while discussing the question of originality in dramatic composition, Taylor said to me, " Look here !   I've made a find !"

With that he took down from the book-shelf a new volume of old plays (he had just added a complete edition of thirty or forty volumes to his library), and pointed out a scene in a play (the name of which I have unfortunately forgotten), which was unquestionably the origin, or, if not, certainly the most remarkable analogue to the Tower Scene in "'Twixt Axe and Crown " that it is possible to conceive.

The Rousbys made their appearance in due course as Bertuccio and Feordelisa.   Rousby made so pronounced a hit, that full houses might have been reasonably anticipated, but the business was bad beyond belief; so " The Fool's Revenge " was with-drawn, and " 'Twixt **Axe** and Crown " took its place.

In this play, in consequence of being placed in a part utterly unsuited for him, poor Rousby retired and took a back seat, while Mrs. Rousby burst forth like a meteor on the dazzled and delighted town, as the Lady Elizabeth.

Up to this period the British public had been accustomed to see a tear a cat quean, swearing " by Gog's Wounds," or " by my father's blood and bones !" or else a terrible horse-marine of a horrible old woman, which even the rare genius of Ristori could scarce render endurable ; hence, when this fair young creature, with her pretty ways, soft musical voice, and gently pleading face, came forth to present the popular Protestant and poetic idea of the Princess Elizabeth, the public heart leaped at her.

Possibly, too, there had been just then a surfeit of the tea-and-saucer drama on the one hand, and of the nude and stupid on the other. Certain it is, however, that the production of this play marked the dawn of the renaissance.

" 'Twixt Axe and Crown " and Mrs. Rousby were the fashion. Fashionable painters vied as to who should have the honour of painting her face ; fashionable sculptors fought for the honour of model-ling her bust, or would have done, had anything so exuberant existed.

Her picture hung upon the line at the Academy.

and a guard had to be established to desire people
to pass on.   There were the Rousby bonnet, the
Rousby cloak, the Rousby robe, the Rousby parasol,
the Rousby Grecian bend, and the Rousby Roman
fall—in fact, there was the Rousby everything to
which by any pretext the name could be attached.

Yet, after all, the popular idol was but a *very*
ordinary young lady, with a somewhat attenuated
figure remarkable chiefly for sharp angles, and wholly
destitute of the noble prominences and graceful un-
dulations so essential to the beauty of the female
"form divine."

She had, however, a sweet voice, with a delicious
soupçon of the brogue, lustrous eyes, superb teeth,
and a lovely face.   These were the qualities which
set the public heart on fire.

As to the art, poor Wybert (who was left in the
cold during the popular craze), had taught her all
she knew.   But with all his skill he couldn't make
her an actress.

She was good enough, however, for the public
(dear stupid British public!) and for the author, and
therefore no one had any right to complain—certainly
not the present writer, who saw the beginning
and the end of this dazzling but unfortunate
career.

The merest ephemeron of fashion, she emerged
from the grub to the chrysalis, flamed forth into a
butterfly—bright, beautiful, brilliant.   She was the
idol of the hour, adored by the men, envied by the
women, had her brief vogue, and was forgotten.

Short as her life was, she **had long** outlived **her** fleeting fame.

A little time before **her untimely death, the poor** soul told me **with** her **own sweet** lips the sad story of **her** rise and **fall ; the sin and** the sorrow which followed. Alas, "the **pity of it !"**

Another of Taylor's discoveries **was an** acute and gentlemanly young American named Steele Mackaye, **who came over** to **this country** full **of** enthusiasm, and permeated **with the fantastic** theory of Del Sarte.

Of course every **theatre in town** was closed **to** the ambitious **neophyte. They always** are closed **to** anyone who aspires to interfere with **vested** interests, unless the aspirant happens to have **a** friend who has a substantial banking account! Mackaye's enthusiasm was contagious. Taylor **was** himself **a** disappointed **actor, so,** at least, he told **me.** His *protégé* had " Hamlet " **on** the brain, **so had the master. He** revised the text, prepared **the play for** representation, and admirably prepared **it, too.**

At length he had **found** the instrument to give his music forth, for **he** had taught himself **to** believe it **was** *his* as much as the bard's ; indeed, in the published edition the name of Taylor shines forth conspicuous **in** all the honours of large type, while the bard plays second fiddle in small pica.

Shut out of London, Taylor **and** his *protégé* migrated to the Crystal Palace, where they produced " Hamlet " half a dozen times, and very well produced it was, **indeed ; the *mise en*** *scène* was excellent. Two new *protégés* of Taylor's divided the honours with the Prince of Denmark.

Miss Helen Barry, then in the flower of mature and majestic beauty, suggested something like the sort of woman Claudius might have imperilled his soul for; while a lovely, but somewhat eccentric young lady, calling herself Miss Carlisle, gave indications of considerable excellence in Ophelia.

There were half a dozen débutants, principally men who had sought "the bubble reputation in the cannon's mouth," and not having found either that or their quietus there, had turned their attention to the stage.

Two or three of these gentlemen came to the fore afterwards, notably Mr. St. Maur, and the future apostle of "reserved force," the unfortunate Charles Kelly, who gave a commonplace but sensible rendition of Claudius, while Mr. Steele Mackaye's Hamlet, if crude, was scholarly, and not without intermittent qualities of considerable excellence.

It was soon after this production that Mr. Taylor proposed to produce his new play of "Arkwright's Wife" at my theatre in Leeds, and I was only too glad to help in carrying out his views.

To Leeds, then, he came, bringing with him Miss Barry, Miss Marion Terry, Mr. and Mrs. Charles Kelly, Mr. Flockton, Mr. St. Maur, Mr. Steele Mackaye, and others.

The play was subsequently produced in town with more or less success, and I have nothing to say about it save to relate an occurrence which took

place during the rehearsals, as a fine specimen of the
amenities which are sometimes to be found upon the
stage among "contending opposites."

There was little love lost between Mr. F., the
stage-manager, and Mr. Steele Mackaye, and they
were continually snarling at each other. The one
despised the other as an amateur, who returned the
compliment by regarding F. as an ill-bred bar-
barian.

The cast was a heavy one, and the author asked
me if I could lend him a couple of my "young
men" (permanent but superior supers) to play two
ruffianly operatives of a dozen or twenty lines
each.

"What do you want them to do?" I inquired.

"To smash Arkwright's machine," he replied.
"These fellahs I've got have been in the army, and
they are society men, too gentlemanly and dilettanti
for this sort of thing. We've been trying them all
the week, but we can't get 'em to put on the steam,
and every morning we get worse and worse."

"Give me the scrip," said I, "and I'll see what I
can do."

That night I took a couple of my "young men"
(one of them is now going about the country as a
star!) and gave them a private drill for an hour or
more, with the result that at the rehearsal on the
following day they "went for" the machine with a
rush so terrific that it absolutely flabbergasted
Taylor's company.

One of his military recruits had just returned

from the Cape, where there had been some hard
fighting.

"By Jove!" he whispered to another, "good
business! Regular forlorn-hope fellahs these!"

Triumphantly regarding Mackaye and the rest,
F. said:

"There, gentlemen, that's what I call acting!"

"What a misfortune," growled Mackaye, "that
Mr. Taylor didn't see these young men before!
He might have engaged a company of supers."

"It's a pity he didn't," retorted the other. "Better
have a company of supers who *can* act, than a company of duffers who *can't.*"

During the following week there was a banquet
given at the town-hall in connection with the opening
of the new bridge, which led directly to the door of
my own theatre.

I couldn't be present, for Mr. Phelps and his
daughters had just arrived *en route* for the Isle of
Man, whither, indeed, they were to accompany me
on the morrow. The old gentleman was staying
with me, and, of course, I had to entertain him.

Mr. Taylor was invited to the banquet as a distinguished guest.

The *Leeds Mercury* was and is a famous Non-
conformist paper, and has done much to further the
cause of education and reform; but it was, and is still,
conducted on narrow sectarian lines. It devotes
columns to dog and man fights; it does not refuse
admission to certain advertisements of a peculiar

MR. EMERY AS ROBIN ROUGHEAD.

character ; nay more, it condescends to admit the advertisements of the theatre (payable in advance) ; but even when I built my new and magnificent "temple," it never noted its existence.

Every artist of eminence appeared ; every London success was produced. Shakesperean plays were revived upon a scale of the greatest splendour ; new plays by Charles Reade and other eminent authors were produced for the first time on my stage ; but my theatre remained unnoted and unnoticed in the columns of the *Mercury*.

It went out of its way, however, to devote a sensational leaderette in all the honours of leaded type to an account of the burning of a little child's skirts during one of my pantomimes in York (forty miles distant!) ; it went for "Formosa" with two savage leading articles ; it went for me personally when I read the "Midsummer Night's Dream" at the Town Hall on the occasion of the Shakespere Tercentenary. For my part, I don't dislike the smell of battle, and I flatter myself I gave quite as good as I took.

Discovering by accident that the proprietors of the *Mercury* had been the custodians of the old theatre (Tate Wilkinson's), and the printers of the play-bills, and that the commencement of their ferocious efflux of piety coincided with the exact period when the keys were withdrawn from their custody and the manager ceased to employ them to print the play-bills, I didn't scruple to publish the fact, and to hit out straight whenever the occasion served.

Taylor sympathized with my wrongs, and now he had a grievance of his own.   He, the foremost dramatist of the day, a distinguished man of letters to boot, had contributed a new play to the literature of the country, had done Leeds the honour of selecting it for the birthplace of his work, and this narrow - minded sectarian journal had absolutely ignored it and the existence of the author.   Those who remember the trenchant Thomas may imagine how he would endure this indignity.

Nursing his wrath, he went to the dinner and— *après ?*

His health was proposed, and in reply he "went" for the *Mercury* and its unfortunate proprietors, who happened to be *en évidence.*

The effect was as if a shot had been fired into a powder-magazine.

Certain it is that he left the enemy discomfited and vanquished, and came away triumphant.

The affair made a mark beyond its small local circle, and was descanted upon at length all over the kingdom ; hence I have referred to it here.

The day after this lively scene he accompanied Mr. Phelps, his daughters, and myself, to the Isle of Man, where he stayed with us for a few days.

The first night of his stay I did myself the plea- sure of acting John Mildmay (a part which I have acted more frequently than any living man) for his delectation.   The next two or three days were devoted to showing him the beauties of Eileen Vannin.   He was so delighted with this sweet isle of the sea, that a month later he returned for the remainder of the season with Mrs. Taylor, his son Wycliff (now a rising painter), and his daughter.

I met them at Liverpool, and escorted them to Douglas, where, for a couple of months, we had a high old time.

His mornings were devoted to brain-spinning, mine to rehearsals, at the end of which he used to call at the theatre nearly every day, and row with me over to Port Skillion, where we daily disported ourselves in the briny.

He was a capital swimmer, and on these occasions was as frolicsome as a boy in his teens, and was fond of recounting his youthful experiences.

It is said that Richelieu prided himself more on his plays than his statesmanship; in like manner, Taylor prided himself more on his play-acting than his play-writing.

From youth to age the play was his passion. Although he came early to the fore and took a fellowship at Trinity College, Cambridge, even then he beguiled the intervals of a busy life by writing critiques on the Norwich company during their periodical visits to the Cambridge Theatre.

As often as they could afford the expense, he and a select party of brother-graduates were wont to travel to town and back by mail (there was no railway then 'twixt London and Cambridge) to see the great productions of the Macready régime at Drury Lane and Covent Garden.

He related with great glee that upon one memorable occasion he and his friends were "stuck" for supplies, and he had to "spout" his watch to enable them to get back to Cambridge.

He was wont to maintain that had it not been for his nose he would have been a great tragedian. Despite that somewhat pugnacious nasal organ, he disported himself year after year with the "old stagers" during the cricket week at Canterbury; indeed, he was one of the shining lights of that famous troupe of amateur actors.

He told me an amusing story in connection with his performance of Miles Bertram in "The Wreck Ashore," which was acted on one of these festive occasions.

In the last scene Miles, who is a pirate and a smuggler, in endeavouring to escape is supposed to be shot by the officers of the Preventive Service.

Usually the bold buccaneer rushes off the stage in the thick of the fight, is shot, and returns with a dab of rose-pink (supposed to represent blood) on his forehead. Then shouting, "Up with the black flag! down with the blue!" he dies, *coram populo*.

Taylor thought he had discovered a splendid substitute for blood in a ripe mulberry.

During the rehearsal he told everybody he came across about his discovery, and at night everyone came to the wings to see the new effect. Prior to the commencement of the scene, he placed his dresser at the centre door, out of sight of the audience, with the mulberry on a plate. At length the supreme moment arrived; Miles fought his way off the stage through a volley of musketry, and was engaged in the act of manipulating the mulberry on his manly brow, when lo! the prompter, who had been dining "not wisely, but too well," mistook the musket shots for the signal for the falling of the curtain, and hurriedly rang down upon an empty stage, thus not only cutting out the death of Miles, but the squashing of his mulberry.

When Taylor found he had been deprived not only of his death-scene, but his novel effect, his rage knew no bounds; he called down anathema maranatha, in every living and nearly every dead language (for he had a copious and florid vocabulary) on the head of the unhappy prompter, and indeed was restrained with the utmost difficulty from mingling his gore with the juice of his precious mulberry.

During this visit to Douglas he and his family came every other night to see the play, and I used to await his criticisms on the following morning always with interest, and sometimes, especially when we acted a poetic play, with anxiety.

Occasionally he "went" for us tooth and nail, always giving good reason for the faith that was in him; occasionally, however, he went into the opposite extreme of admiration, but whether his opinions were adverse or favourable, we always learnt something from him.

During this time he made an elaborate study of my method and resources, and proposed in the fulness of time to write me four different plays with

Wat Tyler, Oliver Cromwell, Michael Angelo, and Peter the Great as central figures.

Alas! we never got further than Wat Tyler, and of that we only prepared the scenario.

Apropos of which, at his death, this scenario was lost.

At length it occurred to me as an inspiration to call on his brother, Mr. Arnold Taylor. This gentleman had only two or three days previously discovered the MS., and was actually on the point of advertising it in the *Times*, when I happened to call in and claim it.

To return to Douglas; nearly every Sunday was devoted to a little picnic confined to the members of our respective families.

On one lovely afternoon as we sat after dinner upon a huge bluff, which overhung the silvery shore hundreds of feet beneath us, the blue cloudless sky above us, the soft western breeze around, the land of green Erin clear to the naked eye, rising like an emerald from the sea, which crept slowly in below with the coming tide, the master produced a MS. play and read it to us.

'Twas a " Tale of the Terror;" but, alas! it was a play with an object, and was written for the purpose of enabling Mr. M. to wear a waxen mask upon his face, so that thus disguised he might deceive his enemy, the wicked marquis; pluck off his mask, and "confound the villain in the hour of his fancied triumph," etc.

I have already said that Taylor was an admirable reader (an accomplishment few authors possess), and he loved to hear himself read.

We listened in silence until he had finished. Then we were more silent still; nothing could be heard but the scream of the curlew winging his distant flight, and the ripple of the waters on the beach below.

At last he said:

"Why the devil don't you speak? and what do you think of it?"

I hesitated. Mrs. Taylor looked at me, and said:

"Say exactly what you think."

"Well, then, I think," said I, "that the first act is equal to anything you have ever done—equal to that wonderful prologue to 'A Tale of Two Cities.'"

His face flushed with pleasure as he eagerly inquired:

"Do you really think that?"

"Yes, really."

"And don't you think the idea of the waxen mask novel and original?"

"No, I don't! It was done by Boucicault in 'Elfie' only two or three years ago, and long before he was born it was done by Monk Lewis in 'Rugantino, the Bravo of Venice.'"

"You don't mean that?"

"I do, though."

"Well, what do you think of the two last acts, anyhow?"

"I think them quite unworthy of you."

" No ?"

" Yes, and more. I think them utterly beneath criticism, and if it were not your work, I would say beneath contempt !"

" By Jove ! you're right, old fellah. I think so myself, so there they go." With that he tore the second and third acts to fragments, and cast them into the sea.

" Now, after that give me one of those weeds, some claret-cup, and let us change the subject."

A few days after this our pleasant holiday came to an end, and the Taylors went one way and we another.

Some months later, going down to dine at Lavender Sweep, I met him by appointment at Victoria Station. He was radiant, and informed me that barely an hour before he had been appointed editor of *Punch.*

A few months later still, having learnt that I was in town on business, to my astonishment and delight he swooped down upon my diggings at the Tavistock in the morning at nine o'clock, and burst out in his impetuous fashion :

" I've come to breakfast with you, and to read you my new play."

" All right ; fire away."

" No, thanks ; breakfast first."

" Order what you like ; Liberty Hall here !"

" Here, then, you fellah : herring-roes on toast— soft roes, mind—salmon cutlets, bacon, and devilled kidneys ; and look alive about it."

After a capital **breakfast** (he was a valiant trencher-man !), he read me " Clancarty."

Had **I only** known then **that the** admirable work might **have been** purchased **for** £300 ! **but it was** not till **long** after that I learnt **the** truth **from the** lips **of** my accomplished friend Miss Ada Cavendish, the original representative **of** the delightful heroine of that delightful **play.**

Soon **after its** production in **town he proposed** that I should **take it on tour in** the **provinces,** paying him **certain** royalties **for the** representation thereof, and undertaking, **in** consideration **of my doing so,** to write the "Wat **Tyler"** play aforesaid.

I could **not myself act** " Clancarty " **as** he desired, but I engaged **Mr.** George Rignold, **an** admirable robust actor, instead ; organized an excellent company, engaged **Mr. Richard** Younge **to** conduct **it,** and sent them forth on their travels.

The play achieved **a** considerable success.

Then came " the little **rift** within the lute," which widened and widened. It **is a sorry story.**

There was a woman in it **(there** always is) ; a lady whom I had never seen, never met, and, in all human probability, never shall, caused the estrangement.

During the second tour of the play, Mr. Taylor had gone to Manchester to preside at a dinner given to Charles Calvert.

To my astonishment he (Taylor) passed by my door going to York, repassed it going back to London ; wrote me an angry and, as I thought, unjust letter, touching the mounting and acting of the play.

Feeling myself wronged, I wrote back in the same strain, perhaps even more angrily, and indiscreetly threw up my rights in the piece, which to this day remain of considerable value.

The breach seemed irreparable, and I had begun reluctantly and sorrowfully to reconcile myself to the fact that all was over between us, when the crowning misfortune of my life touched that large and generous heart, and brought us once more together.

My theatre in Leeds—born of my blood and bones and brains—was destroyed by fire. While the ashes were yet smoking, there came a letter from Lavender Sweep :

" We have seen to-day's *Times.* Remember you have still friends. Here, at least, are two or three. You know I am not rich, but I have a cheque-book and a banking account; both are at your disposal. Don't stand on ceremony. Write or come or both ; there is a knife and fork and a welcome always waiting."

He was as good as his word. I was glad to grasp that honest hand once more, and to smoke the pipe of peace.

The story of our brief acquaintance is told.

Of Mr. Taylor's genius I have already spoken ; of his manliness and generosity much might be said, more than restricted space permits.

His temper was of fire, but his heart was of gold.

Despite his petulance, his intolerance of contradiction, his *brusquerie*, his occasional affluence of adjectives :

> " His life was gentle, and the elements
> So mix'd in him that Nature might stand up
> **And say** to all the world,
>   ' This was a Man !' "

The other day I went to try to find Lavender Sweep. That delightful home—the home he loved so well, the home which he made such sacrifices to obtain—is all gone ; not a stone remains to mark where it stood, and the demon jerry-builder reigns triumphant where once the genial editor of *Punch* and his accomplished wife dispensed their open-handed hospitality.

CHAPTER XII.

TOM ROBERTSON.

" A GENTLEMAN to see you, sir," said the landlady to a lad at Leicester some thirty years ago or more.

The lad had barely turned fifteen, but he was tall and stalwart beyond his years.

He was in sore tribulation, and small wonder ; he had succeeded in obtaining an engagement to act utility at a guinea a week in the Leicester Theatre, with the result that after a remarkable passage at arms with the manager, which ensued immediately on his arrival, he had been instantly and ignominiously dismissed.

A night of never-to-be-forgotten horrors followed. Friendless and hopeless, the river, beside which he wandered for some hours in the darkness of the tempestuous night, seemed to suggest the surest refuge from his troubles. At the supreme moment, however, another idea presented itself—to enlist. Cobbett and Coleridge had done so before him, so there was no lack of goodly precedent. Resolving, therefore, on the morrow to seek out a recruiting-sergeant, he **returned to his** humble lodgings, **went** hungry and **supperless to** bed, and cried himself **(he** was only **a** boy) to sleep.

Possibly **fair** daylight, **a tolerable flow of** animal spirits, **and** a voracious appetite had asserted their **sway, and enabled him** to attack his frugal **breakfast.**

Be that as **it** may, **he** paused, and replied, "**Show the** gentleman in."

A moment later, **another lad,** tall **and** slender, with reddish-brown **hair and reddish-brown** eyes, entered **the room.**

The two lads took **stock** of each other. **The new-**comer was Master **Tom Robertson,** the manager's son ; the other was—myself.

Master **Tom was** a precocious young gentleman, and although **only a** year or two my senior, **he sat** upon me relentlessly. Although he didn't say **so in** so many words, he speedily convinced me **of the** turpitude of my conduct **in** endeavouring to obtain **a** guinea a week under false **pretences.**

" My good sir," **said he,** "you **don't** know the governor, else you'd have **been** aware that under certain circumstances—especially upon the opening night **of** the season—it is absolutely essential for him to let the steam off. If you had only accepted those few doubtful compliments with equanimity (as you ought to have done !), this fuss would have been avoided. Besides all this, you have committed an outrageous assault upon the governor, who had to go on for your part at a moment's notice. **He** was strongly inclined to take **you** before the beaks

for assault and battery, but my mother has taken
compassion on your youth and inexperience. She
thinks, for everybody's sake, it would be better for
you to carry out your engagement, and take a
month's notice, commencing from yesterday."

To my untutored mind this proposal appeared a
perfect godsend, and I jumped at it; indeed, I
was so impressed with the magnanimity of the
managerial mind, that I left no stone unturned to
evince my gratitude, and worked day and night at
anything and everything allotted me.

The members of the company were all very charming people, and were very kind to the poor novice.

Mr. Sam Butler, the tragedian (an admirable and
accomplished actor), was especially kind, and took
great pains in coaching me up in my parts, especially
in François in "Richelieu," which he desired me to
play with him.

From this time forth the elder hope of the
Robertsons and I became great chums, and took
long walks together, during which, with the modesty
of youth, each ventilated his favourite shibboleth
about art.

Both were bound to become great tragedians, of
that there could be no possibility of doubt; both
were also to be dramatists, and were to write
tragedies, of course—in fact, we devised one there
and then, based upon a local cause *célèbre*, in which
love and jealousy were mixed up; but we never
got beyond the plot, being at variance as to the
dénouement.

I wanted the murderer to die **by** poison, and his victim to come **to life, marry her** lover, and live happy ever after; but the dramatist of the future held out **for** first principles. **He** insisted that the murderer should be hanged *coram populo;* **that at** the moment when he was "turned off," the ghost of his victim should appear, clad in white, like the "Castle Spectre," through a transparent cloth at the back of the gibbet, lighted up with blue fire.

Evidently my *collaborateur* was of the same mind with the late lamented **Crummles,** when **he** dilated to Nicholas Nickleby upon the advantages accruing from the tub and **the pump.**

"My dear boy," said **Tom,** "**we** have all the stuff **in** the theatre—the George Barnwell gibbet, **the** Jack Ketch rope, and the rest of the props."

Upon my suggesting that an execution was incompatible with the dignity **of the** classic drama, **we** agreed to differ, and that tragedy was never written.

We next devised **a** piece **of** another description, suggested by the wonderful performance of Monsieur Gouffé, the man-monkey, **who** was acting with a circus company at **the** amphitheatre in Humberstone Gate.

We went to see this remarkable personage in "Jocko, the Brazilian Ape," and were so impressed by his tragic death-scene that we concluded to write a *pièce de circonstance* to give greater scope to his undoubted ability.

Upon going round to interview the renowned performer, Tom opened fire in French, but was

speedily cut short in the most unmistakable White-
chapel patois, after this fashion : " Stow it, cully ;
none of your kid here! I ain't to be 'ad. Wot's
your little game ?"

Upon explaining our views, monsieur replied that
" the fakements are all rumbo, and I don't want no
new-fangled slums, nor yet any adjective swells
a-coming to take a rise out of me, so you'd better
take your 'ook."

As we retired in graceful confusion, we both
arrived at the conclusion that monsieur only needed
the prehensile appendage to be in reality that which
he simulated so admirably.   His face and form were
unmistakably Simian, and his standard of intelligence but one stage removed from the brute he
impersonated ; indeed, if ever the Darwinian theory
needed corroborative testimony, it might surely have
been found in the person of Monsieur Gouffé.

And thus our second attempt at collaboration
vanished into air.

A capital company of travelling comedians were
acting at the fair, and whenever we could get out of
the bill at the theatre, we used to run down and pay
stolen visits to the itinerants, many of whom have
since blossomed into famous performers.

It is strange how what actors call the " business "
of plays travels from town to country, over sea and
land.   These good people were perpetually playing
the farce of " Lovers' Quarrels," "conveyed " by Sir
John Vanbrugh from Molière.   Years after, I saw
Coquelin and others doing exactly the same business,

MRS. KENDAL (MADGE ROBERTSON) AS
LADY CLANCARTY.

garters and all (Honi soit qui mal y pense), in " Le Dépit Amoureux," at the house of Molière.

During my month's probation I was entrusted with a number of important parts, and had almost begun to believe that my backslidings had been condoned.

Vain hope! It is true that at the end of the month my manageress suggested that I should stay, but she coupled my staying with the stipulation that my salary should be reduced to twelve shillings a week.

This was not very inviting, but half a loaf is better than no bread, so I stood it as long as I could.

Doubtless arriving at the conclusion that Satan ever finds some mischief for idle hands to do, the M.S. of "Susan Hopley" was given me to copy.

Those who are familiar with my unfortunate caligraphy may readily realize the treat which was in store for the unfortunate prompter.

Upon mooting the question of compensation, I was informed that I was already amply compensated by the receipt of my munificent honorarium; but that, in consequence of my detestable and illegible scrawl, the management would not call on me to copy any more MSS.

From Leicester we went to Sheffield (I paid my own fare out of that noble twelve shillings a week!), and here Orestes and Pylades parted company.

At that period Master Tom's ambitious aspirations prompted him to regard with jealous eyes anything approximating to rivalry. I was taken out of

the part of François *sans cérémonie*, and Master
Tom was put over my head. The grief and mortification I suffered from that humiliation I find, even
at this distance of time, difficult to describe.

In consequence of this injustice our budding
friendship came to an abrupt termination, and my
disaffection ripened into a rebellion which culminated
in my leaving the company at a moment's notice.

Two or three years later, the managerial régime
of the Robertsons came to an end, and the family
migrated to London, and thence to various provincial theatres, where their proficiency stood them
in good stead.

It was at this period that Tom Robertson commenced that weary fight with fortune against which
he struggled manfully for so many years.

Our acquaintance, which had terminated so
abruptly, was renewed thuswise. The fickle goddess, who had so persistently frowned upon him,
had smiled upon me, and I had been successful
beyond my deserts.

At the end of my second season in Bath and
Bristol, I passed through London *en route* to Canterbury and Rochester, where I was engaged to fill
out a few weeks during the summer.

On the evening of my arrival in town, a friend
took me to the Wrekin in Broad Court, for the purpose of showing me the place to which Edmund
Kean was brought upon the memorable night when
he finally broke down at Covent Garden.

The setting sun flooded the almost empty **room** with a lurid light as we entered. Exactly opposite sat two seedy, unshorn-looking young fellows smoking their **pipes.** One of them held an inverted pewter pot in his hand, **draining the** last drop **of porter into** the spittoon. The **noise of the** opening door evidently attracted his **attention.** As he looked up our eyes met, and we recognised each **other.** It **was** Tom Robertson. His companion **was his** life-long friend, Fred Younge.

After all these years I can see that **picture now** as clearly as I saw **it then.** Tom whispered something **to** his companion, who whispered back again. Thought-reading **was** then unknown, **yet,** although I didn't hear one word **of** this conversation, **I** instinctively divined what they had said, **and years** later I learned from Robertson's own lips **that my** instinct was not at fault.

After an awkward pause **we** fraternized and passed the evening together, comparing **notes as** to our respective careers. His tragic aspirations had been cruelly disappointed, and **the** disappointment had left behind a bitterness towards **all** successful histrions, especially tragedians, which never left **him** to the day of his death.

It was fortunate for the world that he was a disappointed actor ; had he been a successful one, he would never have been a famous author. Before he abandoned acting, he made an effort to carve out an opening for himself in another department of the art. He devoted much time and attention to the study of

French character, but with dubious success. No
man knew more of the rudimental principles of his
craft; but no man with such fertile and abundant
resources ever achieved so little.

Although he succeeded in obtaining engagements
at various minor theatres, success obstinately and
persistently eluded his grasp.

Probably, of all the parts he ever attempted, the
only one in which he achieved even a moderate
success was an eccentric idiot of a cavalier in a by
no means bad play, called "Love and Loyalty,"
written by Robson, the Crystal Palace forger, which
was produced by James William Wallack at the
Marylebone Theatre, and was upon one occasion
transferred to Drury Lane, for the benefit of that
renowned impresario, E. T. Smith.

It is popularly believed that, given a certain
amount of culture and intelligence, nothing is so
easy as to act, whereas, in point of fact, nothing is so
difficult. All the culture, all the intelligence in the
world are utterly useless without the special gifts
which are essential and indispensable to make an
actor.

These gifts Robertson did not possess. He had
the power to conceive, but he had not the capacity
to execute. He could tell other people what to do,
could show them how to do it, but he could not do
it himself.

He could write plays, he could stage-manage
them, he could teach people to act, he could do anything in connection with the histrionic art but act.

Hence it was that he concluded to turn his attention to stage-management and authorship, and he
did not hesitate to encounter even the drudgery of
the prompter's box to enable him to master the
object he had in view.

When Charles Reade and Mrs. Seymour formed
a company to tour the provinces, they were so fortunate as to secure his services in this capacity.

For a considerable period he fulfilled the same
duties in the company of Mr. C. A. Clarke, a well-
known manager, who in his time had been one of
the numerous secretaries of Alexandre Dumas, *père*.

In the days when Robertson had become the
great society dramatist, Clarke was wont to relate
with infinite glee a characteristic anecdote of his
sometime prompter.

During the season at Windsor the houses had
been very bad, and in order to give a fillip to the
business the manager had obtained the bespeak of
some of the lordly "flunkeys" of the royal household.

When he returned from the Castle radiant with the
glad tidings of his success, Robertson was conducting the rehearsal of the play for the night, and was
apparently not in the most amiable mood.

" What play have they selected, governor?" inquired a dozen eager voices.

" The comedy of ' Money,' " replied the manager.

" More d——d coat-and-trouser pieces!" exclaimed
the irate apostle of the future fashionable drama, as
he dashed the prompt-book to the ground.

At various periods Robertson took engagements to superintend amateur performances at certain country houses. I have often heard him say that, upon these occasions, it was amusing to note the petty jealousies which prevailed among these noble amateurs.

"The theatre's bad enough," said he, "but the actors ain't in it with the swells. Crimean heroes, fellahs who were in 'the thin red line at Inkerman,' or in the thick of that bloody business on the banks of the Alma, squabble like women, fight about a line or two, and stigmatize each other as duffers and impostors! Of course, of course! A fellah has only to rub his shoulders against the wings even of an amateur theatre to become thoroughly demoralized."

At this period he began to turn his attention to journalism. Even here, for a time, he found all doors closed against him.

Occasional stories for the *London Journal*, and publications of that class, served to help to keep the wolf from the door.

On one occasion he met an actor friend, to whom he gave one of these stories in type to read.

"Do you recognise it?" he inquired.

"'It's Clari, the Maid of Milan,'"* replied the other.

"Of course, of course, you know it, but those duffers of editors never have heard of Howard Payne, or Clari either," replied Tom.

---

* A drama by Howard Payne, in which the ballad of "Home, sweet Home" was first introduced.

At last he succeeded in penetrating the journalistic ranks, and one evening he came to me at Sadler's Wells Theatre flourishing an early number of *Fun*, in which some contribution of his had been accepted. He was radiant with delight.

It was at or about this time that he became connected with the Strand Theatre, then open as a commonwealth, under the direction of Mr. James Tully, the composer, and Mr. Allcroft, who succeeded in gathering around them a combination of young people destined hereafter to become famous. These were George Honey, Belford, George Hodson, H. J. Byron (whose first burlesque, "The Lady of Lyons," was produced here), Leicester Buckingham, Edward Gomersal, Johnny Clark, Charles Bernard (afterwards a famous manager), the redoubtable Tom himself, and the beautiful Miss Herbert, Miss Featherstone (afterwards Mrs. Howard Paul), etc.

It was during this time that Miss Henrietta Hodson (now Mrs. Labouchere) made her first appearance on the stage as the apparition of the "bloody child" in the burlesque of "Macbeth."

How the managers held their heads above water, how the actors kept the wolf from the door, ate bread and cheese, smoked tobacco, quaffed beer, and wore clean linen (although a little of that went a long way in those days!), is one of those mysteries which remain to this day unsolved and unsolvable.

When I had a vacation and a pound or two more than I knew what to do with, I used to run up to the happy hunting-grounds, and catch a glimpse or

two of the beautiful kingdom of Bohemia, perchance
more beautiful to an occasional wayfarer like myself
than to the perpetual dwellers therein.

After dinner, or the more fashionable theatre,
perchance the opera, I always dropped in at the
Strand for the finish.

When the play was over, we usually adjourned to
a well-known hostelry opposite Somerset House,
where many a time and oft "we have heard the
·chimes at midnight."

Hope deferred had made his heart sick, and the
·constant burthen of Robertson's theme was that
women had better be brought up to take in washing,
and men taught to make shoes—anything rather
than enter the hateful precincts of the buildings
where modest merit was trampled out of existence,
and where only impudent impostors and pretentious
idiots flourished.

When he had "let off steam" after the paternal
fashion, he would soften down, subside into "I don't
mind if I do," and admit that there was something
good in the world, even the theatrical world, after
all.

The years came and went, and he still remained
at the foot of the ladder, gazing indignantly "at the
dazzling and starry life beyond his reach."

Among the climbers upwards he now rubbed
shoulders with George Augustus Sala, Henry J.
Byron, Frank Talfourd, the brothers Brough,
Leicester Buckingham, Andrew Halliday, and scores
of others who have since become famous.

Among other expedients to keep the pot boiling, he now became the literary man of all work for Lacy, the publisher.

French's list, to this day, attests the industry and fecundity of poor Tom at this period. Here may be found his adaptation of " Ruy Blas," " Ladies' Battle," " Faust and Marguerite," " The Duke's Device," and a score of other works, for all of which he received but journeyman's wages ; in fact, I doubt if he ever received more than a couple of guineas an act for any of them.

At or about this time he became a member of a certain well-known literary and artistic club, compounded principally of young and disappointed aspirants for fame in the art of dramatic writing.

Obviously he knew more about histrionic art than any of his compeers ; hence he posed as an oracle, and they listened as to a Gamaliel.

At this period the men who really understood the canons of criticism, the men who had seen all the great exemplars of art, could be counted on the fingers of one hand. Occasionally severe, they were always scholarly, and never, or hardly ever, unjust. Certainly, never ungentlemanly.

Now commenced a new departure. Continual disappointment caused Robertson to dip his pen in gall, and he led a new crusade against English art and English actors, more particularly poetic actors. His superior knowledge enabled him to detect blots, and to point out holes in the armour of the giants. His youthful colleagues followed suit, and amongst them they ran amuck at everything and everybody in their way.

These gentlemen had all the zeal and all the proverbial discretion of proselytes. They modestly maintained that Shakespere was an antediluvian bore, Knowles was a dotard and a driveller, Bulwer a prig and a pretentious duffer. All managers were the born enemies of authors.

As for the Bard, he could be acted for nothing ; hence it behoved this band of brothers to hit out against the defunct and stupid old twaddler whose dry bones had for three or four centuries been twined around living men's necks and had actually deprived them of their daily bread !

Then came the onslaught on the Adelphi guests. Poor old Adelphi guests ! how their ghosts must have grimly smiled could they have seen the Gaiety guests, resplendent in the baggiest of bags, the Berlinest of Berlins, and the Blucherest of Bluchers, during the Bernhardt régime three or four years ago.

Next came the advent of Fechter, undoubtedly a man of genius, a man whom it was impossible to praise too highly. His appearance, with its extremely dubious commercial results, enabled the apostles of the new régime to heap insult upon insult upon English art and English actors.

Young gentlemen, with the down not yet fledged on their lips, who knew as much of art as the present writer does of Sanscrit, maintained that French art was the beau-ideal of perfection, and that English actors, with rare exceptions, and those principally amateur friends of the writers, were not artists at all. The self-constituted mission of these airy youths was to deride, to ridicule, and to hold up to contempt everything noble and manly—everything which generations of educated men and women had been taught to esteem and admire.

Some eighteen or twenty years ago Charles Reade wrote thus of this genus :

"When little men, with little heads, little hearts, little knowledge, little sensibility, and great vanity, go into a theatre, not to take in knowledge and humanity, but to give out ignorance and malice—not to profit by their mental superiors, but to disparage them—they are steeled against ennobling influences, and blinded to beauties, however obvious.

" But the retribution is sure.

"' Depreciation' is the writer's road to ruin. Men rise in our difficult art by the divine gift and the amiable habit of appreciation ; to appreciate our gifted contemporaries is to gather unconsciously a thousand flowers for our own basket.

" The depreciator detests and envies his gifted contemporaries, and so gathers nothing but weeds and self-deception. The appreciator makes a name, a fortune, and a signature.

" The depreciator tickles his own vanity, but gets to admire nothing, feel nothing, crush nothing, and be nothing but a thing without a name !"

Some of the persons here glanced at have grown older and wiser, and know better than they knew five-and-twenty years ago; they have learned to appreciate as well as to depreciate.

The tadpoles have developed into full-grown frogs; the Dizzys of that period have become the Beaconsfields of this; they have ceased to be Radical, and are now sedately Conservative—nay, some of them are actually beginning to deplore the absence of some of the elder actors, whose mature and virile art they formerly held up to derision.

One thing must always be said in their favour —they were always loyal and faithful to their friends.

With scarce an exception they stood by Robertson through thick and thin, and hailed him as the incarnation of a new Avatar.

As for him, one of the best signs of his native goodness of heart was the loyalty with which he clung to his old comrades. During his period of storm and strife, his boyish chums, the brothers Younge (Richard and Frederick) had migrated to Australia with G. V. Brooke and Coppin.

Upon returning home, they found all avenues closed to them; but Tom took Fred Younge by the hand, and did not scruple to confide to him (though he was supposed to be a low comedian) the horsy and asinine hero of " Caste."

Some time prior to the production of this play, we dined at the Savage (then under the Piazza) with Byron. We were all doing ample justice to the good things before us, except poor Byron, who was a martyr to dyspepsia.

Younge reminded the others of some youthful escapade at Scarborough.

"Do you remember," said he, "that memorable haul of herrings—a shilling a hundred? How we pitched into them! I ate a score myself. I never met such herrings!"

"And the herrings never met such appetites!" grimly responded Byron. "Ah! I'd give all I've done since to have the hope, the health, and the appetite of those days!"

After dinner we went to Drury Lane to see "King John." I went for pleasure; they for business, having each to write a notice of the performance.

We met Chatterton in the rotunda. He was no stranger to the antagonistic feeling which they entertained towards him and his management, and peremptorily declined to admit them, alleging that every seat was engaged.

As they retired to the vestibule, he called me aside, and whispered, "The best seats in the house for you, dear boy, and C." (a friend who was with me), "but not a square inch for those adjective substantives!"

When I returned to Robertson and Byron, they were absolutely dancing a breakdown of delight at not being condemned to witness "this diabolical performance of this diabolical play"!

I have cited this anecdote as an apposite illustration of the unreasoning dislike which both these authors entertained at that period for the poetic drama and its expositors.

Robertson's antipathy was accentuated by his scorn and contempt for managers.

It is perhaps scarcely to be wondered at, considering the indignities he had endured at their hands. I met him one day in the Strand, a mysterious brown-paper parcel in his hand, head aloft, hair long and unkempt, teeth grinding, nostrils dilated, eyes aflame.

" What's up ?   House afire ?" I inquired.

" No, no ; but *I* am!   I've just been reading this play—a splendid play, a magnificent play—to Sefton Parry!   What do you think he said ?"

" Don't know."

" Why, he said it was ' rot'!   What do you think *I* said ?"

" Can't guess."

" I told him that until that moment I was in doubt as to whether the play was a good one or not ; but now that he had pronounced it to be a bad one, my assured conviction that he was such a blazing idiot had convinced me that the play was really a good one !"

That play was " Society."

This work had been hawked about from pillar to post ; no manager in London would even look at it, when at length it had the good fortune to attract the attention of the late Alexander Henderson.

This astute personage gave it its initial performance at the Prince of Wales's Theatre, Liverpool, where I saw it in May, 1865.   It was capitally acted, and, despite its crudities and absurdities, made an immediate mark.

Its production in town speedily followed. **Mrs.**
Bancroft states that she produced "Society" entirely
on her own initiative. Byron assured me that he
recommended it highly. However that may be, it
is certain that Robertson owed his first step on the
ladder of fame to that man of dubious antecedents,
Alexander Henderson.

Then came the friendly **aid** and native sagacity **of**
the Miss Marie Wilton of that period.

The production of "Society" marked **the dawn of**
a new era in dramatic **literature. It was said of**
"The Beggars' Opera" that **it made** Rich gay and
Gay rich. Similarly **it** might be said of "Society"
that it was the stepping-stone **to Tom** Robertson's fame, and the foundation of **Marie** Wilton's
fortune.

Then followed a continual succession **of those**
deftly fashioned drawing-room charades not inaptly
designated "cup-and-saucer" dramas, which **for**
years were the vogue with fashionable London.

For years the *haut ton* **jostled with each** other **as**
they struggled in **and** out **of the** most detestable
little hole ever dignified with the name of a theatre,
for the purpose of assisting in that which the art of
Robertson and the cultured skill of Marie Wilton
and her accomplished colleagues elevated into the
apotheosis of the commonplace.

The author knew what his public wanted, and he
gave it them. Whenever he suffered his dramatic
instincts to carry him away, whenever he was in
sight of a great situation, he pulled up and reduced

his art to the standard of his auditors' intelligence.

Conspicuous examples of this may be found in the second and third acts of "Caste," when that redoubtable replica of Rawdon Crawley, yclept George d'Alroy, goes to the wars, and when he returns with the milk-can.

The most notable illustration, however, of this "effect defective" is to be found at the end of the second act of "Ours," where, in a supreme moment, the actor's art is dwarfed down to the braying of a brass band and the hoarse roar of multitudinous voices behind the scenes.

Let the reader contrast this emasculation of a great dramatic idea with the end of the fourth act of the much-maligned "Lady of Lyons," and then see how small and puerile the commonplace appears beside the outburst of human emotion, which sets every heart afire, when the wretched Melnotte takes that heart-rending farewell of the woman he has so loved, so wronged.

"Ours" was Robertson's next effort, and that was also produced for the first time in Liverpool in August, 1866, and was transferred to London three weeks later, where it ran till the production of "Caste" in April, 1867.

The ambition of his life was to write a great popular drama, but he never succeeded in achieving that object. "Shadow Tree Shaft," in which he was assisted by the great practical skill of the veteran dramatist of the minors, Mr. J. B. Johnstone, was

MR. AND MRS. S. B. BANCROFT.

produced in this same year (1867), at the Princess's
by George Vining, and failed disastrously. The
" Nightingale" at the Adelphi, and " For Love" at
the Holborn, shared a similar fate. " A Rapid
Thaw," produced at the St. James's Theatre during
the management of Miss Hubert, turned out to be,
in the argot of the theatre, " A Severe Frost," and
collapsed altogether after an inglorious existence of
six nights, and has never since seen the light.

" Caste," however, proved a triumphant success,
and was only withdrawn in the following year (1868)
to make room for " Play."

Despite the repeated and disastrous failures before
referred to, Robertson's work was now in great
demand, and in 1869 he produced within two days
of each other, January 14th and 16th, " Home" at
the Haymarket, and " School" at the Prince of
Wales's. A month later he produced " Lady Clara
Vere de Vere " at Liverpool, for the German actor,
Bandman, and his accomplished wife, who had both
recently made a success in " Narcisse" at the Lyceum.
The success of " Lady Clara" was so doubtful as to
induce Bandman to immediately withdraw it from his
repertoire.

Baffled, but not beaten, Robertson produced it at
the Gaiety, a month later, under the title of
" Dreams." Miss Robertson (now Mrs. Kendal)
distinguished herself highly in the heroine, Alfred
Wigan failed most signally in the hero, while John
Clayton achieved the success of his life in the
Duke.

One felt inclined to say, "Give us the yah-yah swell, with the plums in his mouth, and the English heart in his body, to the pretentious prig of a foreigner." For all this, the play was but a *succès d'estime*, and has now disappeared altogether from the acting drama.

Other plays of Robertson's, produced at other theatres, were even more unfortunate, and a play which Sothern produced with me—the very name of which I have forgotten—dropped almost still-born.

Indeed, with the exception of "Home" and "Garrick," adapted for Sothern from the French, out of the magic circle of the Prince of Wales's Theatre, and the admirable troupe of comedians whose idiosyncrasies he had carefully studied (even, as it is said, the younger Colman, Reynolds, and Morton studied the specialities of the matchless Lewis, Emery, Quick, Munden, and other great actors of the Georgian era), Robertson never achieved a success worth speaking of.

Much attention was directed to the alleged plagiarisms of Reade and Tom Taylor; but those of Robertson attracted comparatively little attention. Jack Randall in "Birth" is a distinct prig from Vapid in "The Dramatist;" "Home" is taken bodily from "L'Aventurière;" "Garrick" from "Sullivan;" and "School" from Benedick's "Cinderella;" but no one appears to have recognised the genesis of "Caste," or, if so, they have kept the knowledge to themselves.

Those who desire enlightenment on the subject

may satisfy their curiosity by referring to "La Vie d'une Comédienne," by Théophilus Barrière.

The ugly duckling is ever the pet of the maternal duck, and the author still retained a lurking fondness for the unfortunate "Dreams." To give it another chance of survival, he arranged with Mr. Fred Younge to produce it in the country with the "Caste" company.

My audience was generally made the *corpus vili* for these experiments, and Robertson came to Leeds to superintend the rehearsals.

On the last day of his visit, I came over to see him. He, Younge, and I dined together, and a very delightful afternoon we spent, "acting our young encounters o'er again."

The cruel malady which ultimately brought him to an untimely grave as yet had scarcely made a sign ; the rift had broken in his stormy sky ; all was bright and cloudless ; the future promised gleams of happiness to come ; he was a boy again.

After dinner I induced him to explain the mysterious pantomime, and its whispered accompaniment, which took place when we three had met at the Wrekin so many years before.

"Now," said I, "on a certain summer's evening ever so many years ago, a young man entered the Wrekin—a young man——"

"From the country, with hair half-way down his back," interrupted Younge.

"And a shirt-front like a bow-window," continued Robertson.

"All right." said I. "I perceive you recognise the picture. Doubtless you remember the other two young men and the empty pewter. Well, one of them turned round and whispered something to the other. You recollect that ?"

"Perfectly."

"I didn't hear a syllable that you uttered, but I know what you said as well as if I had heard it. If I guess rightly, will you tell me ?"

"Certainly ; go ahead."

"Well, you said, ' Here's another impostor, with clean linen and a five-pound note in his pocket, while our united resources won't run to another pint of porter !' "

"You've hit it, dear boy ; you've hit it, word for word !" roared Tom—whereat we all roared in unison.

That evening I saw him off to town ; at his desire despatched an insurance ticket for the journey to his wife. Then we shook hands and parted, and that was the last I ever saw of Tom Robertson.

Fate had been cruel to him. It had accorded him a stormy youth, a tempestuous manhood, a career of perpetual trial, struggle, and privation ; and—when, after years of disappointed hopes, he had reached the goal of his ambition ; when fame and fortune and domestic happiness awaited him— he was cut off at the zenith of his golden prime.

CHAPTER XIII.

It is so long since I first became acquainted with the subject of this paper, that I have a difficulty in recalling when or where we first met.

Whether it was at the Garrick, the Arundel, at Charles Reade's house in Mayfair, or upon some first night (he was always *en évidence* on first nights), I cannot now recall. I only remember that it was in my *première jeunesse;* that I thought him a delightful young old fellow, and that, from that time until now, when the end has come which must come to us all, we remained on terms of friendly intimacy.

During my managerial days, Mr. Simpson was secretary to the Dramatic Authors' Society, a position which brought us into continual contact.

At a period in life when most men convert their "swords to ploughshares," their mansions to "hives for humming bees," he took a new lease of life.

He loved to surround himself with young people, but was always the youngest fellow in the company.

Let who will tell a story ne'er so good, "dear

old Pal" would cap it with something smarter and brighter, improvised for the moment, or culled from the varied and vivid experiences of half a century.

The only mature emotion he permitted himself was his paternal regard for his adopted son, Mr. John Clayton, in whom he took all a father's pride, and from whom he received a son's devotion.

The regard of these two for each other was a tender and delightful thing to witness.

For years Palgrave Simpson's Sunday mornings were the pleasantest things of the kind in town. Alas! they are all over.

"Where be your gibes now? your gambols? your songs? your flashes of merriment, that were wont to set the table on a roar?"

He was essentially a modern-idea'd man, and one of the iconoclastic order.

I remember being shocked with his description of his first play.

He was taken as a boy to the Norwich Theatre (the Simpsons hailed from Norfolk) to see John Kemble's farewell in Cato.

One would have thought the noble youth would have been impressed with "The Last of the Romans."

Not a bit, the irreverent dog stigmatized "Black Jack" as being a tiresome, asthmatic, antediluvian old duffer—with a feeble falsetto voice.

It was idle to argue with him on this subject; he simply laughed me to scorn, and held to his guns.

One of his earliest stage acquaintances was the

gentle Edward Ball, since known to fame as Edward FitzBall of that ilk.

Fitz's first play—of a series of five or six hundred, more or less—was acted in Norwich, and Palgrave "assisted" at the occasion, and was more impressed with it, and the local tragedian, than he was with Cato or Kemble.

Being left in fairly affluent circumstances, he went to make the grand tour, and was so pleased with Continental customs that he remained abroad till approaching the meridian of life.

At length being overtaken by a serious reverse of fortune, he devoted himself to light literature, writing for the magazines, etc.

From boyhood he had an ingrained taste for the drama, and he now concluded to try his hand at dramatic composition.

To render himself proficient in the art of construction, he articled himself for a term as a pupil to Eugene Scribe, from whom he learnt the rudimental principles of dramatization.

He returned to England armed with a number of plays, principally of the lighter order, under the impression that he had only to present himself, and the door of every playhouse in London would open to their future lord and master. Like many aspirants before and since, he was woefully disappointed.

He was not, however, easily daunted, and at length, after two or three years, he found his "Open, sesame."

Thereby hangs a tale :

During my last engagement at Newcastle-on-Tyne, my friend, the late Sidney Davis, gave me a comedy in three acts, called " Passing through Fire," which some thief has since stolen! This by the way!

The play was from the German of the Princess Amelia of Saxony, and I wanted Pal's advice about placing it.

Having carefully read it, he said, " It's a capital piece, but it isn't strong enough for three acts; besides which, I've done it already in one; in point of fact it was the first piece I ever got produced," and going to the bookshelf he handed me a copy of a charming little one-act piece, entitled " Poor Cousin Walter."

" It's worth telling how I got that piece done," he continued.

" I had tried everywhere, and failed everywhere, when at length a mutual friend gave me an introduction to Leigh Murray, who at that time was confined to the house with a virulent attack of quinsy—so virulent, indeed, that it was expected to prove fatal.

" Now, Leigh and I were neighbours in Brompton, and I passed the crossing opposite to his house daily.

" The sweeper was a poor cripple, and I always dropped him a copper.

" This operation, combined with my peculiar appearance, my beard, my swarthy complexion, my cloak, and the felt hat which I affected in the winter, attracted the attention of the **Murrays,** who christened me ' The Benevolent Brigand.'

" Well, **when I** called **to** present my **letter of** introduction, **Mrs.** Murray, who came to receive **me,** could scarcely restrain herself from **laughing in my** face.

" ' Excuse **me one moment, sir,'** said **she, as she** ran upstairs.

" ' Who **do you** think **it is, my dear ?'** she asked of Leigh.

" ' **Don't know,'** he gasped—for **the poor** fellow could scarcely **speak.**

" ' Why, whom but **the " Benevolent** Brigand." '

" **The** idea **so tickled** Leigh that **he** burst into **a roar** of laughter, which **burst** the quinsy, **saved** his life, enabled him **to play ' Poor** Cousin Walter,' **and** gave me my first **introduction to the stage."**

I think Simpson's **next production** was " Second **Love "** at the Haymarket, a play **which** is **one** of the most delightful pieces **of** the kind **in** existence.

After this came " Daddy Hardacre," an admirable adaptation from **the French,** remembered chiefly **by** the brilliant achievement **of** that **fiery** but pigmy genius, **poor** Fred Robson.

Simpson had a facile and **a** prolific pen, more remarkable for neatness and elegance than strength. To speak **truly,** he never arose to power, but everything he **touched** denoted the gentleman and the scholar.

As a mere work of constructive skill, nothing **on** the English stage can excel his admirable dramatization of Mr. Edmund Yates's " Black Sheep," a

work which only failed to attract through Charles
Mathews's execrable attempt at Stuart Routh.

There were strong moments, though, in the acting
of the other parts. Mrs. Charles Mathews, who had
been a tragedienne in her own country, doomed
by adverse circumstances to pose herself here as a
comedienne, was strong as fire and true as steel in
Mrs. Routh ; and, barring his nasal mannerism, so
was Johnny Clark, as Jim, the street arab.

Two or three of the plays, written in collaboration
with Herman Merivale, it goes without saying, are
distinguished by power as well as by skill ; but the
only work of Palgrave Simpson's which still holds
the stage is his admirable adaptation from Sardou,
entitled " A Scrap of Paper." Two masters, in their
way, had tried their hand at this work, viz., Watts
Phillips and Charles Mathews ; but their adaptations
are forgotten, while Simpson's lives, and will certainly
continue to live, so long as Mrs. Kendal's admirable
art remains to vivify it.

His Continental experiences had made him such a
peripatetic cyclopedia upon all things pertaining to
the genesis of the French and German drama, that
he was a terror to our pirates.

It was no use Mr. Barnaby Bouncer announcing
his new and original comedy if Pal happened to be
in the way.

He rarely or ever spoiled the prigger's game the
first night, but if one happened to call the next day
to make an inquiry, the " seer " would smile benig-

nantly, put his hand on one of his numerous volumes, and point out the original.

He had acted a good deal as an amateur, and prided himself not a little on what he believed to be his proficiency in the actor's art.

His crack part was Grampus, in " The Wreck Ashore," which, in my juvenalia, I remember to have seen him act at the Lyceum, in connection with Byron, Brough, Leicester Buckingham, and others.

He had a difficulty with his *r*'s, which somewhat detracted from the manliness of Grampus, who became, under his treatment, a mild, inoffensive, and gentlemanly freebooter.

At one time Pal had serious thoughts of taking to the stage, and he went about the country with the Wigans, acting with them at Liverpool and elsewhere ; but, like Byron, he was a blighted being, and abandoned the task in disgust.

At first intended for a clergyman of the Established Church, he drifted into the realms of freethought, and became a pronounced agnostic.

Years ago, however, he had an awakening after a serious illness.

All ways lead to Rome, and for many years he had been drifting in that direction.

Recently, in a serious moment (a rare thing with him), he told me of the premature death of a mutual friend (a young author of rare promise), whose last moments were so soothed and sanctified by the consolations of the old faith, that he (Simpson) had himself turned to the Rock of Ages, and had there found refuge for his doubts and fears.

He had, in fact, been converted by a brother of the Oratory, who, like Cardinal Howard, had been a man about town and an officer in the Household Brigade.

"Father Sebastian," said he, "is the noblest, finest fellow in the world. Let me introduce you. I want him to convert you. No! not to convert you, but to take you back to the fold."

When I smiled and said something sceptical, he burst out, "Don't laugh, my boy; don't laugh. D——n it all, you must save your soul alive!"

Let us hope his soul is saved, anyhow.

Nearly two years ago he lent me a couple of volumes of Balzac, which, by an unfortunate accident, I had omitted to return.

The last time I ever saw the dear old boy was at the Prince of Wales's Theatre, the first night of the "Jilt," July 29th, 1886.

He had long been a martyr to bronchial asthma, and was evidently breaking fast.

After a hurried chat, he begged me to return his "Comédie Humaine."

I was going out of town, and it was not until my return long after that I bethought me of my promise. Talk about coincidences—here is a strange one :

On the 19th of August, 1885, these two volumes were packed and directed to be sent by parcel post.

By some fatality they got mixed up with a heap of other books, were thrown aside, and were only accidentally exhumed the very day before he died.

"I'll go up to Simpson's to lunch to-morrow, and take the books with me," said I.

"You'll never lunch with poor Mr. Simpson again," said a lady on the other side of the breakfast-table as she handed me the morning paper, in which I read the following paragraph :

"DEATH OF MR. J. PALGRAVE SIMPSON.—We regret to announce the death of this well-known dramatic author, which occurred yesterday. Mr. John Palgrave Simpson is perhaps best known to the public as the author of the dramas, 'World and Stage,' and 'Second Love,' the latter of which is very popular in America, and has been translated into several foreign languages, and as the adapter of 'A Scrap of Paper.' He was born in Norfolk, according to 'Men of the Time,' early in the present century, and received his education first under a private tutor, and afterwards at Corpus Christi College, Cambridge, where he took his degree of Master of Arts. Although intended for the Church, he entertained a great objection to taking holy orders, and instead travelled for many years on the Continent, residing at several foreign Courts. A 'severe reverse of fortune' occurred to him, and as he was now obliged to work for his livelihood, he betook himself to literature, contributing articles for many years to *Blackwood* and *Fraser* and *Bentley's Miscellany*. It was not till

1850 that Mr. Simpson began to write for the stage, a department of literature in which he achieved considerable success. He has produced about sixty pieces of different kinds. Besides the dramas we have mentioned as coming from his pen, he also wrote 'Sybilla; or, Step by Step,' 'All for Her,' 'Alone,' and 'Time and the Hour.' Collaborating with Mr. Herman Merivale, he is also responsible for 'Court Cards,' 'A School for Coquettes,' and other plays. Among his latest works is a life of Weber, compiled from materials collected by the son of the great composer, and a novel called 'For Ever and Never.'"

Except the introductory lines, this paragraph was written by Mr. Simpson himself!

Surely a more modest epigraph was never written.

When I took his beloved Balzac to Alfred Place, as I walked down the lonely and deserted street I could almost fancy that it was peopled with ghosts in the gloaming.

Charming Marie Litton's dainty face seemed to peep out above the window-blind of the house opposite. Big jolly Pellew, with his everlasting "Have a weed?" glided noiselessly on one side, and poor Claude Dangois on the other; while up above in the silent chamber, behind the library, lay him whom we had all known and loved so well.

His trusted friend and servant told me that only a few days before his death Mr. Simpson

insisted upon going down to the Spa at Tunbridge
Wells.

On his arrival he was well enough to dine at the
table d'hôte; next morning he was taken dangerously
ill, and was immediately ordered home.

Then, and not till then, a premonition of the end
seemed to seize him.

On Thursday, August 18th, 1886, he received the
last sacrament. He had a restless night; on Friday
morning at five he fell asleep, and never woke again.

At six o'clock he passed away without a sigh—
without a sound.

The medical certificate states that his death was
caused by "asthma, chronic bronchitis, and exhaus-
tion."

On the following Tuesday, a few relatives and
friends followed "Dear old Pal" to St. George's
Cemetery, where, after eighty years' pilgrimage on
earth, he rests in the hope of a life beyond the
grave.

As I left the churchyard I shook hands with John
Clayton, and bade him good-bye.

That good-bye was destined to be good-bye for
ever.

Barely twelve months elapsed before this fine
manly fellow followed his friend and father to "that
bourne from whence no traveller returns."

Poor Jack!

> " He should have died hereafter ;
> There would have been a time for such a word."

I learn from an authoritative source that Mr.

Simpson left behind him a diary of thirty volumes of remarkable events connected with the inner life of the Drama, extending over the past thirty years.

When his will was made in 1869, he directed that these treasures of dramatic history were to be destroyed at his death.

He had, however, of late years repeatedly avowed his intention to alter that clause in his will.

As he never did so, it is feared his executors will have no discretion in the matter, and will feel bound to adhere to the letter of the testament.   Let us hope not.

F. ROBSON AS JEM BAGGS IN "THE WANDERING
MINSTREL."

INTERMEZZO.

THE SOCIAL STATUS OF THE ACTOR.

This paper, which was called forth by a remarkable contribution of Mr. Burnand's to the *Fortnightly*, appeared originally in *The National Review*.

As it bears especial significance to the position occupied by the actor in the social scheme, I have ventured to place it here—midway between the record of "The Victors and the Vanquished."

Mr. Burnand has had the temerity to affirm that the actor's calling is burdened with a stigma which has always deprived him of social status, and still debars him from being received in society on the same footing with the "briefless barrister, the poor clergyman, or the humblest officer in her Majesty's service."

Let us examine how far this assertion accords with the facts.

In the time of Elizabeth, when the actor's art first took bodily form and shape in this country, and the players were the mediums for informing the public mind with the noblest dramatic literature the world has produced, our great master (himself an actor)

33—2

made the prince of scholars and of gentlemen describe the players thus : " They are the abstract and
brief chronicles of the time ; after your death you
had better have a bad epitaph than their ill-report
while you live." More distinction attached to the
name of gentleman then than now. Yet the great
actors bore their coats-of-arms, and in their leases
and wills were designated gentlemen. The fact of
Ben Jonson's being a bitter bad actor was no bar to
his becoming Poet Laureate.

Were I disposed to discuss the fight which commenced between the players and the Puritans, three
centuries and a half ago, and which is still waging,
I should probably find as much to say on the one
side as the other ; for I am an Englishman before I
am an actor, and I know how much England, and
the world, owe to the progress of that noble though
narrow-minded faith.   For the present I confine
myself to stating that though the Puritans succeeded
in closing the play-houses, no " social stigma " debarred Mohun, Hart and others from bearing
commissions in his Majesty's service, and fighting
for their King ; nor did Davenant's relations with
the players debar him from succeeding to the
Laureateship, or from being the faithful servant and
confidential emissary of the ill-fated Charles, and of
his wife, the unfortunate Henrietta Maria.

At the Restoration, most assuredly, Tom Killigrew's connection with the stage never interfered with
his intimate relations with that graceless scoundrel,
the " Merry Monarch," and his Court.   I do not cite

the King's friendship for Killigrew as an honour to
the stage ; I merely mention it as an illustration of
the position he occupied in the " society" of the
period.

Colley Cibber's being an actor did not deter him
from gaining the laurel wreath in an age of giants,
when there were such men as Pope, and Swift, and
Bolingbroke in the land.

No "social stigma" deterred the University of
Cambridge from bestowing upon Thomas Sheridan,
in full conclave, the honorary degree of Master of
Arts ; and five-and-twenty years later, in 1746, the
sister University of Oxford evidently did not consider that Holman had brought discredit on his
alma mater by becoming an actor, inasmuch as the
powers there gave him his degree long after he had
gone upon the stage.

The circumstance that Richard Brinsley was the
son of Tom Sheridan the actor, and was himself
manager of a theatre, did not prevent him from
becoming the intimate friend of Pitt, Fox, and the
Prince Regent, nor from serving his country with
distinction in three successive Parliaments ; nor am
I aware that the knowledge that the Sheridans trace
their descent from an actor has ever reflected the
slightest stigma on the Queens of Beauty and the
Kings of Brains that gifted family has bequeathed
to the nation.

Quin's being an actor neither prevented him from
being selected as tutor to George III., nor from
being king of the little world of fashion at Bath ;

while as for Garrick, a well-known anecdote may
serve to illustrate his position in the society of his
time.   During an important debate in the House of
Commons, it was ordered that "strangers do leave
the House."   Roscius alone remained behind. Some
fox-hunting booby, espying him, demanded that
"this House be cleared of strangers;" whereupon
Pitt rose on one side of the gangway, and was
followed by Fox on the other, each declaring "that
if the honourable member persisted in offering this
insult to the man whom the House so esteemed and
honoured, the one would move, and the other would
second, the adjournment of the debate."   Such was
Garrick's social status during his life, and we are
told by Johnson that "his death eclipsed the gaiety
of nations."

It were a thrice-told tale to recount the honours
paid to the memory of this great actor, and to that
of the eminent actress, Mistress Oldfield, by the
noblest in the land when their remains were transferred to their last resting-place amongst the illus-
trious dead in the Abbey.

It is also worth remembering that the fact that
George Canning was the son of an obscure country
actress did not prevent him from becoming Prime
Minister of England.

Getting nearer our own time, let us see how the
"social stigma" affected the Kembles.   Roger, the
father, was a poor strolling-player and manager, who
acted in barns, and the like, and who was compelled
to "dodge" the law, in order to act plays at all.

Out of his miserable income he strove, and struggled, and starved, to send two of his boys to Douay for a college education. The eldest child, Sarah (afterwards "The Siddons"), at one period of desperate trouble, was driven to take refuge in the degradation of domestic servitude. Yet this family of strollers ultimately became personages of most distinguished social eminence.

The Rev. Julian Young tells us that his father, Charles Mayne Young, was on visiting terms with half the aristocracy of the kingdom. Miss Owenson and Miss O'Neil were daughters of humble country actors, but I have never heard that the public were, on that account, prejudiced against the writings of Lady Morgan, or the social status of Lady Beecher; and I have yet to learn that the honour of the great house of Derby has been in any degree sullied by its alliance with Elizabeth Farren, the daughter of a strolling player.

The high distinction achieved by Charles Kemble when the Queen commanded his return to the stage; the repeated honours paid to Macready, to the Keans, Charles Mathews, and Phelps, to Fanny Kemble and Helen Faucit, in the past; and in the present, the tributes to English art which accompanied Mr. Irving's triumphal march through America; the high claims to social distinction accorded to every eminent actor living, appear strangely at variance with Mr. Burnand's theory of the "social stigma."

Of course, he will maintain that these honours

have merely been accorded to certain individual
artists. I admit it ; but these individual artists are
representative people, and whether the President of
the United States makes a morning call on Mr.
Irving, or Professor Ruskin compliments the actor or
the authors of " Claudian," they are simply paying
homage to the art of which the actor and the authors
are, for the time being, representative. Similarly,
when the first gentleman in England invites a
number of distinguished actors to Marlborough
House, he pays a natural compliment to the art the
whole world loves and admires.

While grudgingly admitting that there always has
been " a privileged few among the actors, and among
other citizens of the Great Republic of Art and
Letters, who have been admitted to the assemblies of
the great, and whose hospitality the great have
condescended to accept in return," Mr. Burnand
maintains that, in this respect, at the present day
" the stage has retrograded."

But let us hear what an impartial authority has
to say on this subject. In the pages of the very
magazine in which Mr. Burnand fulminated his
jeremiad, Baron F. Rothschild states : " The social
distinctions with which the great painters, sculptors,
musicians, *and theatrical artistes of the day* are overwhelmed, the universal desire to assimilate them
with the daily drift of one's life, is a proof of the
estimation in which art is held." Now this is the
deliberately recorded conviction of a man who is
ensconced in that fashionable fortress, which, it is to

be feared, a great many of the audacious comedians have carried by storm.

In the opinion of Mr. Burnand, the fact of a man's being a clergyman, a briefless barrister, or an officer in the army or navy, is in itself " a passport to society" which the actor does not possess, however accomplished he may be. Heaven forbid that I should seek to depreciate any of these honourable professions. I merely seek to point out that they are not, of themselves, an " Open, sesame " to the charmed circle of society. Surely Mr. Burnand cannot have forgotten that, not so very long ago—say, when the " socially stigmatized " Garrick, Foote, and the elder Colman were visiting " Sir Somebody This," " My Lord That," or " The Duke of T'other," at their country houses—the poor chaplain was invariably condemned to sit below " the pale spectrum of the salt."

Only the other day, any man who could pay the fees and eat his dinners at Lincoln's Inn could be a barrister. But Mr. Burnand will scarcely venture to maintain that the mere possession of this easily-acquired honour will induce society to open its arms to these worthy fellows, and invite them to five o'clock teas, carpet dances, and fashionable dinners? Were he to walk with me to-morrow to Lincoln's Inn, he would scarcely assert that two or three poor, half-starved gentlemen, whom I can point out to him, will be accepted in " society " merely because they happen to wear a wig and gown over their threadbare garments; and I am equally sure he

would never dream of telling me that my poor friend
Brown, the curate at fifty pounds a year, to whom a
dinner is an event, and a new coat a godsend, or
that Jones the subaltern and Robinson the midship-
man, struggling to live on three half-crowns a day,
will be accepted in " society," merely because the
one happens to serve God and the others to serve
the Queen.   I know barristers who have given up
the law (or it has given them up), and who have
become actors.   *Au contraire,* I know a very bad
actor who has become a very good barrister, and
who has a very large practice.   I know priests of
various denominations who have stepped out of
the pulpit on to the stage ; and I know several
officers, in both branches of the service, who have
gone in for acting, or what is called " acting management."

Mr. Burnand allows that, despite the " stigma "
which he alleges surrounds us, people born of
theatrical families are often honest, humdrum, decent
folk, who go the even tenor of their way, unconscious of evil, and uncontaminated by the vicious
examples around them.

" To the genius, the talents, and the *private worth*
of our eminent actors in the past and the present,
the stage owes its lustre—but they owed nothing to
the stage."

But is this logical ?   Let us see how it applies to
any other art or science.   Carried to its legitimate
conclusion, it means, if it means anything, that the
poet owes nothing to poetry, the painter and sculptor

nothing to painting or sculpture, the legist **to juris-**
prudence, or the scientist to science !

To return, however, from vague abstractions to
actual facts, let us see how far this theory holds good
as applied to the stage.

In the past, as I have already shown, the Kembles
were a family **of** strolling players of **the lower order.**
Macready was the grandson of an obscure Dublin
tradesman.   **Edmund Kean was a child** of chance.
In the present, Helen Faucit, Mrs. Kendal, Mrs.
Bancroft, and the Terrys, are daughters of country
actors—people who had **to** fight a hard battle in
bringing up their children.   Henry Neville **and**
Thomas Thorne come in the same category.   I
have heard David James boast that he was a supernumerary in the Princess's Theatre, while Messrs.
Irving, Wilson Barrett, Barry Sullivan, Toole, and
Lionel Brough, are self-made men, who **avow,**
with honest pride, **that they owe** their fame, their
fortune, everything they possess, to the stage.

And now, having, I hope, disposed **of** the theory
of the "social stigma," **I** will come to what Mr.
Burnand says about the actress, which is a much
more serious matter.   He alleges, in sober, serious
earnest, that the profession of the stage is one in
which "if a girl remains pure in heart, it is a miracle
of grace !"   An allegation of so sweeping a character
as this comes strangely from one whose nearest and
dearest relatives are members of the profession to
which he himself is indebted **for** such fame and
fortune as he has achieved.

This amusing gentleman's cap and bells are always *en évidence*, hence it is difficult to take him seriously, besides which, his opinions are heavily handicapped by his somewhat dubious experiences as author, actor, and manager—experiences which have scarcely been acquired in the highest school of art or artists.

Burlesque, at the best, is hardly an ennobling study, nor are those who devote themselves to caricaturing the nobler work of greater men exactly the class of people whose opinions can be permitted to pass unchallenged.

I am constrained to admit that there are certain places which are honoured by the designation of theatres, which, if called by their right names, would be more correctly described by a more Elizabethan or Oriental phrase. There are women who come on the stage to show their diamonds and their fine dresses ; there are creatures who court the glare of the footlights to enable them to display as much of their persons and as little of their costumes as certain managers will permit. But I refuse to regard them as types and representatives of English actresses.

Certain more or less distinguished members of the aristocracy, male and female, occasionally figure as respondents and co-respondents in the Divorce Court ; yet what would be thought of the man who, on the strength of these " base exceptions," would have the audacity to maintain that if " a girl remained pure amongst the English nobility, it would be a miracle of grace"? No one can take up the record of the police courts, any week out of the fifty-two, without finding some offence charged against one or other of the clergy. Yet, notwithstanding this, a publicist would scarcely have the mendacious effrontery to stigmatize the ecclesiastical calling as one which places its members out of the pale of society.

Mr. Burnand apostrophizes a pair of imaginary parents, and improvises a supposititious and wholly improbable, almost impossible case, in which he *imagines* a young girl, who has never before been on the stage, and who is able to obtain an immediate engagement in "a large London theatre." Surely no one can know better than he does, that even the ballet, the poor despised ballet, who regard the "Lottie and Tottie" interlopers with loathing and contempt, and who, in the majority of instances, are decent, honest, hardworking girls, have to undergo a long and tedious training before they are permitted to appear in public.

For even the pantomimes, special engagements are made months in advance, and there are only two West-End theatres where, at present, it is possible for a young lady who has never been on the stage before to obtain an opening of the humblest description, even as a supernumerary. The first is the Princess's, and the second the Savoy. In the first the supernumeraries consist, on the one hand, of old actors and actresses, some of them of great ability, whom reverse of fortune has brought

to this hard pass; on the other, of ambitious young
aspirants of the better class, who, fortunately for themselves, undergo a course of artistic training under the
able tuition of the manager.   In this theatre the
daughter of a distinguished literary man, son of a
yet more distinguished sire, has recently succeeded
in obtaining an engagement to play small parts.
Will it be asserted that, if this young lady's father
(whose knowledge of the inner life of the theatre is
profound) deemed it within the verge of possibility
that his child could be contaminated by the surroundings, he would suffer her to cross the threshold
of that or any other theatre ?

As to the Savoy, upon calling one day at Mr.
D'Oyley Carte's office on business, I was by
accident shown into a room where I found upwards
of five-and-twenty young girls, who impressed me
by their demeanour and appearance; they seemed
charming, modest, well educated, and were all more
or less accomplished musicians.   Some of them (so
I learnt afterwards) were daughters of poor clergy-
men, doctors, and retired military men, while others
belonged to the middle class.   From this class came
the plaintiff in the *cause célèbre* Finney *v.* Gar-
moyle, and from the same source the chorus of the
Savoy is continually recruited.   The "atmosphere
of moral contagion" which surrounds this theatre
may be surmised from the following illustration.   A
few months ago a certain young gentleman who
occupied a private box threw a bouquet on the
stage, containing a note with an impudent proposal

to one of these young **girls.** **He** was immediately
taken by the neck, and thrown out into the street
without the slightest ceremony, **save** that he was
recommended to go to Bow Street for a remedy for
this summary process **of** ejection—a remedy of
which, hitherto, he has steadily declined to avail
himself.

Let us walk from the Princess's **to the St.** James's,
from there **to the** Haymarket, and **thence to the**
Adelphi, the Vaudeville, the Savoy, and the Lyceum,
and I **will** ask **Mr. Burnand to** accompany us, in
order that he may point out to his imaginary parents
in which of **these** theatres their charming daughter
(always supposing that **she** succeeds **in** getting an
engagement) " will unconsciously deteriorate in tone
until the fixed lines of the **moral** boundary have
become blurred and faint."

A stage-manager who is irritable **and** dyspeptic,
and whose "breeding lacks the repose which marks
the caste of Vere de Vere," when he has been on
the stage for six or eight hours is apt occasionally to
" let out " when confronted with a drunken carpenter,
an incompetent property-man, a rebellious ballet, or
a stupid squadron of supers. It is highly reprehen-
sible for these wretched managers, or stage-managers,
to forget themselves, especially before ladies ; but,
after all, as a very charming young Venetian lady
once observed :

> "We must think men are not gods,
> Nor of them look for such observances
> As fit the bridal."

Having summed up his case against the London theatres, Mr. Burnand proceeds to state that "for a young lady travelling it would be simply impossible, unless accompanied by her mother, or by some trustworthy relative." This sentence is rather involved, but I will take the obvious meaning. I believe I am not in error when I state that Mr. Burnand's personal and actual knowledge of travelling with a company extended only over a very short tour, during which he distinguished himself as Captain Crosstree in his own sprightly burlesque of "Black-Eyed Susan." Now, as I have been actor and manager of many of the principal theatres for twenty years and upwards, and as mine was the very first company (except the Haymarket and Lyceum) that ever went on "tour," it may be assumed that I am fairly well qualified to describe the routine of a travelling company's weekly journey.

The acting manager places a notice in the porter's lodge, and in the green-room, desiring the ladies and gentlemen to be at the station a quarter of an hour prior to the departure of the train. The baggage-man calls, both at theatre and lodgings, for the baggage. In exceptional cases (late journeys, etc.) cabs and omnibuses are prepared for conveyance to and from the station. The railway people always provide two carriages—or three, if necessary—consisting of first and second class compartments for the through journey. No strangers are ever permitted to enter the carriages. Married ladies and children always have a compartment to themselves; the lead-

F. C. BURNAND.

ing lady and single girls generally group **themselves together.** **Some of** the gentlemen adjourn **to** the smoking-carriage, others **to their books** or **papers.** When the company **arrive at** their destination, **the** agent in advance awaits **them with a** list of lodgings, terms, etc. The baggage-man **conveys the** baggage to the theatre or lodgings, and there is an end of **that** journey. It was an unwritten **but** perfectly **under-stood law in my** company, **that no single** gentleman ever occupied apartments **in a house in** which any single lady **of the company was located.** *Verbum sap.*

Having **proved** that **it is not only** possible, but that **it** may be exceedingly pleasant, **for a** young lady to see infinite varieties of **hill and dale, wood and** water, quiet hamlets and **populous cities, in goodly company,** I come now **to** the **rank and file of the** theatre.

Mr. Burnand's allegation that **no** special training is required is simply preposterous. To attain any distinction in **the** higher range of art **it is** essential that the aspirants should understand the principles of elocution, and the **art** of intoning verse rhythmically; they should be able to dance and fence, for the mere **art** of moving with ease and grace is in itself one of the most difficult accomplishments to acquire. Even for the most frivolous form of **art** (burlesque), the artist must know how **to** sing and dance. Besides, there is the study of the text, long and fatiguing rehearsals, etc. Of course, it goes without saying that there **are** idle loafers who are under the impression that they are actors ready-made—that they have only to show themselves on the stage to carry everything before them. The doctrine of "the survival of the fittest," however, soon makes short work with them. "Drones hive not" with the sagacious manager, and the loafer makes way for the conscientious, industrious student, who works, and waits, and watches for his chance, which is often a long time in coming.

Actresses are no more free from faults than other women ; but, in nine cases out of ten, they are more industrious, and frequently more conscientious. As with other women, vanity and ambition are their foibles. It is, indeed, astonishing how often they resist temptations which would enable them to gratify the one and achieve the other. It is true that they envy each other's little triumphs ; but only let adversity assail a rival, and envy and uncharitableness give place to sympathy and loving-kindness.

In the majority of instances they are devoted daughters, faithful wives, and the best of mothers.

Unfortunately, black sheep are to be found in the theatre as well as everywhere else, for

> "Where's that palace wherein foul things
> Sometimes intrude not ?"

But when the black sheep are found out (especially in a country theatre), they do not (if they remain) have a very pleasant time of it.

Take the actors and actresses, with all their follies and their faults, and I affirm that they will compare favourably, and more than favourably, with a similar number of any particular section of the community, for propriety of conduct, humanity, and benevolence.

Finally, I maintain, despite Mr. Burnand's dictum to the contrary, that never was there a greater demand for educated and accomplished young girls than now, when the position of a successful actress is attended with so much social distinction and such large emoluments. The difficulty which besets the neophyte is the absence, in consequence of the abolition of the great provincial stock companies, of all opportunity for obtaining the requisite experience, without which it is impossible to gain even the slightest degree of proficiency. To propound a remedy for his unfortunate state of affairs would take me beyond the scope or limits to which I am here restricted.

Some years ago, when unexpectedly called upon to address the Church Congress at Leicester on the relations between Church and Stage, I presumed to point out, to a distinguished assemblage of ecclesiastics, "that the theatre had long been out of leading-strings, and that the actor who appreciated his art, and who respected it and himself, objected to being patted on the head with one hand, and being snubbed with the other." I repeat now, that the actors do not care about being patted on the head with one hand, while the theatre and the art they love, the art to which they owe everything, is being aspersed with the other.

BOOK II.

THE VANQUISHED.

CHAPTER I.

THERE have been victors and vanquished from the beginning of time, as there will be to the end.

The fierce delight of battle inspires the conquered as well as the conqueror, but when the fight is done, for the victor, there is the return to the fond wife, the exultant mother and the joyous children. There is the triumphal march, the trophies, and the tributaries following his chariot-wheels in captive bonds ; the loud-mouthed roar of the "shouting plebeians," the banquet, the music, the garlands of roses, and the wreaths of laurel !

When dead, the city pours forth its myriads to follow him to his grave ; the lying cenotaph testifies to his spurious virtues ; the servile senate decrees a votive statue to his memory, and the venal historian deifies him in his glowing pages. In like manner, poetry, painting, sculpture, and music, are but the handmaidens of the successful histrion. For him there is the present glory of the hour face to face with the public heart; for him is the living ecstasy of the rosy wine of life, crushed nightly into foaming golden goblets, the smile of beauty, the plaudits of the delighted crowd, the princely honorarium, the social triumph, the homage of all hands and hearts!

But woe—woe to the vanquished! For him naught remains but poverty and obscurity, blighted hopes, and sometimes a broken heart.

If, for a moment, a little moment, he is enabled to catch some brief glimpse of life's exultant morning, when victory hovered over those now discrownèd brows and illumined them with some rays of the light of her glory; if once more in his dreams he hears the plaudits of the multitude commingling with the voices of too partial friends and proclaiming him the foremost of his time and calling, the waking only serves to accentuate the bitterness of the present misery.

The ill-omen'd cry, " Væ Victis!" rings ever in his ears till the great silence comes, and with its

> " Generous fulness lends
> Home to the homeless, to the friendless friends."

So mote it be. Such are the conditions of the fight for fame and fortune, and—

> " Man is man, and master of his fate."

Hence the writer seeks no maudlin sympathy for the vanquished whose story he is about to tell; he merely seeks to show that though they fell, they did not fall ignobly ; that they, as well as the victors, formed component parts of " the very age and body of the time ;" above all, he seeks to keep their memory green in the faithful hearts who loved them living and who mourn them dead.

CHAPTER II.

THE GARRICK OF THE NORTH.*

SOME years ago I "picked up" at an old bookstall, in the market-place at York, a rare and valuable etching of Mrs. Siddons, together with a rude outline proof-engraving of a tall, slender, angular, remarkable-looking, dark-complexioned young man, with very pronounced features.

The man was attired exactly like Mr. Irving as Eugene Aram, in the dark-coloured coat, vest, and continuations of a hundred and thirty or forty years ago; and the resemblance was so striking, that had it not been for the faded and discoloured paper, evidently more than a century old, on which the plate was printed, I should certainly have set it down for an admirable likeness of that popular actor.

After vainly endeavouring to ascertain the original, the plate was consigned to one of my numerous portfolios, with the Siddons, and other curios.

* Although Frodsham does not come within the category of " Players whom I have known," I have an hereditary knowledge of him, through my prolonged connection with the York Circuit; hence I have not hesitated to include this lost genius in my record of the " Vanquished."

A few months later, in overhauling my treasures for the delectation of Charles Reade, I directed his attention to my " mysterious man in black." After carefully inspecting the plate for some time, Mr. Reade, who knew everything, turned to the adjacent book-shelves, and taking down a volume of the memoirs of my eccentric predecessor, Tate Wilkinson, published in 1790, he read as follows :

" I am now speaking of an exuberant flower of the drama, possessed of voice with melody, and merit, to an eminent degree. He had strong feelings, and tears at will ; and had he been a few years under the correction of a London audience, and attentive to his good advisers, he would, in all probability, long before this, have been in his meridian, perhaps at this time a setting sun.

" There is a coarse picture at York, in the print-shops, which is not only very like his person, attitude, etc., but is what a picture of real worth should be. It is a strong conveyance, without giving elegance, which he by no means ever attained, though his admirers claimed for him what he certainly had not. The said trifling print does not make him *outré* as to awkwardness, but it exactly conveys Frodsham's manner and mode as an actor."

" Rely upon it," said Reade, " this was the unfortunate Frodsham, the Garrick of the North, as Hamlet."

Mr. Reade was right, for I afterwards discovered, beyond all doubt, that this rude engraving was the 'counterfeit presentment" of the eccentric genius, who out of sheer obstinacy and false pride fretted his fiery life out on the boards of the Yorkshire theatres when, according to the general testimony of his contemporaries, had he consented to put his " Pegasus in harness," and to serve under the banner of Garrick (undoubtedly the greatest genius of that or any other age, not only as actor and manager, but as tutor), the pupil would have run his master hard in the fight for fame.

Prior to his *début* in York, little is known of the subject of this sketch, save that he was a gentleman by birth and breeding, and that he was reputed to be the scion of an ancient family of the town of Frodsham, ten miles from Chester. The coincidence of names, though remarkable, is by no means impossible, since the late Mr. Gomersal (the Napoleon of Astley's, so humorously embalmed in the Bon Gaultier ballads) informed me that he was born at the village of Gomersal, near Leeds. Frodsham was educated at the famous school of Westminster, where he appears to have made some desirable acquaintances.

Genese mentions that when Miss Frodsham was acting at Peterborough some time after her father's death, the Bishop of that city called upon her, and entertained her at the palace on the ground of having been an old friend and schoolfellow of Frodsham's at Westminster.

Although but a youth of one-and-twenty when he joined the company of players on the great Northern Circuit in 1758, he must have either had consider-

able previous experience or great natural aptitude,
or both, inasmuch as a year after his arrival he had
acquired possession of nearly all the principal parts
in tragedy and comedy. To be sure, it took some
time before an antediluvian actor named Crisp, who
had played Hamlet over half a century, could be
induced to cede the Prince of Denmark to the youthful tragedian ; and for a considerable period after
that, this obstinate old gentleman barred the way
to Richard, Lear, Sir John Brute, etc. Frodsham,
however, did not, as we players say, act "a bad line
of business." Besides Hamlet, Othello, Macbeth,
Romeo, Edgar, Richmond, Jaffier, Castalio, Alexander, Lothario, Osmyn, Young Norval, in tragedy,
he played Benedict, Lord Townley, Young Mirabel,
and Don Felix in high comedy ; and of lighter
eccentric characters, Bayes, Marplot, Dick (Appren-
tice), Lord Hardy, Colonel Balby, Plume, Sir Calla-
ghan O'Brallaghan, and Captain Macheath (with the
music), all of which he enacted for a rural guinea a week.

A guinea a week for " tragedy, comedy, history,
pastoral, pastoral comical, historical pastoral !" Only
think of that, young gentlemen, you who step out of
universities, marching regiments, or counting-houses,
or perhaps from behind counters, and air your pretty
faces, and fine clothes, and too frequent imbecility,
at two, or three, or four, or five guineas a week to
begin with, in metropolitan theatres. " Other times,
other manners," with a vengeance ! Although a
guinea a week went much farther in those days
than now, it is difficult to realize that a man could

eat, drink, sleep, wear broadcloth and clean linen, on so miserable a pittance; hence, I suppose that Frodsham had some private means, as we never hear of his being in an impecunious condition. However slender may have been his emoluments, it is certain that the northern players acquired the high reputation which afterwards distinguished them, principally through him, inasmuch as he stands first in a list of celebrities whose names will be remembered so long as the annals of the British stage endure.

Gifted, however, as were his successors, he achieved a local prestige which none of them ever reached— not even the Siddons, the Jordan, or John Kemble himself. This remarkable popularity cannot be accounted for by merely exceptional ability, however great that might have been; it arose in a great measure from exceptional circumstances, as I shall endeavour to show. From Old York to London was not infrequently a longer journey in point of time then than the voyage from New York to London is now. It was not unusual for paterfamilias to make his will before tempting the perils of the king's highway—hence the journey was seldom or ever taken, and Old Ebor remained almost as much a metropolis as when she disputed the supremacy with London herself. The nobility and gentry of the north flocked into the beautiful old city for the winter and summer seasons; and one of the most potent attractions was the theatre, which was crowded nightly by the *élite* of the great northern families. The London actors rarely or ever came

to York, **the good people of York** rarely **or** ever
went **to** London; consequently they had no opportunities for forming standards of comparison between
their own popular **favourites and the** more distinguished players of the metropolis. **No** wonder, there-
fore, that Frodsham, **with** his youth, his interesting
appearance, his reputation **for** birth and breeding,
his remarkable ability, and the glamour with which
the stage surrounds the great creations **of** the poets,
leaped at once into public favour, and became the
idol **of** the northern playgoers. The ladies were
the great supporters of the drama, and **of** them
Tate Wilkinson, **a** man of the world and an admirer
of the sex, says:

"The ladies **of York,** without any compliment,
have a grace, a manner, a decorum, not often **met**
with out of London (Bath excepted), for **York** certainly boasts a pre-eminence when the boxes are
crowded that dazzles the eyes of a stranger; and no
wonder—for as London and Bath cull the choicest
beauties **from** the three kingdoms, so does antient
York City allure them from Hull, Leeds, Doncaster,
Wakefield, Pontefract, and every part of that noble,
spacious, and rich county."

As for the men of the county families, we have
only to read the comedies of the period (or "Tom
Jones" may save us the trouble) to enable us to
form a pretty accurate idea of their conduct, character,
and occupations at this period. No marvel that
amongst a rising generation who could not open
their mouths without emitting an oath, and who

devoted their time principally to gambling, racing,
cock - fighting, badger - drawing, bull - baiting, and
drinking, the accomplished young tragedian should—

"Like a star i' th' darkest night stick fiery off indeed."

Wilkinson expressly tells us that :

"The public were so infatuated (and, indeed, he
was so superior), that he left all others at a distance,
and the audience too blindly, and too partially (for
his own good) approved all he did beyond comparison. When in full pride (before he wilfully sank
himself) I do not think any actor but Garrick would
have been liked so well ; and even Garrick himself
would not have passed current without some old
maids' opinions at a secret cabal—when Frodsham
would have been voted superior, and under the rose
appointed the man for the ladies ; nor would that
decision have been from elderly ladies only, as he
had often melted the youthful fair ones of the tenderest mould, whose hearts were but too susceptible
whenever Frodsham was the lover."

So much for his popularity with the fair maids of
York ; now for Wilkinson's own opinion :

"He was naturally a good actor in spite of himself, for though London improves and matures, and
is the most enviable theatrical situation, yet genius
will be found in every rank, soil, and station, and
Frodsham had a quick genius, aided by a liberal
education. . . . With proper cultivation he would
have been a good substitute for Barry. . . . Had he
been caught at a proper time, while wild, by such a

DAVID GARRICK.

man as Garrick, and if Mr. Garrick would have taken
pains with him, the York hero would have done
honour to London. . . . His Edgar, in the mad
scenes, was the best I have ever seen ; his Hamlet
and Jaffier I never saw equalled but by Mr. Garrick
and Mr. Barry."

This is the unbiased verdict of a contemporary,
and a rival ; for Tate avows, with the utmost candour,
that the York people, in 1754, would not stand him
in any of Frodsham's characters, *e.g. :*

" I was daily abused for attempting Mr. Frodsham's part of Othello. When the day came, I was,
after dinner, taken so dreadfully ill, that I never
expected to play more. Frodsham was not to be
found to supply my place, and the audience were
dismissed. . . . I performed Oakley and the Appren-
tice, which in Dublin had pleased so much ; but at
York I was unfortunately much disapproved. I was
shocking after Frodsham as Dick."

A wiser head than that of this indiscreet young
man might well have been turned by all this fulsome
adulation, which, if it did not bear fruit in the immediate present, yielded an abundant crop of mischief
in the by no means distant future.

In 1758, when he was in the very zenith of his
popularity, he took advantage of a holiday to pay
his last visit to London. The day of his departure
was one of lamentation for his admirers, who were
convinced if Garrick once saw their favourite he
would never return to the stately old city by the

Ouse ; and I am disposed to think that he himself
was under the impression that he had only to show
his face in town to be immediately snapped up by
one or other of the London managers.

On the night of his arrival he went to Drury
Lane, and paid his money like a man to the pit, to
see his great rival in Hamlet. Next morning he
left his pasteboard at the Palais Royal (as Garrick's
splendid mansion in Southampton Street was called).
The card was merely inscribed " Mr. Frodsham,
from York." This curt inscription doubtless piqued
the great-little man's curiosity, and he desired his
free-and-easy visitor to be shown into the library at
once.   Now it must be premised that the York actor
was not only young and vain, but self-opinionated
to an abundant degree ; on the other hand, Roscius
had a habit of " sitting upon " people ; consequently
the two gentlemen met with their " armour on."
Garrick was very patronising, and Frodsham returned the other's condescension by being superciliously affable, expressing his opinion on plays and
players, and on the plays of Shakespeare more
particularly, with a serene self-belief to which Garrick
was quite unaccustomed.   Doubtless he expected
the country actor would make his approaches " with
bated breath and whispering humbleness," requesting
permission to be heard, etc. ; finding, however, that
he made no advances of this kind, the great impresario at length broke the ice thus :

" Well, well, Mr. Frodsham, I suppose you've
seen a play since your arrival in London ?"

"Oh yes! I saw you play my own crack part last night, sir."

"Oh, indeed! And how did you approve? I hope I pleased you, sir?"

"Why, yes, certainly, my dear sir—vastly clever in several passages, but I can't say I was struck with your entire performance."

This took Garrick's breath away, and he afterwards avowed that he never had such "a rise" taken out of him in all his life, as by this outspoken and audacious young country actor. The great man gasped and stammered:

"Why—now, now, to be sure now—I suppose you good people in the country—pray, pray, now, Mr. Frodsham, what sort of a place do you act in at York? Is it a room, or a riding-house, occasionally fitted up with scenery? Eh, eh?"

"Neither, sir," replied Frodsham with dignity. "A theatre—a splendid theatre, Mr. Garrick."

"Ah, to be sure, my Lord Burlington told me so. By-the-bye, come and see my Sir John Brute to-night" (and he gave him an order for the pit); "then come and breakfast with me in the morning, and we'll have a trial of skill. Mrs. Garrick shall be judge between us. Good-day, Mr.—York—good-day. I must be off to rehearsal. Remember breakfast—breakfast at ten to-morrow."

Frodsham was punctual to the moment next day, and did justice to Mrs. Garrick's substantial repast; after which David opened fire with—

"Well, well, Mr. Frodsham, what do you think of

35—2

my Brute? Eh, eh? Now, no compliments—tell
Mrs. Garrick; was it all right? Would it go down
at York?"

"Well, sir," replied the young coxcomb serenely,
"I can't undertake to say. Our audiences are con-
foundedly exacting.* For my own part, I was
delighted. Sir, I didn't expect it from your Hamlet.
You see, I am accustomed to play Hamlet myself,
sir; but tragedy is my forte, while comedy—my
good sir—comedy is yours. Your Brute, sir—
d——n it, Mr. Garrick—your Brute was the most
brutal thing I ever saw in my life! I don't mean
from an artistic point of view. No, no! there, sir,
it was perfect. But you stood on the stage in your
drunken scene, flourishing your sword; you placed
yourself in an attitude (I'm sure you saw me in the
pit), and with your eyes fixed on me, you seemed to
say, 'D——n it, Frodsham! did you ever see anything like that in York? Eh, sir? Eh?'"

Garrick, who was accustomed to swallow flattery
by the hogshead, did not accept the rival Hamlet's
doubtful compliments with perfect equanimity. He
hemmed and hawed, pretended to laugh the matter
off, and then said:

* I remember an experience of my own in Yorkshire, somewhat
analogous to this. We had produced, in a very splendid manner, and
at great expense, at my new theatre in Leeds, Boucicault's "After
Dark," which crowded the Princess's for a whole season, during George
Vining's management. There was a bad house on the first night, and
I was contemplating the performance from the back of the pit, very
ruefully, when one of the regular *habitués*, a fair type of the intelligent
Tyke, approached, and by way of consolation, accosted me with, "Ah!
Musther John, you may well look ashamed o' yoursen. This sort o'
muck may do for London, but it wunna do for Hunslet Lane!"

"Well, well, now for a taste of *your* quality ; now a speech from Hamlet, Mr. Frodsham, and you, Mrs. Garrick—ahem ! ' bear a wary eye,' my dear."

Nothing loth, with the utmost *sang froid*, Frodsham recited Hamlet's first soliloquy.

When he had finished, Garrick said :

"Well, well, hey now ! There is stuff about you, but you see you want some of my forming ; and really, in some passages, you have acquired tones that I do not by any means approve."

" Tones, sir," replied the country actor. " Tones ! I flatter myself, Mr. Garrick, I *have* tones ; but you are not familiar with them. Now, sir, *you* have tones, very odd ones, and Mrs. Cibber has tones, very strange ones, which I do not by any means approve ; but I suppose, in time, I might get used to them, as I might to your Hamlet !"

Despite all we hear of Garrick's vanity and jealousy, he must have had many noble qualities.

I am under the impression that if some "young man from the country" were to call on any of our London managers nowadays, and ventilate candid and uncomplimentary opinions about their acting, he would be shown to the door with as little delay as possible. Instead of which, as soon as David could recover his breath, he replied :

" Why now—now you're a d——d queer fellow, Frodsham ; but, for a fair and full trial of your genius, my stage shall be open to you, and you shall act any part you please. If you succeed, we will then talk of terms."

Surely, here was a frank and generous proposal, and if this bumptious young blockhead had had the grace to have accepted it, the current of his whole life would have been changed. I suppose, however, Garrick's patronising condescension put the other's back up, for, with characteristic modesty, the airy youth responded :

" My dear Mr. Garrick, you are mistaken if you think I came here to cadge for an engagement. I am a Roscius myself in my own quarters, and I judged it a proper compliment to wait upon a brother genius ; but I neither want nor wish for an engagement, nor would I relinquish the happiness I enjoy in my dear old York for the first terms your great city of London could afford !" And with an imposing obeisance to Garrick, and another to his beautiful wife, the insolent young puppy made his exit, leaving the rival Roscius absolutely dumb-founded at his impudence.

Of course, this modest young gentleman's visit to town would have been incomplete without an interview with that rough diamond, David's rival, Rich, of Covent Garden, who was as remarkable in his way as Garrick was in his.

Although a shrewd, clever man of business, Rich's education had been grossly neglected, and his language was vulgar and ungrammatical to the last degree. Either from this cause, or from habitual inattention, or perhaps from an insolent affectation, which he mistook for a rough-and-ready kind of wit,

he pretended to forget people's names, and con-
tracted a vile habit of addressing everybody as
" Muster." Garrick he called " Muster Griskin ;"
Shuter, " Muster Shuttleworth ;" Barry, " Muster
Barleymore ;" and Wilkinson, " Muster William-
skin." Foote he persisted in calling " Muster
Footseye."

On one occasion, after being repeatedly accosted
in this manner, the English Aristophanes became
quite furious, and demanded to know "why the
d——l he was not addressed by his proper
name."

" Don't get lumpy, don't get lumpy, Muster Footseye," said Rich ; " sometimes, you know, I forget my
own name."

" I know," replied Foote, "that you can't write
your own name ; but I'm d——d if I can conceive
how you can be such an ass as to forget it."

Frodsham found the renowned pantomimist (he
was said to be the greatest harlequin in the world !)
surrounded by his usual troupe of cats. There was
one perched on each shoulder, one on each knee,
and two or three others purring about his legs. In
the intervals of petting his favourites, he was teaching a young lady to act. Superciliously looking at
his visitor from head to foot with a large reading
glass, he took snuff ; next he blew his nose like a
foghorn, then he dismissed his pupil, and began :

" Well, Muster Frogsmire, I suppose you've come
from York for an engagement, and you want me to

larn you how to act.   Did you ever act Richard,
Muster Frogsmire ?"

"Yes, sir."

"Why, then, you shall see me act," says Rich;
and, strutting about like a turkey-cock, and making
the most hideous grimaces and contortions, he began
to spout—

"Now is the winter of our discontent."

A little of this went a very long way with Frodsham, who cut his would-be tutor short with, "Sir,
my name is *not* Frogsmire; I don't want an engagement; and I don't want to be taught to act; but I
do want to wish you and your cats a very good-
morning."

So saying, he stalked out of the room, leaving the
despot of Covent Garden purple with rage.

Whatever may have been Frodsham's aspirations,
it is quite clear that his arrogance and presumption
had effectually closed the doors of Drury Lane and
Covent Garden against him.   'Tis an ill wind, however, that blows no one any good, so there were
great rejoicings in the North Countrie when he
returned, especially when it was found that neither
Garrick nor Rich had chained and secured the York
Roscius.

When he afterwards discussed his visit to the
London managers with his friend Tate Wilkinson,
he could not be persuaded that he had requited
Garrick's courtesy with impertinence, or that he had

been impatient and insolent to Rich. On the contrary, he always maintained that "David knew he was speaking to as good a gentleman as himself, and an actor of equal ability. While as for Spangleback" (so he called Rich), "Sir," said he, "he's a boor, and isn't fit to carry guts to a bear. He's an ignoramus, who not only knows nothing of Greek or Latin, but who knows nothing of his own language; in fact, he knows nothing of anything except his infernal cats and his beastly pantomimes!"

Whether the manager (Baker), in honour of his return, increased Frodsham's salary, there are now no means of ascertaining, though surely in the fulness of time he must have got beyond that munificent stipend of a guinea a week. In each town he certainly had a benefit, which was, at that time, a delightful and dignified institution. It is bad enough now, but then it involved eating innumerable and periodical pecks of dirt, and enduring an amount of personal degradation which appears absolutely incredible. In York, Norwich, Hull and other important cities, "it was at that time the custom" (and a beastly custom it certainly was!), says Wilkinson, "for the performer, whether man or woman, to attend the play-bill man round the town, knock humbly at every door, honoured with or without a rapper, and supinely and obediently leave a play-bill at every shop and stall, and request the favour of Mr. and Mrs. Griskin's company at the benefit."

"Good God!" exclaims Tate, in a burst of honest

indignation. "What a sight to actually behold **Mr.** Frodsham, a gentleman, with fine natural talents, and esteemed in York as a Garrick, *the Hamlet of the age*, running after or stopping a gentleman on horseback, to deliver his benefit bill, and beg half-a-crown (then the price of the boxes)."

Nor was this the climax of degradation. After the play, on the benefit night, the beneficiare had to "return thanks," and if married, both husband and wife had to appear.

It is alleged by Wilkinson, that upon the occasion of one of Frodsham's benefits (doubtless towards the end of his career, when he was entering on the downward path) he spoke a comic epilogue, and actually carried his wife on and off the stage *on his back*.

A pleasant situation this, for the wretched wife; a refined exhibition for an intelligent audience; above all, what a proud position for the "Hamlet of the age" to occupy!

Of course we know but too well that despite the great social distinction of Quin, Garrick, Sheridan, Foote, Mossop, etc., they were not infrequently exposed to indignities from the fashionable ruffians and rakehelly Dundrearys of the period; but these players, as Garrick once said boldly in the teeth of a howling mob who sought to intimidate him, were "above want, and superior to insult." Besides, they did not wear their swords for nothing; they not only knew how to use them, but were quick to resent outrage, and to punish impertinence. Yet here was a man of their own order, young, ardent, and ambitious, who by his own act and deed **brought** this shameful discredit on the whole fraternity. One is tempted to ask, Was the wife a cripple? **Were** the audience demented? Or was the man himself mad or drunk? It is only charitable to assume that he was both! Amongst other charming customs of **the** period, **we are** told "admittance behind the scenes was allowed, **not only** at benefits, but in general to the gentlemen (?) who frequented the boxes;" hence I shrewdly suspect that this disreputable exploit arose from a scandalous wager, or something of the kind, between the mad actor and his drunken friends behind the scenes.

The "too susceptible fair ones" must surely have felt deeply mortified and insulted by this escapade. If they were so, they were generous, for they soon forgave their favourite, and remained faithful to their Frodsham to the last.

It redounds to the credit **of** honest Tate Wilkinson that the very moment he became manager of the great Northern Circuit in 1763 he abolished all these degrading customs. They died hard enough though, elsewhere, for seventeen years later we find no less a person than Mrs. Siddons, on the occasion of her farewell to Bath (to which fashionable city she had retired after her failure in London), producing "five reasons" for again tempting Fortune in town, in the shape of five bouncing bairns, whose "shining morning faces" appear to have proved a potent attraction on the occasion.

Frodsham's conduct to Garrick shows that he could be as arrogant as he was eccentric and egotistical. " There can be no doubt," says Wilkinson, " that the applause he commanded and received intoxicated his brain, as much as the plentiful potations of Burgundy with which, and with other pleasant spirited draughts, he too soon finished his early days of life and fame."

It was the fashion of the day for men of the first quality to drop down dead drunk under the table after their fourth or fifth bottle. We have it on record that even " the heaven-born Minister," that model of continence, William Pitt, before he commenced to demolish a political opponent, was not infrequently accustomed to retire behind the Speaker's chair to " clear himself " of his superfluous port after the " high old Roman fashion." What marvel that this ill-advised and weak-minded young actor went headlong to the devil in such goodly company ? When once he commenced his downward career he went at a galloping pace, and, alas ! he soon reached the end of his journey.

Exactly ten years after his return from London he made his last appearance in his beloved York.

On the evening of October 19th, 1768, he played Lord Townley in Vanburgh's comedy of " The Provoked Husband."

It is said that he appeared in high spirits, and it was remarked that he had never acted better.

At that time it was the duty of the principal actor to " give out," at the end of the first piece, the per-

formance for the following night. On this occasion
Frodsham came forward and said, " Ladies and
gentlemen, on Monday evening will be presented
the tragedy of ' Coriolanus,' to which will be added "
(looking seriously around, and placing his hand upon
his heart) " ' What we must all come to.' "

Those were the last words he ever spoke upon the
stage.

Three days afterwards he was dead !

Twenty years later, Tate Wilkinson, who survived
his unfortunate friend exactly thirty-five years,
chronicles his premature death in these quaint, yet
touching terms : " His mind, his superabundant
good qualities, were all warped and undermined by
nocturnal habits. In the morning he had to take to
the brandy bottle, to patch himself up for the day.
In the afternoon he had recourse to the same stimu-
lant to pull himself together for the night, and the
end was that he died enfeebled, disordered, dropsi-
cal and mad, at the age of thirty-five."

Verily, " The gods are just, and of our pleasant
vices make instruments to scourge us."

Here was a youth of brilliant parts, of exceptional
and extraordinary endowments, a scholar, a gentleman, the idol of the hour, admired by the men,
adored by the women, an actor capable of holding
his own beside " the choice and master spirits of the
age," lost, utterly lost by his own folly.

Garrick, who also survived Frodsham eleven
years, frequently stated to his friends that he had

" never met so strange a mixture of eccentricity and genius as in that mad actor from York."

The whole history of the English stage presents no more remarkable illustration of the ephemeral and evanescent character of an actor's fame than the shadowy outline I have here attempted to limn of the wasted and inglorious life of this unfortunate young man.

One is almost tempted to imagine that Roscius had his provincial rival in his eye when he penned these touching lines :

> " For he who struts his hour upon the stage,
> Can scarce extend his fame for half an age ;
> Nor pen nor pencil can the actor save—
> The art, and artist, share one common grave !"

Had it not been for his brief accidental acquaintance with Garrick and Tate Wilkinson, the very existence of poor Frodsham would by this time have been forgotten.

In the " Thespian Dictionary," published two years after the death of the famous Northern manager, the name of the York Roscius is conspicuous by its absence ; and in the very city where once it was " familiar in men's mouths as household words," it was only through the casual recognition of Charles Reade that I discovered that my " mysterious man in black " was the once famous

" GARRICK OF THE NORTH."

CHAPTER III.

G. V. BROOKE.

"Full fathom five" Gustavus **"lies !"**

No history **of** the English-speaking theatres of the nineteenth century, whether in Great Britain, America, or Australia, will be complete without some record of the meteoric career **of the** ill-fated Gustavus Vaughan Brooke.

Born **in** Dublin about **half a century** ago, and educated at Trinity College, **he** became stage-struck while yet a boy. Obtaining an introduction to the manager of the Theatre Royal, **he** persuaded that autocratic personage **to** permit him **to** attempt William Tell and other parts which **he** had seen Macready act. It is needless to say **that** the poor tyro failed signally ; he, however, gave sufficient indications of promise to encourage him to hope that he might ultimately become an actor. Soon afterwards we hear of his opening and "shutting" at the Victoria, as Virginius. Subsequently he went **into** the country, and got an engagement upon a modest salary in the Great Northern Circuit, which opened

the doors of all the great theatres to him.   He soon
emerged from the crowd, and, while still a youth,
was received as a sort of semi-star in Manchester,
Liverpool, and other large towns.

When I first met him in Manchester, there were
three theatres there—the newly erected Theatre
Royal, at that time considerably in advance of any
theatre of its size in or out of London ; the old
Queen's Theatre (where I was acting) ; and a wooden
edifice, which had been converted from a circus into
what was called the City Theatre.

Probably all the actors, and all the amateurs calling themselves actors, now engaged in the various
Metropolitan theatres put together, could not form
three companies so efficient as the three companies
at that time acting in Manchester.   The best one by
many degrees was that which appeared at the wooden
theatre.   The principal members of this troupe were
Gustavus Vaughan Brooke, "Lord Foppington,"
Browne (the greatest and most versatile comedian I
have ever seen in my life), William Davidge, Henry
Bedford, and Sam Emery.

A fortnight or three weeks after this occurrence,
in going home one night, I met Mr. James Browne
and Mr. Barry Sullivan (now, poor fellow, lying
in articulo mortis, but then leading actor at the
Theatre Royal), and adjourned with them to the
tavern immediately opposite the City Theatre.   Our
principal topic of conversation was the arrest of
Brooke as he was going on the stage that night.
It was his benefit, and the manager had been obliged

G. V. BROOKE AS OTHELLO.

to get him out of durance to enable him to keep faith with the public. While we were discussing the incident, a row was heard outside, and a handsome young fellow entered the room in animated altercation with a cabman about his fare. The stranger, who spoke with a delicious Dublin brogue, was fair-complexioned, with an oval face, fair hair, and blue eyes. He stood about five feet ten or higher, was broad-chested, straight as a dart, and apparently was about five-and-twenty or thirty years of age. His dress was peculiar to eccentricity. He wore a drab cloth overcoat with a cape, a large blue silk muffler was twisted carelessly round his neck, and a white hat was perched on one side of his head. Although I had never seen him in my life, I felt instinctively this must be Brooke. I was not left long in doubt upon the subject, for when he came to our end of the room Sullivan introduced us to each other, and a delightful time we had of it till we broke up about two in the morning. Brooke and I had many common points of interest—notably one. Three years before, he had been in management at Kilmarnock, and the pecuniary outlook was so dubious that, being unable to pay his lodgings, he had been turned out, and was compelled to take up his quarters in the dressing-room at the tumble-down old theatre, which was over a stable. Two years afterwards I passed through the same ordeal in the same locality, and we laughed heartily enough as we compared notes.

After this I read with interest in the newspapers of his *début* as Othello at the Olympic—then under the management of Captain Spicer. There was a very bad house : the audience were unsympathetic, not to say antagonistic, and the new actor made no headway at all until he reached the second act. My friend Walter Lacy informed me that up to this period Brooke took no pains to conceal his contempt for the cold-blooded audience. A happy accident, however, broke the ice.

The newspapers of the day teemed with accounts of the gallantry of the Emir of Algeria, Abd'l Kader ; more particularly of an exploit in which he had rescued a number of women and children from being roasted alive, by riding through his blazing camp, sabre in hand, cutting the tent-ropes, and carrying away the poor creatures clinging to his saddle-bow.

In the quarrel scene, as Othello came rushing down between the combatants, exclaiming, " Hold ! for your lives !" as his scimitar swept through the air it collided with their swords, making a fiery circle in its flight. The picturesque grandeur of the action, and the magnificence of the pose, so struck a fellow in the gallery that he roared out, " Abd'l Kader, by G——!" This exclamation touched the keynote of sympathy : the house rose at it, the pit sprang to its feet, the boxes swelled the general chorus of applause, and from that moment the success of the actor was assured.

When he made his exit, half the house got up and made their exit also, leaving Iago and Cassio to finish their scene by themselves ; while they (the auditors) discussed the new tragedian in excited tones at every **bar within** a hundred yards **of** the theatre. From the commencement of the third act till the curtain fell upon Othello's death the play went like a whirlwind. Next morning the **actor** "awoke and found himself famous," **and henceforth** the little theatre in Wych Street was **crowded** nightly.

Captain Spicer behaved most liberally: Brooke's original salary was £10 a **week; but** after the very first performance it was increased to £60. Nor was this all: the management of Drury Lane **and** the Haymarket contended for him, and offered fabulous terms: he, however, remained faithful to the flag under which he sailed.

He was now the talk of the town, and ran through a succession of his great parts with continued and increasing success. His admirers alleged that **he** was the greatest Othello since Kean, that he **was** also the beau-ideal of Romeo, Claude Melnotte, and Ion. I confess that to me it is difficult to realize the idea of his superlative excellence in such opposing individualities as Ion and Othello. **As** far as I know, the only original part he ever created was Philip Augustus, in Dr. Marston's noble play of "Philip of France and Marie de Meranie," in which Miss Helen Faucit also created the character of the heroine.

At the period of our intimacy his acting was, to my thinking, more distinguished by vigour than subtlety or refinement; but there was a noble ardour and a majesty of motion about him which carried everything triumphantly before them, and which I have rarely seen equalled since. In the artifices of

the histrionic art he was pre-eminent ; he " took the
stage " like a lion—indeed, his every movement was
rhythmical, and was distinguished by a leonine grace
conspicuously absent in the angular attitudes of certain weak-kneed and wooden-jointed actors of later
days.

In Othello he certainly eclipsed all living actors
save Edwin Forrest, who towered head and shoulders
above them all, not even excepting the much-be-
slavered Salvini ; in Virginius, after Macready's
retirement, he remained unrivalled.

A great future was now before him ; the ball was
at his foot, the game was his own ; but, alas ! for
lack of common prudence, his fall was as rapid as
his rise had been phenomenal.

From the beginning to the end of his chequered
and romantic career he lacked ballast, and was
always but too prone to be led astray by the latest
sycophant, especially if the sycophant happened to
wear a petticoat. Instead of " shunning vain
delights, and living laborious days," his youth and
high spirits led him headlong into the vortex of
dissipation, which surrounded and soon dragged him
down.

Sometimes he sought relief from these ignoble
occupations in rowing and boating. One day he
rowed up the river from Earl's Wharf Pier to
Putney and back ; a jovial dinner and skittles and
other diversions followed ; then it became necessary
to " put on a spurt " to get back in time for the performance. It was his first appearance in town as

Sir Giles Overreach ; there had been no Sir Giles
in London since Kean's day, and it was characteristic of the man that Brooke treated so fiery an
ordeal so lightly. When he arrived at the theatre
it was long past the time of commencement ; the
audience (a densely crowded one) were already
impatient ; it was three-quarters of an hour late
when the curtain rose, but the delay was condoned,
and he was received with unusual enthusiasm. He
wore a new dress that night ; the heat was over-
powering, and he was in a bath of perspiration,
arising principally from the hasty pull down the
river. At the end of the first act he desired his
dresser to strip off his singlet ; the new canvas
lining of the dress was damp ; a chill struck to his
lungs ; by the time he reached his great scene in the
fifth act he was totally inaudible, and his failure was
as complete in Sir Giles as his triumph had been
assured in Othello.

Instead of resting and nursing himself, he tried to
fight off his malady with drink ; but he got worse
and worse, collapsed utterly, and left the theatre.

The manager of Drury Lane still believed in him,
sought him out, offered splendid terms ; he pulled
himself together, and, fortified by the accursed
whisky-bottle, attempted to retrieve his fallen fortunes. There was an enormous house ; great things
were anticipated ; but alas ! of the brilliant and
accomplished tragedian, there remained only what
George Lewes cruelly described to be "a hoarse and
furious man, tearing a passion to tatters with the

melody of a raven." **Yes!** the magnificent voice
which had once struck the chords of every passion,
that had thrilled every heart, had gone for ever.
Even in its decline it still remained a marvellous
organ, so long as he knew how to use it. This
engagement culminated in a miserable *fiasco*, in
consequence of which he quitted the theatre in disgrace, and sought refuge in an obscure tavern in the
immediate vicinity.

Contemporaneous with these events, Mr. Phineas
T. Barnum had despatched one Mr. Wilton Hall to
Europe, to secure Jenny Lind for a tour in America.
Having accomplished this mission to the satisfaction
of his chief, Mr. Hall was once more despatched to
England to hunt up novelties to exploit in the
States.

Upon arriving in town this gentleman heard, of
course (for the subject was rife on all men's tongues)
of Brooke's sudden rise and equally sudden fall ; and
it occurred to the astute American that Gustavus
was still a young man, that amendment was not
impossible, and that what he had done before he
might do again. Presenting himself at the H——
late in the day, he found the wretched object of his
quest still in bed, and roaring out for a "pot of four
half!" Upon explaining his business, he met with
but scant welcome, for the unfortunate tragedian's
mind was unhinged by his reverses, and he had
arrived at the conclusion that his career was over.
Hall, however, would not take "no" for an answer.
Instead of a "pot of four half!" he called for a

bottle of Cliquot; under its benignant influence he soothed the fallen star, and in an hour's time it was arranged for him to leave the place on the morrow. Next day, at twelve o'clock, **Hall** came **with a** brougham, paid the tavern bill, and took Brooke **to** splendid lodgings in Belgravia. The day after, he was taken to a West-End tailor and "figged out" in the height of the mode; and a few days later, to the astonishment of everybody, Gustavus was to be seen every afternoon lolling about in his chariot among the fashionable mob in the Ladies' **Mile**.

After **a** month's recuperation, the tragedian and his mentor sailed for New York, where a series of engagements in all the principal theatres was speedily arranged. The tour commenced far away **down** South; the climate agreed **with** Brooke, who recovered his voice—that is, as much as he ever did recover it; he "struck ile" immediately, **and** once more leaped into fame and fortune—the first **tour** alone yielding a profit of £20,000.

He had left England a beggar; after two or three years' absence he returned a wealthy man: he had been expelled from Drury Lane with ignominy, he returned in glory; he had been hooted from the stage, he was now received with the loud triumph of a conqueror: he was engaged for twenty-four performances; he gave forty-eight to houses crowded from floor to dome.

His progress through the provinces was **one** triumphal march: he entered every town in a magnificent coach drawn by four horses and driven **by** two outriders in scarlet ; crowds followed him with cheers from the hotel to the theatre, from the theatre home again (sometimes making asses of themselves by taking the horses from his carriage and taking their place) ; the newspapers exhausted the language of adulation, and editors and reporters bowed down before him as if he had been a demi-god ! Deputations of mayors and aldermen besought him to honour their towns by giving an additional performance ; dinners and suppers were given to him, or he gave them ; presentations of plate were made to " the greatest tragedian in the world "—which, however, " the greatest tragedian in the world " had to pay for—besides which he presented tickets for soup, coals, blankets, and tickets for the play to the deserving poor and their children, who in Ireland were taught to pray for " father and mother and Gustavus Brooke " !

While in Birmingham, the Hon. George Coppin, the famous Australian comedian, manager, and M.P., saw Brooke act, and engaged him then and there for two years in Australia and New Zealand at £100 a night, paying all expenses besides. This engagement also was a triumphal success, and at the end of two years Gustavus was rolling in wealth. By the same time he had, unfortunately for himself, quarrelled with Hall, and they parted company—the worst day's work Brooke ever did in his life.

At this period he might have retired with forty or fifty thousand pounds ; but in an evil moment he was induced to enter into partnership with Coppin

in the management of the Theatre Royal, Melbourne,
and of a great public pleasure-garden called the
Melbourne Cremorne. The moment he went into
management his luck began to turn; he had no
knowledge whatever of finance, and failure followed
failure. Things got from bad to worse; he returned
to his old pernicious habits; at last, having lost
every shilling he had in the world, over head and
ears in debt and in danger of arrest, he was compelled to fly the country! When he arrived in the
colony, he was received as if he had been a member
of the royal family; deputations came aboard to
meet him. When he landed there were crowds,
carriages and horses, bands of music, and triumphal
arches, to accentuate his welcome. When he left,
he slunk aboard at dead of night, like a thief, and
lay hidden behind the smoke-stack of the *London*
till she quitted the harbour. When he left England
he was a man of fortune; when he returned after an
absence of seven years he was penniless!

To mend matters, he had taken to himself a young
wife (Miss Avonia Jones), of whose ability he entertained a much higher estimate than the public ever
did.

During his absence taste had undergone a strange
transmutation in the old country, and Charles
Fechter was the fashionable idol of the hour; the
criticasters had declared that he was the apostle of
the future, that he had taught us how Shakespere
should be acted (with a French accent), that all
English art was commonplace, old-fashioned, vulgar,

and, indeed, defunct. These sapient gentlemen could not now stultify themselves : **Fechter** had failed miserably in Othello—*ergo*, Brooke must not succeed. Upon his re-appearance as " the valiant Moor" upon the scene of his former triumphs, he was assailed with a general chorus of vituperation that was amazing; according to the consensus **of** critical opinion he was now vulgar, coarse, extravagant, scarce fit for a booth at a country fair. Indeed, a distinguished man of letters absolutely had the good taste to declare to **me that the** initials " **G. V. B.**" ought to be interpreted " Great Vulgar Brute !" Others went further, and alleged that **he** was drunk upon his opening night ! **As a matter of** fact, he had never been more sober in his **life.** **For** two months prior to the commencement **of** his engagement **at** the " Lane," he had lived quietly in the bosom of **his** family **at Dublin,** went early **to** bed and early to rise, and was in better form on the night **of** his re-appearance in London than when he first won all hearts **as Othello.** **On this** occasion the public unfortunately were " as easily led by the nose **as asses are,"** **and** they accepted the *ipse dixit* of the **papers as gospel.** Poor " **Gus** " was further dragged down by the failure of his wife, a young, **crude, in-**experienced actress, and his collapse was disastrous and complete. When he went into the country, the bad news **had preceded him, and he failed** nearly everywhere. **At** or about **this period we** met a great deal, and he acted at my theatres in Leeds, York, and Hull, with varying success.

At length family matters took his wife to America, and he was left to his own resources in this country, with deplorable results.

When we next came in contact with each other, by a remarkable coincidence **we** were both again acting in Manchester. This time the venue was changed ; he was at the Queen's, I was at **the** Theatre **Royal.** One day he called upon me, and told me he **was** going to Leeds, where at that time I was building my **new** theatre, subsequently destroyed by fire. He asked me **to act** for his benefit at the minor theatre ; of course, I gladly acquiesced, and it was arranged that I was to play Othello to his Iago.

What I am now about to narrate could not possibly be published at the time of its occurrence, but it may **not** be amiss after all these years to chronicle a sad but remarkable event.

Upon arriving **in** Leeds to rehearse, I saw **no** sign of him till the fifth act of **the play, when** he informed me that he had only that moment received the startling news that **his wife** and George Coppin **would** arrive in Liverpool the next day ; the one was returning from America, **the** other was coming from Australia for the express purpose of re-engaging Brooke and rehabilitating him in the colony.

As usual, when left to himself, poor " Gus " had committed numerous indiscretions. Amongst others, he had involved himself in an unfortunate connection, and was quite unmanned in contemplating the situation in which his folly had placed him.

When I got to the theatre at an early hour that night, to my astonishment I found him (for we occupied the same room) already dressed for Iago. Except that he seemed a little more dignified than usual, there was nothing remarkable about him; it was only when we got on the stage together that I found he was *Bacchi plenus!* My impression is that had he been acting Othello no one would have discovered his infirmity; indeed, it was impossible for him to go wrong in the Moor, but he had never mastered the words of Iago textually, and was always afraid of being caught tripping with the text. The continued effort of memory muddled him, and unfortunately let the audience into the secret. He stuttered and stammered, and even mixed up his soliloquies in the most *mal à propos* manner. Instead of saying at the end of the first act:

> "I have 't; it is engendered; hell and night
> Must bring this monstrous birth to the world's light!"

he substituted the conclusion of the soliloquy in the next act:

> "'Tis here, but yet confused—
> Knavery's plain face is never seen till used!"

whereupon some over-zealous Shakespearian in the pit blandly exclaimed, "No; it is you who are confused, Mr. Brooke." This interruption disconcerted Gustavus, and put him entirely wrong.

In the quarrel scene of the second act he broke down altogether. The most notable feature of his picturesque costume was a breastplate of white buck-

skin, elaborately prepared with pipe-clay, after the
fashion in which soldiers' belts are got up. When
the interruption occurred which led to the collapse,
Brooke advanced amid a tempest of yells and groans,
and evidently getting a little mixed in his metaphors,
and under the impression that he was acting for my
benefit instead of my acting for his, exclaimed,
"'You common cry of curs, whose breath I hate,'
I don't care the cracking of a rotten gooseberry for
you; I am here to-night to do honour to the legitimate drama in the person of my friend, John
Coleman, and I can lay my hand upon my heart and
say——" and as he suited the action to the word
there arose a pillar of pipe-clay which filled the stage,
and evoked, I think, the loudest roar of laughter I
ever heard in a theatre.

After this I persuaded him to drive home, under
charge of my man, while the stock leading man
finished the part of Iago; then, putting on steam, I
rushed through the last three acts to the best of my
ability.

I had arranged for Gustavus to be brought back
just as the curtain fell. During the interval he had
tubbed and soda-watered, and "Richard was himself
again." He was in mourning for the death of his
mother, and was clad from head to foot in black,
black-gloved, etc. I thought I had never seen him
look so *distingué*. Placing him hastily at the pro-
scenium wing, on the left-hand side, I said :

" Now, Gus, will you trust yourself entirely to
me ?"

"I will do anything you wish me to do, John," he replied.

"Stand here, then," said I; "listen to what I am about to say, and, for God's sake, don't stir hand or foot till I bid you."

Then, in response to the call, I went before the curtain, and addressed the audience thus:

"Your voices are very eloquent on my behalf; let me entreat you to use them a little on behalf of my friend. For the past week I have looked forward to this night with pleasure, but the pleasure of renewing my acquaintance with you was as nothing compared to the honour I anticipated in acting this part beside Gustavus Brooke, whose Othello I considered, in my boyhood, one of the great achievements of the English stage. Well, to-night has been a great grief and a great disappointment to us all; but if you knew the cause I am sure you would condone all the shortcomings which have occurred. No one in this building is more conscious than my poor friend that he has failed in his duty to the poet, to you—and, above all, to himself; but you who are indebted to him for so many pleasures of memory, you who have so often seen him at his best and brightest, can well afford to be generous now. He is about to leave us for a distant country: in all human probability we shall never see his face nor hear his voice again; he hears every word I am saying, he is anxious to be reconciled to you; you cannot, will not, must not, part from him in anger. I ask you, for the sake of old times, to give him one parting cheer, one parting God-speed!"

As I spoke the last words I stepped to the wing, and led him to the centre of the stage. Then occurred a scene which I shall never forget as long as I live; the house rose like one man, and cheered with a mighty voice that shook the building **to its** base. **Men** and women waved their hats and handkerchiefs, and **sobbed and** cried aloud. **He was** himself carried away by **the** general emotion; clasping my hand fervently, he made an attempt to speak, but I plucked his arm under mine, and we retired together amidst the continued acclamations. As we passed out of sight **of the** audience, he fell weeping on my shoulder; **then he** gasped **out,** "God bless you, old fellow!" We had five minutes' serious talk before we said good-bye, and when **we** parted that night we parted for ever.

As I was about to undress, the manager came to my room in a state **of** great perturbation, and told me that the editor of the only local paper which at that time devoted its attention to the drama had gone away disgusted at the period of the breakdown in the second act, and that the sub-editor had confidentially informed him (the manager) that a "slating" article was in type for publication on the morrow.

Now, this one part of Othello is the bow of Ulysses; at any rate it is the only part that ever "takes the backbone out" of me for the next day; besides which, it had been a night of horrors, involving almost superhuman exertions on my part to keep the audience in hand and carry the play to a successful conclusion. In addition to all this, I had to be in the express to London at two o'clock in the morning; it was now twelve. The publication of this article at the period would have been a pleasant welcome for the poor wife on her arrival in the Mersey, and would certainly have put an end to Brooke's engagement with Coppin. The paper would go to press in an hour; there was nothing for it but action, prompt and decided; so as soon as I had got the beastly black stuff off my face, I drove down to the office of the *E——*. The editor, who was a personal friend, had gone home. He lived a mile and a half out of town; I drove without a moment's delay to Mount Valery. He had gone to bed. I knocked him up, explaining my business. At first he was surly as a bear with a sore head at being awakened from his first sleep, hard as nails, and obdurate as the devil; but he yielded at length to my entreaties, and gave me a note authorizing the sub-editor to expunge the article. Previous to its suppression they gave me a " pull " of it, and it is somewhere in one of my scrap-books now. Assuredly I slept none the less soundly on my way to town for my share in that part of the night's performance.

And yet, if the article had appeared, perhaps Coppin might not have engaged Brooke for Australia; in that case he might not have sailed in the *London*. And yet, those who love him best must feel now " 'Tis better as it is."

I never heard from him again except once. I

MRS. MOWATT AS ROSALIND IN "AS YOU LIKE IT."

wrote him for my **prompt-book of** " Othello," which **I** had left behind **on that** eventful night. He replied, taking **an affectionate** farewell, **but** asking if he might keep **the** book for my **sake.**

Coppin engaged him **for** Australia, and **went on in** advance **to** sound **the note** of preparation. **The** people **of** Melbourne **were agog** with anticipation, eager **to forget** and forgive, **and anxious for** their old **favourite to renew** his **former** triumphs.

At the moment of our **parting Brooke** solemnly promised **to turn over a new leaf, and I** have every reason to believe that **he did so.** It is certain that **for** months **prior to his** leaving England he had been **both** temperate **and abstemious.**

His sister, who through life **had been** his guardian angel, accompanied **him to** Australia. **They** sailed from Gravesend **in the** *London*, the **very vessel** which had brought him home. The story **of that** fatal voyage has been told quite often enough, **and** told better than **I can** ever hope **to tell it.** Strange **to** say, however, **I** encountered **in** the very Manchester where **we** had **first met** a sailor—one of the survivors **of** that **ill-fated** expedition—who told me that **poor "Gus"** had endeared himself to everybody on **board by his** modesty and manliness. His sister was lying below, sick and helpless. **At** the last moment, when **the** men who escaped took to **the** boats, they urged him **to** accompany them ; **but he** put them gently aside and said, " No, thanks ; you are **very** good, **lads ;** but **I** can't **leave** her." **As** they were moving away he said, "When **you** get to

Melbourne, remember me to the boys." For answer
they gave a parting cheer. .As they pulled off they
saw him leaning over the rail, his bare feet paddling
in the rising waters, a sad, sweet smile upon his face,
his wistful eyes fixed upon them till the ship faded
out of sight, and darkness fell upon the deep.

That picture of the poor player standing alone, as
it were, amidst the quiet crowd, calmly awaiting
death with the dogged spirit of their island race, is
almost too awful to contemplate, even at this distance
of time. Were they thinking of home, friends, or
kindred? Was he recalling his lost youth, his
wasted manhood, or was he dreaming of the young
wife whom he had left behind, and who died so soon
after of a broken heart? Did he see some phantom
audience rising before him as the doomed ship sank
beneath the wild waves that sounded his requiem;
or had his simple faith in that supreme moment
found shelter in the blessed hope that lifts the
sinner's soul to heaven? Let us hope so.

His epitaph is "writ in water;" were it "graven
on granite," had I the writing, it should run thus, in
the lines of our great master:

> "Nothing in his life
> Became him like the leaving it; he died
> As one that had been studied in his death,
> To throw away the dearest thing he owed
> As 'twere a careless trifle."

So best! Had he survived the terrors of that
awful time, who knows what fate might have held
in store for him? As it was—

> "Death cometh not to him untimely who is fit to die."

Praise and blame are alike now; yet I venture to
apply to him **Lord Rosebery's** noble *apologia* for
Robert Burns: "Too much has been made **of errors**
which were the generous faults of a generous **mind,**
and **we** do not love him the less for feeling that he was
not altogether removed from our lower humanity."

For myself,—because **I loved** him, I have paid
this poor tribute to the memory **of a man** who never
had an enemy in this **world,** except—himself!

Since this paper originally **appeared in** *Longman's
Magazine,* it has been **appropriated** ("convey the
wise **it** call") by nearly **every journal in** the empire
and **in America.**

The only acknowledgment **the author** has **ever**
received has been "a little cheque" from **the pro-**
prietors of the *Melbourne Age,* and the following
communications, which he is privileged to publish:

[COPY.]

" 35, York Street, Portman Square,
" March 5, 1886.

" DEAR SIR,

"I have read with much pleasure your
interesting paper on poor Gustavus Brooke—that
rough genius with good sterling qualities—whose
sad end, and the early death of his young wife,
caused me much regret. I have to thank you for
the kind mention of myself.

"**As** a fact, however, my agreement with G. B.
was £25 a week, to play alternate nights. On the

pronounced success of the first night I played him every night, and of course doubled his salary.

"Yours very faithfully,
"(Signed)   HENRY SPICER."

" John Coleman, Esq."

[COPY.]

"March 9, 1886.
" DEAR SIR,

" Yes, Brooke played with Mrs. Mowatt, the American actress, in my piece, 'The Lords of Ellingham.'

" The play was written almost in my boyhood, and offered no grip for poor Brooke's vigorous hand. I was very glad, after a few nights, to restore him to a line of parts in which he could show his mettle.

" His Othello was almost faultless. His majestic carriage and magnificent voice caught the audience from the first, and his success was never for a moment in doubt, though we had enemies in the house, and even in my own company, who, in the interest of a rival house, had tried to induce Brooke to break his engagement, and who would have been glad to see him fail.

" He was, however, at heart a true gentleman, and acted throughout most loyally to me.

" That is the chief reason of the interest with which I have always regarded his memory, and of the pleasure with which I read your kind and manly tribute to his general character.

"With respect to his first night in 'Othello,' a circumstance occurred such as I have never since seen—the p:t rising, *en masse*, in the midst of the cene, cheering and waving hats, etc.

"It was where Othello, learning too late Iago's treachery, breaks down with horror and remorse, exclaiming : 'Oh! Fool! fool! fool!'

"Believe me,

"Yours very faithfully,

"(Signed) HENRY SPICER."

"John Coleman, Esq."

The author's friend, Mr. E. L. Blanchard, has also placed at his disposal the following interesting note :

"On the night of Monday, April 9th, 1866, was produced at the Surrey Theatre a new historical drama in five acts, written by Mr. Watts Phillips and entitled 'Theodora, Actress and Empress.' In discharge of a journalistic duty I was present when the curtain rose on the play, and occupied a seat in the stalls, nearly at the extremity of the third row on the right-hand side of the auditorium. Next to me was Mr. Leicester Buckingham, at that time the dramatic critic of that short-lived daily newspaper, the *Morning Star.* We were both interested in the success of the play, not merely on the author's account, but because the heroine was represented by Miss Avonia Jones, the widow of G. V. Brooke, the tragedian, whose sad end was still a subject of mourn-

ful comment. During the overture I had rapidly
related to Leicester Buckingham how I had encountered the widow in deep mourning, accompanied
by her agent, Mr. E. P. Hingston (who brought
Artemus Ward to England), wandering about
Gravesend on a cold Sunday morning of the preceding January, seeking for one of the survivors of
the ill-fated steamer, the *London,* from whom she
might possibly gather information concerning the
position of her husband when the vessel foundered
in the Bay of Biscay on its outward voyage to
Australia. I explained how I had been enabled to
put the poor bereaved lady on the right track, for I
knew the bold mariner, who had escaped so miracu-
lously in one of the boats, was Thomas Gardner, the
son of the landlord of the Terrace Tavern, and I
had heard him relate in the coffee-room of that
hostelry only the previous night the stirring story of
the rescue which came at last after he had been
tossed about by the stormy waves for forty-eight
hours. I told the result of the interview—how we
heard that the Dutch portion of the crew, twenty-one
in number, had refused to work, and how these men
went to their berths and remained there, so that the
passengers had to work at the pumps for many hours
with the English seamen. Attired in a red Crimean
shirt, bare-headed and bare-footed, G. V. Brooke
had exerted himself incessantly. He was reminded
that the labour was useless, and when last seen,
about four hours before the steamer went down, he
was leaning with grave composure upon one of the

half-doors of the companion-way leading to the
cabin. His chin was resting upon both hands, and
his arms were on the top of the door, which he
gently swayed to and fro while he calmly watched
the scene. One of the passengers who saw him
said : 'You have worked wonderfully. Mr. Brooke,
and behaved more bravely than any man on board.'
To the steward, who came up and spoke to him,
Brooke exclaimed : ' If you succeed in saving yourself, give my farewell to the people at Melbourne.'
These were his last words."

CHAPTER IV.

CHARLES DILLON.

EXCEPT Edmund Kean, no English actor ever resembled so closely the great Frederick, in conduct and character, and in strange and perpetually varying vicissitudes of fortune, as the erratic and ill-fated Charles Dillon.

The French and the English Lemaître both fought the battle of life from hand to mouth; both emerged from obscurity; both leaped into fame and fortune; both, alas! ended their chequered careers in poverty and obscurity.

The bent of their genius was identical, and the Englishman gained much of his popularity from essaying certain characters which the Frenchman had created; *par exemple*—Paillasse, Maurice (" La Dame de St. Tropez"), Le Docteur Noir, Don César, Ruy Blas, etc.

Both evoked smiles or tears with equal facility, both thrilled their audiences with passion, or melted them with pathos, and it may be truly said of both these gifted men, that their capacity was as unique as their versatility was boundless.

The Frenchman, however, had one advantage over his English compeer : the one passed his dazzling and starry life upon the Boulevards, the other was unfortunately, for the greater portion of his life, relegated to the backwoods.

The barest record of the trials and struggles of the English Lemaître would have been more replete with interest than ninety-and-nine romances out of a hundred.

It would have revealed a childhood of poverty and misery—a youth devoted to trudging half over England, ragged, and almost barefoot—acting in barns and shows, at wakes and fairs, at what he called "dukies" or penny "gaffs," in slums of King's Cross, the New Cut, or Drury Lane ; a manhood which culminated in the management of the most fashionable London theatre of the period, where, for two entire seasons, he was the idol of the populace and of the fashionable world ; a maturity which ended in the street of a petty provincial town, whose best claim to be remembered hereafter will be from the fact that he died there.

I cannot pretend to give even the faintest outline of this meteoric career. I can only recall the impressions of a personal acquaintance which commenced in my youth, illustrated by certain incidents which occurred during the period of our early intimacy.

In my boyhood I lived at Westbourne Green. We dined at six, and as soon as I had bolted my dinner I usually "made tracks" for some theatre.

The Marylebone, being the nearest, frequently came in for my stray sixpences, or less frequent shillings. Upon one especial evening I made the best of my way to Portman Market, attracted thither by the announcement of Elton (the poor fellow who was soon afterwards drowned off Holy Isle, in the wreck of the *Pegasus*) as Virginius.

When I had parted with my sixpence, and an additional twopence for a playbill, I found that, from some cause or other, Elton could not appear, and "The Dog of Montargis," with the "renowned' Coney and Blanchard, as Landry and Eloi, the dumb boy, were substituted for Elton and "Virginius."

This was a disappointment; still, a play is always a play to a lad of fourteen; besides, "The Dog of Montargis" is a very good play of the kind. I had never seen it, and it was admirably acted; at least, I thought so then, and I am disposed to think, even at this interval of time, that my boyish impression was a correct one.

The principal performer, the "dawg," was a magnificent Mount St. Bernard, who went about his work as if he had been born to it. He licked his dead master's face, rang the bell, carried the lantern, led the way to the forest, seized the murderer by the throat, and strangled him, to my great satisfaction.

The heroine of the drama, Miss Clara Conquest, was the most charming of village maidens. She was a brunette, with a plump, beautifully-balanced figure, dark curling hair, bright sparkling eyes, with just the *soupçon* of a cast in them, which rather enhanced

their sprightliness, teeth like pearls, a mouth like
Cupid's bow, a saucy tiptilted nose, and the daintiest
feet and ankles I ever beheld.

Macaire was a wonderful "bowld" speaker, one
Mr. Mark Howard.

The Seneschal was the famous "Bogey" King,
so called because he was the mildest man in the
world, with the most sepulchral voice.

Blaise was Tom Lee, the Irish comedian from
Drury Lane, a capital actor.

Landry, the villain, as I have said before, was
acted by Coney, a great, hulking fellow, who carried
his shoulders up to his ears, and shouted incessantly,
but who, nevertheless, fought a capital broadsword
combat.

Blanchard, who played Eloi, the dumb boy, was,
at that time, a singularly handsome, symmetrical
young fellow, and an elegant pantomimist.

The hero of the night, "The murdered Aubri,"
was enacted by an abnormally ugly young man,
whose name did not appear in the bill. This gentleman had a huge, cavernous mouth, with protruding
and irregular teeth, a corrugated nose, snake-like,
glittering eyes, a head of long, lank black hair,
growing very low down on a broad but receding
forehead, over the brows of which two great bumps
projected. In fact, to maintain the semblance of a
forehead at all, a quantity of the front hair was
shaven off, and as evidently he was not an adept in
the artifices of the toilet, the blue-black mark clearly
indicated the exact locality of this tonsorial operation.

But when **Aubri** had been on the stage five minutes, I lost sight of his plebeian appearance in my admiration of his ability.

He moved with ease, grace, and distinction. In his one great, indeed, his only scene—the scene of the murder—his sword-play was magnificent; his pathos and his passion were alike admirable. Such was my first impression of Charles Dillon.

His subsequent performances at this period did not strike me so favourably. The parts in which I saw him placed him to singular disadvantage. They were Lothair (" Miller and his Men "), El Hyder, and Philip, in his own adaptation of Bulwer Lytton's ' Night and Morning."

For years previous to this he had combined the functions of author, actor, and stage-manager, and had starred at the " minors " in his own pieces of " Marco Sciarra, the Brigand of the Abruzzi," " The Maid of Zaragossa," " The Mysteries of Paris," etc. All wild, exaggerated youthful productions, but containing strong lines and powerful situations enough to make the fortunes of half a dozen West-End dramas nowadays.

From this time I saw no more of him for a considerable period; but as he was persistently coming to the fore, I heard of him continually, and soon learnt that he had gone into management in the country.

The first time I came in personal contact with him was at Wolverhampton.

While acting at Stafford a good many years ago, seeing that G. V. Brooke was announced as Othello,

and Dillon for Iago, the members of the company
(all youthful enthusiasts), out of their slender salaries,
chartered a coach and pair, and drove over to Wolverhampton to see them act. I went round behind the
scenes to call on Brooke, and to ask the customary
courtesy of admission for our little party. Dillon,
who was dressed for Iago, came forward and introduced himself very affably.

He was, I thought, very much improved in appearance. He had now mounted the huge black
moustache which hid the cavernous mouth, and he
ever after sedulously cultivated that hirsute adorn-
ment.

His Iago was quite as good as Brooke's Othello,
and they were both as good, or better in these parts
than any actors I have ever seen since.

Miss Clara Conquest (my pretty brunette with the
twinkling feet) had now become Mrs. Dillon, and
she made a very interesting Desdemona ; the Emilia,
I am ashamed to say, I have forgotten. Harry
Widdicomb was Roderigo, and the late Mr. F. B,
Egan, a veritable son of Anak, and the handsomest
man I have ever seen, was the Cassio.

When the play was over, Brooke, Dillon, and
Widdicomb took us to the Peacock, entertained us
right royally, and sent us on our way rejoicing.

Two or three years elapsed, and I saw no more of
Dillon.

One morning, while strolling along the Market
Place at Norwich, after rehearsal, I encountered an

elderly man attired in a shabby clerical suit of black
It seemed to me as if I ought to have known him.
That *soupçon* of swagger, that broad receding forehead, those two swelling bumps projecting over
either brow, the iron-gray hair shaved upward
towards the poll, those snake-like eyes, that rugged
irregular nose, that abysmal mouth—where could I
have seen them before ?

Where, indeed ? The stranger evoked an impression, not a recollection ; an impression which
vanished as I passed by, and went for my " consti-
tutional " amongst the quaint nooks and interesting
relics of olden time which abound nowhere more
than in that delightful old city.

When I got home, just as we were sitting down to
dinner, a card was brought up, bearing the inscription, " Charles James Church, B.A., Balliol College.
Oxford."

I desired my visitor to be shown up, when, lo !
the B.A. turned out to be the seedy-looking gentleman I had met in the Market Place.

He was an actor as well as a B.A.   He had been
at the theatre the night before, had seen my Othello,
and had called to pay his respects to the Youthful
Tragedian of the Norwich Circuit ; a circuit to which,
he said, he had been formerly attached.

Now this gentleman did not look much like a
B.A., but he looked very hungry, and—dinner was
on the table.

The rites of hospitality are sacred, so we called
for another knife and fork.

Our guest made himself at home, and did ample justice to our frugal repast.

Over his after-dinner **pipe he talked** incessantly : grew eloquent about his friend the "divine" Edmund Kean, and other distinguished actors ; **glanced** modestly at his own peaceful triumphs at college **or** theatre ; aired his acquaintance with **politics,** poetry, **and the drama ;** talked like a senior wrangler ; quoted Cicero **and** Demosthenes ; and altogether impressed me with his erudition.

He also impressed me with his apparent aversion to **soap and water,** and the paucity of his **linen.** Objectionable as were these peculiarities, they merely struck me as being the offspring of the eccentricities of genius. Since then, strange **as it may appear, I** have seen other actors and other B.A.'s (and eminent ones, too !) with whom a little linen and a **little soap** and water went a long way.

Evidently my new acquaintance, **not to put too** fine a point upon it, was "**hard** up." By-and-by, when he had had a glass or two of whisky and water, he began to quote Juvenal, and became a bore. So I brought our interview to an end. Then, as we say in the theatre, he "came to cues."

He was on his way to town and lacked a few shillings to make up his fare.

This difficulty being got over, he presented me, as a mark of his esteem and gratitude, with a new little French book (in a yellow cover, prix 1 fr. 25 c.), by Lamartine.

It was something about a wonderful dream of

"The Parliament of Man—the Federation of the World," evoked by smoking a pipe or two of haschisch.

I had been vainly endeavouring all the afternoon to recall who it was that my visitor reminded me of. At the moment of his departure the recognition dawned—I may say leaped upon my mind.

"Pardon me," said I, "Mr.——"

"Church, sir, Church."

"Precisely. Well, Mr. Church, do you know that you remind me in the most surprising manner of Mr. Charles Dillon ?"

"Not in the least surprising, sir, considering that I happen to be the unfortunate father of that unfilial son !"

"Good gracious ! You don't say so ? Pray sit down, sir, and have another glass of whisky and water."

Nothing loath, Mr. Church sat down again, and returned to his potations, while he gave me a scene from "The Stranger."

With a fine flow of Brummagem, he informed me that "he had taken a serpent to his bosom, who had betrayed, dishonoured him ; that he had been left a lonely, blighted, broken-hearted man; that the ungrateful boy, on whom he had looked forward to be the prop of his declining years, had brought his gray hairs with sorrow to the grave ; had assumed the badge of infamy ; had taken the name of his deadliest foe ; but that a time would come," etc. The time *did* come—with the end of the bottle of whisky,

CHARLES DILLON AS OTHELLO.

when it occurred to the **B.A.** to take **his departure,**
invoking maudlin benedictions **in Latin and Greek,**
and prognosticating a glorious future for **me.**

Years after, Dillon himself **told me** that **he cer-**
tainly had the misfortune **to be** indebted **for his**
existence to this vagabond, **who, by-the-bye,** instead
of being a B.A., was a distinguished **painter** (and
glazier !).   **How** the **fellow** acquired his knowledge
of the classics **no one** ever knew ; **he** certainly
never graduated **at** Balliol.   **He had** turned stroller
in some small company where **he** met **Dillon's**
mother, **whom** he abandoned **and** left to **starve.**
The poor **woman,** while **the lad** was but a **child,**
found a friend and benefactor, and **her** son a **father,**
in Arthur Dillon (a theatrical agent and **a** popular
actor at the Surrey), whose name Charles **ever after**
bore, and whom he loved **with** filial devotion.

A few months after **I first** formed the acquaintance
of my friend, the distinguished painter **and** glazier
aforesaid (who, **by** the way, made periodical descents
upon me in divers places, until at length I intimated
that his room was preferable to his company !), **I**
went **to** Sheffield, where I encountered Dillon for
the second time.

Apropos of Sheffield, he told me afterwards that
he commenced his managerial career there with
Bulwer's comedy **of** " Money," **which had never**
before been acted in the town.

The theatre was crowded with an excited audience,
who followed the play with eager interest.

The "king of the gallery," as he was called, was a chimney-sweep, who elected to guide and control the opinion of the gods. This fellow was a personage to be feared and "squared," for his hostile verdict was simply damnatory to any play or players, or even to the management itself. Being strongly exercised in his mind as to the persistent interruptions of the Old Member in the Club Scene, when the irate old idiot had for the sixth or seventh time called out, "Waiter! snuff-box!" the sweep got up and roared from his perch, "Oh, shut up! Mesther Dillon, let yon owd rooster ha' his d——d snuff-box; bundle him out, and get on wi' t' play."

When I commenced my engagement at the Adelphi Theatre, Dillon was concluding a six weeks' stay at the Theatre Royal. At this time his Belphegor was being much talked of. Indeed, it was so popular in Yorkshire and Lancashire that the part was practically prohibited to any other actor. During all the time I was in Sheffield I never attempted it, except on one memorable occasion, to which I shall hereafter refer. As this particular part was the one with which Dillon's name was so intimately associated, it may not be out of place to mention the circumstances connected with its original production.

It was first acted by him to a wretched house of something like ten or twelve pounds, and the sight disheartened him; but he found, as many other actors have often found, that his scanty audience represented the heart, the blood, and brains of the theatrical public.

The sparsely-peopled pit gathered themselves together, and began to listen **with** interest. He " went " for them, and they **" went "** **for him ; and,** despite the wretched house the piece **was an extra-** ordinary, a triumphant hit.

Upon its next performance, during **the** following week, the theatre was crowded from floor to ceiling ; as, indeed, it was for years afterwards, whenever and wherever he was announced for Belphegor.

During my engagement, having a night's holiday, with the actor's usual craze for the enjoyment thereof, I went to the other theatre to see Dillon in " The Black Doctor."

It was summer, and the performance was supposed to commence at eight o'clock.

Upon my arrival, at about **a** quarter past, I found the bold Charles strutting **up** and down the **side** of the theatre, with his everlasting cigar in his mouth, attended by a select troop of parasites, to whom he was recounting his latest funny story, pausing **be-** tween whiles to look into the pit to see " how many more grinders had dropped in."

I went up, and reminded him of our meeting in Wolverhampton. He looked **at** me incredulously, and **said :**

" Good God ! you're not that boy ? Well, by Jove ! you have shot up. All right, sonnie, you'll have the boxes all to yourself, so in you go, and **I'll** get dressed."

He had been playing to enormous " business " **for** a month, but had re-engaged again, and yet again, and although then at the height of his popularity, had outstayed his welcome.

There was a wretched house.

He walked on for Fabian in the street trousers and boots I had seen him in ten minutes before—in fact, he had only slipped on a blouse and "made up" his face, and yet how admirably he acted the part throughout, how splendidly he played the mad scene! I came to be critical, I remained to cry; so there was an end to my criticism.

During the performance he sent round and asked me to meet him at the inn opposite when the play was over.

Now I must premise that two or three months previously I had produced for my benefit at New-castle-on-Tyne a drama which I had adapted from Dumas' novel of "Monte Cristo." It was a crude, boyish thing, but my own—although I must confess that the idea was suggested to me by seeing the French players at Drury Lane, when the memorable row occurred which led to two or three English actors, who ought to have known better, being lugged off to Bow Street.

When we met at Sampson's, Dillon astonished me by opening fire thus:

"Young shaver, I've a crow to pluck with you. You've cribbed a copy of my 'Monte Cristo.'"

When I could recover my breath, I assured him that I had never even seen his "Monte Cristo." He replied:

"Well, if you haven't, Sydney Davis" (a distin-

guished actor of that period, and brother of the
Newcastle-on-Tyne manager) "has. He was with
me in Dublin, and played in the piece with me."

I indignantly retorted :

" He may have played in your piece, sir, but he
has never played in mine."

And so we parted with a little temper on both
sides.

Two or three nights afterwards he took his benefit,
with the following modest programme :

The play of " The Cavalier;" the Princess's drama,
" The Violet ; or, Napoleon's Flower," and " Monte
Cristo "!

At our theatre we played "Othello."

As we did not commence till eight o'clock, by the
time I had got the black off my face it was well-nigh
twelve.

At this moment Richard Younge, who played
Iago, came to my room, and invited me to go up to
the Royal to see " Monte Cristo." I replied, " It's
useless going now ; the play will be over by the time
we get there."

" Ah ! you don't know Dillon !" replied Younge.
" Anyhow, come and chance it." So away we
went.

When we arrived at the theatre, about a quarter-
past twelve, the curtain was just falling on the
prologue, so we were in time for the last three
acts.

A capital piece of the kind, and, as far as Dillon
was concerned, a capital performance ; but the other

people were here, there, everywhere, nowhere ; a
circumstance which did not surprise me when I
learnt that the prompt-book had been lost, and the
play had been acted without a MS., and even without a part, Mr. and Mrs. Dillon telling the people,
at their only rehearsal, that they came on here and
went off there, and that they had to say "so-and-so."
This was the only actual practical illustration of the
pernicious practice christened by poor Tom Robertson "ponging" that ever came under my personal
observation.

On this occasion, although the curtain did not fall
till past two in the morning, the audience sat it out
to the last.

My next meeting with Dillon led to a few hasty
words, "all on account of" "Monte Cristo ;" and
thus commenced a misunderstanding which ultimately led to disastrous results for both.

Next season, in conjunction with my friend Mr.
Johnson (the comedian of the Lyceum), I took
the Theatre Royal, Sheffield, and Dillon went into
opposition at the other theatre ; and a very stupid
opposition it was for both parties. For two years
temper and petty jealousies embittered the conflict ;
and we were continually defeating Dillon or being
defeated by him.

At that period, if we had only coalesced and put
our forces together, with his artistic ability and my
commercial aptitude, we might easily have made our
fortunes.

The idea struck me so forcibly that I made friendly

overtures, and invited him to come and act at Bolton, where I was making a summer season.

He came, as usual, without properties or dresses, and laid mine under contribution.

We had rows about rehearsals, to which he would never come, unless literally dragged to the theatre ; but he was so agreeable, had such a flow of anecdote, such remarkable and romantic experiences, that I really became fascinated by him ; but, as to business, I could not bring him to book, and nothing ever came of his visit.

A month afterwards he appeared, with a scratch company, as Belphegor, at Sadler's Wells, then under the temporary management of young Webster, Ben Webster's nephew.

This young gentleman had sufficient influence to coax John Oxenford up to the wilds of Islington, even in the dog-days.

The genial John came, he saw, and was conquered by the country actor. Next day there appeared a flaming article in the *Times*, and Dillon was famous.

Three months afterwards he was manager of the Lyceum.

Now, it must be remembered that at this time "there were giants in the land :" the memory of Macready was still kept green ; Phelps was at the height of his popularity at Sadler's Wells ; Charles Kean was the favourite of the Court and of the public, and had an enormous following at the

Princess's; the Wigans were drawing all fashionable London to Wych Street; the new Adelphi was just opened; the Haymarket still enjoyed a great prestige; Drury Lane had Charles Mathews and the pantomime; yet, notwithstanding these potent attractions, Dillon's success was immediate and pronounced.

With ordinary prudence, he might now have become one of the first, if not *the* first manager in London. Apart, however, from his erratic mode of conducting his business, he unfortunately commenced his enterprise with borrowed capital, was overwhelmed with old debts, and had not even the scintillation of an idea on the subject of finance.

Besides these drawbacks, his defective early training, his eccentric mode of dress, his disregard for the *convenances* of society, perpetually asserted themselves, to his serious disadvantage. When out of the theatre he was never happy unless when loafing around the nearest bar with congenial companions, who swallowed his stories (which were by no means bad ones) and his libations with equal avidity.

In this respect he was wonderfully like Edmund Kean and Lemaître, who, at the height of their prosperity, preferred the society of their old "pals" to that of peers and princes.

It must be admitted, however, that Dillon "bore his blushing honours meekly," and that he never was so affable in his life as during this brief spell of prosperity.

The only extravagance he ever indulged in was a brougham, which was usually ordered at ten, to bring him to the Lyceum, but it was generally two or three hours later before he started. It was again ordered to take him home to dinner, but was invariably kept waiting all the afternoon, while he oscillated 'twixt the Albion and the Strand, when it was not infrequently dismissed altogether. Then he would adjourn to his own room in the theatre, where, over a rumpsteak and a pot of stout, with a few intimates he would discuss his last or his next performance, until it was time for the doors to open, when he would take a stroll round the Strand, to smoke his cigar, and to see the people flock into the pit; a habit he could never get rid of to the last.

At the end of his first season he went straight to Drury Lane, where he appeared as Richelieu, Hamlet, and Othello. From thence he went to Manchester with his company.

We met there, and he proposed that we should go into partnership for "a flutter," as he termed it, at Sheffield.

If the affair turned out to our mutual satisfaction, we were to talk about my putting a little coin into the Lyceum.

We had by this time each our special band of partisans, and if the Guelphs and the Ghibellines would only unite, and come to the theatre, we were bound to make a great thing of it.

An agreement was duly prepared, in which, among

other things, it was stipulated that we were to alternate Othello and Iago, Jaffier and Pierre, the Corsican Brothers and Chateau Renaud, Romeo and Mercutio, King John and Falconbridge.

He elected to open in " Richelieu."

Unfortunately, with the commencement of the partnership our misunderstandings began.

Rehearsal was called at ten.

Ten, eleven, twelve came, still no sign of Dillon. If we meant to open that night there was nothing for it but for me to rehearse the play, so as to be ready to play the part myself if necessary.

Of course, I rehearsed my own stage " business," which was totally different to his, and the result was that when he at length turned up at seven o'clock, there was a disreputable performance and a dreadful breakdown.

Through the " mull" of " Richelieu," we had indifferent houses for the next two or three performances, but on the first and second nights of " Othello " we were crowded in every hole and corner.

From that moment my partner was a changed man, and became unbearable and unendurable.

The following week he altered the programme, and insisted upon closing the theatre on Wednesday and Thursday, involving the firm in a loss of fifty or sixty pounds—a liability which he repudiated in the most airy manner. This circumstance brought our short partnership to an abrupt and disagreeable termination.

From that moment to the day of his death we never spoke again.

During his second season at the Lyceum he took **large** sums, but as fast as they came in they were appropriated by creditors. The result was disastrous, and his management ended, like that of his predecessor, Charles Mathews, in Basinghall Street.

In these **days of** long runs it may not be uninteresting to recall the work done, and done well, too, during those two seasons.

The opening bill was " Belphegor " and the burlesque of " Perdita." After a run of six weeks, " Belphegor " gave place to " The King's **Musketeers**," a production which, for elegance and good taste, remains unsurpassed.

Edmund Falconer's play of " **The** Cagot " enabled Dillon to distinguish himself in a congenial and sympathetic original part, besides which he appeared at intervals **as** Othello, Hamlet, Claude Melnotte, Richelieu, Virginius, William Tell, the Black Doctor, and Citizen Sangfroid in " Delicate Ground."

These plays, combined with a magnificent production of " Conrad and Medora " carried him with a flowing sail up to February 16th in the following year, when " A Life's Ransom " achieved a considerable success.

Of minor productions I note Mr. John Hollingshead's first farce, " The Birthplace of Podgers," and another by Edmund Yates and poor Pat Harrington called " Doing the Hansom."

The season terminated with a performance of " Richelieu," which recalls a somewhat amusing occurrence. This play was frequently acted upon alternate nights with " The King's Musketeers," in which, it will be remembered, the great Cardinal plays a somewhat subordinate and ignoble *rôle*.

One of the members of the company was Tom Stuart, "the caged lion," as he was irreverently called, from his having been heard one night in the Haymarket Green Room, while contemplating his imposing outlines in the mirror, during the intervals of a wickedly bad " heavy father," to apostrophize himself thus : " Ah, Tom, Tom ! here you are a caged lion, but the time will come when you shall stalk abroad, and the wide forest shall tremble at your roar !"

Well, this gentleman played Richelieu in " The Musketeers," while Dillon played the Cardinal in Bulwer's play.

" Ah, well, well !" growled Tom ; " we play " Richelieu " every night. Charlie does the old buffer one night, I do him the other ; and, by goles, I think I get the best of it !"

The muster-roll of Dillon's first season attests the production of two original works, two Shakespearian plays, two revivals of Bulwer Lytton, two of Sheridan Knowles, three romantic dramas, half a dozen farces, and *two* magnificent spectacular burlesques, either of which, supported by such a cast as they then obtained, would, independent of any other attraction, crowd a West-End theatre for an entire season nowadays.

During the last campaign an original play by Leigh Hunt was produced, called "Love's Amazement;" another by Westland Marston, called "A Hard Struggle," and an adaptation from the French of Madame Girardin.

Of Shakespeare, "Macbeth" and "As You Like It," in which Helen Faucit appeared, and "Othello." Besides these great works, Whitehead's play, the "Cavalier," Kotzebue's "Stranger," and Casimir de la Vigne's "Louis XI." "John Bull," "She Stoops to Conquer," and "Wild Oats" were acted in conjunction with the burlesque of "Lalla Rookh," which was produced on a scale of Oriental splendour.

This season, if not so prolific of events as the first, showed, notwithstanding, the goodly record of two original works, three Shakespearian productions, three legitimate plays, three standard comedies, two or three original farces, and one spectacular burlesque, besides various revivals from the first season.

Be it remembered, none of these works were pitchforked upon the stage ; they were all done excellently, and many of them were elaborate and sumptuous productions.

When Dillon quitted the Lyceum, he left behind him a few people who have since made their mark upon "the very age and body of the time," notably

Miss Marie Wilton, who made her first appearance in town upon his opening night, as Henri (" Belphegor "), and **Perdita, in** Brough's **burlesque,** " The Royal Milkmaid ;" Toole, who played Fanfaronade and Autolycus; Calhaem, who played Leontes ; Edmund Falconer, and **F. B.** Chatterton.

Toole went to the Adelphi ; Calhaem clung to the fortunes **of Falconer at the** Lyceum and Drury Lane, of which he became manager, in conjunction with Chatterton, **who** afterwards became lessee of Old Drury, the Princess's, and Adelphi ; while Miss Wilton crossed over the way to the Strand, of which for years she remained the cynosure, until she went to the Prince of Wales's, **where her** subsequent career marked an **epoch in** the annals **of the** modern stage.

A year **or two later I was engaged to act for the** Christmas and the week following at Sheffield.

At or about this period **an** unfortunate dissension had occurred between Mr. and Mrs. Dillon, which at last led to their total estrangement.

To my astonishment, I received a letter **from the lady,** applying **for an engagement, and I engaged her at once** to play the opposite parts **in my** pieces.

During **my second week, the** manager urged **me** to play " Belphegor." Upon my observing that I did not wish to trespass on Dillon's *donnée*, he pointed out that as I was no longer in management, I had a right **to fight for my own hand; that the play,** especially in conjunction with Mrs. Dillon, would be sure to attract a great house.

Ultimately I yielded to his wishes, and the result was exactly what he had prognosticated. We were crowded from floor to dome.

It so happened that the lady dressed in the room adjacent to mine. I had barely got upstairs after the play, when there arose from the next apartment a scream, which startled and alarmed me. It was followed by the thud of a heavy fall. Then, silence !

I knocked at the door again, and yet again. It was no time for ceremony, so I burst it open.

There lay stretched upon the ground the pretty little brunette of my boyhood, now a wan and woe-worn woman. Yes ; there she lay, pale, rigid, and senseless.

Beside her was a telegram with these words :

" Charles Dillon sailed to-night from Queenstown for America."

The fact was that Dillon's creditors had become as unreasonable and impatient as they had hitherto been rapacious, and his flight to America had been precipitated by his morbid dread of being arrested.

He had the utmost difficulty in scraping together the money for his passage, and as he had no engagement to go to, he went out on pure speculation, which is about the worst thing an impecunious actor can do anywhere.

Amidst a terrible tempest which arose during the voyage, a violent lurch of the vessel flung him from one side of the deck to the other, breaking his leg in two places, so it came to pass that when the unfortunate man landed in New York without a dollar, he was also a cripple.

It was some weeks before he could move, and when at length he was enabled to crawl out, it was with the greatest difficulty that he could obtain an engagement at all.

The theatre in which he made his appearance was " out of the track of ships," and on his opening night it rained in torrents, consequently there was a wretched house.

When he came limping on the stage he met with a most chilling reception, but he pulled himself together, and by the time he had got to the end of the first act of " Belphegor," the audience felt that a great actor was before them.

The press, however, was anything but gracious in its recognition ; the theatre was unpopular and out of the way, and the engagement was financially a failure.

His necessities placed him at the mercy of the managers, who invariably had the best of him, and I fear his demeanour was not ingratiating ; hence all the time he was in America he was in perpetual hot water.

His arrangements were so badly managed, that from New York he went direct to San Francisco, where he found himself announced for both theatres,

JOHN L. TOOLE AS BARNABY DOUBLECHICK.

and there was the very deuce to pay between the
rival managers, with little money for Dillon.

From "Frisco" he went into the mountains of
Nevada, where he acted in tents among the diggers.
From thence, back at a bound to Boston, Philadelphia, and Chicago. Even if he had taken large
sums of money, these dreadful journeys would have
swallowed up every cent.

From America he made his way to Australia and
New Zealand. In Australia he did a little better.

At this time he was at his best, and with a little
skill and prudence might easily have amassed a
fortune. But he was so erratic, so undependable,
that he never gave himself the ghost of a chance
anywhere, or at any time.

Mr. Charles Wilmot, manager of the Grand
Theatre, Islington, gave me the other day a characteristic illustration of the fatal facility with which
Dillon kicked the ladder from under his feet on
every occasion.

While Wilmot was managing the theatre at Dunedin for Miss Julia Mathews (remembered here
chiefly for her sprightly performance of "The Grand
Duchess"), Dillon came to fulfil an engagement, and
was announced to open in "Virginius." He put in
an appearance at rehearsal (of course, an hour late),
ran through a few scenes, and, as usual, disappeared,
leaving the company to finish it as best they could.

At nightfall, when the time of commencement
approached, Virginius had not arrived. Now the

theatre was the joint property of two publicans; each Boniface had a bar, and no one could enter the temple of Thespis without passing through one or other of these shrines of Bacchus. Away went Wilmot to bar No. 1, where he found the missing "star" in company with one Ben Canter, a costumier, from Vinegar Yard, who had found his way to this remote region. The tragedian was complacently stroking his imperial, and regarding his "counterfeit present- ment" as Belphegor, in an old copy of the *Illustrated London News*, which Canter had brought down to show him.

"Time to begin, Mr. Dillon!" said Wilmot.

"Coming, my boy, coming. Look here! isn't it marvellous I should meet this old villain in these 'diggins'? He used to dress us at the Marylebone when I was a lad. Still more marvellous that *this* should turn up at the Antipodes! It was taken during my first season at the Lyceum, sir. I re- member the night well. It was the night when Charles Dickens came round to me with John Oxen- ford, and said, 'Charley, my boy——'"

"Really, Mr. Dillon, I must remind you that the stage is waiting."

"'Let the forum wait for us.' There isn't much of a house; I've been counting the beggars as they dribbled in."

"They come in late, sir. There will be a splendid house by-and-by, if you'll only get dressed."

"All right. Have a drink?"

Against his inclination, poor Wilmot was obliged

to imbibe. At last he coaxed the recalcitrant tragedian (not without making a halt at the other bar) to his dressing-room.

"Now, my dear, where are the 'props'?" blandly inquired Dillon of his *compagne de voyage*.

"I haven't the faintest idea," replied the lady, "unless you left them behind in the last town."

"Good heavens! You don't say so? This is a lively look-out! Wilmot, what is to be done? I can't go on without 'props,' you know. You had better dismiss the house."

"Heaven forbid!" replied Wilmot. "But do you really mean to say, Mr. Dillon, you have neither properties nor dresses?"

"Not a rag for Virginius! Better dismiss, I tell you."

"Dismiss the devil!" roared the manager. "Wait a moment."

So saying, he ran to his lodgings, which were in the immediate vicinity, and returned with his own fleshings, sandals, and a Roman shirt, into which Dillon struggled as well as he could, while Wilmot went round to the wardrobe to see if he could find a toga. There was only one in the theatre, and that had been already appropriated by Appius Claudius, who could by no amount of persuasion be induced to relinquish it.

"No, sir," exclaimed that noble Roman, "Virginius is only a centurion : I am the first decemvir, and was born in the purple. I have lived in it, and mean to die in it." And die in it he did in due course, when Virginius strangled him in the last scene.

Away rushed poor Wilmot back to his lodgings again, whence he emerged with a sheet which he had plucked from his bed, and which Dillon had to arrange as the *toga virilis* as best he could.

Later in the play, when he had to don his fighting gear, one of the supers was obliged to be stripped of his armour. It may easily be surmised that under the circumstances the Dunedin public were not profoundly impressed with the great metropolitan tragedian.

This, it is to be feared, is only one of the many instances which marred his progress through the colonies.

After an absence of some years, he returned to England physically weakened, and, I fear, not otherwise improved by these sordid experiences; besides which, his voice was unfortunately affected by some subtle malady, which at any moment paralysed the vocal chord, and left him suddenly speechless.

After the fatigues of the long voyage he needed rest and recuperation. Could he have gone to some quiet home, and given himself up entirely to domestic influences—could he have found some shrewd sympathetic friend to advise him and look after his interests—I believe, even then, it would not have been too late to have retrieved everything.

The London public, and the populations of the great towns, were prepared to receive him with enthusiasm, but, impelled by the direst necessity (for he landed at Liverpool almost penniless), he was driven into the hands of Mr. Knowles (the Manchester manager), who advanced certain moneys, and who, being a man of purely commercial mind, stipulated for prompt, and, indeed, immediate repayment.

For upwards of a quarter of a century Knowles's Christmas productions had excelled in splendour most of the metropolitan pantomimes. Unfortunately, this year he had met with a failure, and the idea occurred to him that Dillon might enable him to recoup his losses. In a weak moment, before he had recovered either his strength or his voice, the unfortunate tragedian was induced to open in " Lear." The result was disastrous. The bad news spread in every direction, and preceded him wherever he went, and failure followed upon failure.

During his prolonged absence Mrs. Dillon had requested me to bring her only daughter on the stage, and I had felt it a pleasure, a duty, to comply with her request. He now wrote, thanking me for my action in the matter, and begging me to let bygones be bygones, and I was only too delighted to say, " Yes; with all my heart."

Later on he applied for an engagement at my theatre in Hull. I was glad to accede to his request, and looked forward to a pleasant time, during which we might " act our young encounters o'er again." I had announced him for Macbeth.

He did not turn up at rehearsal, but that did not

surprise me, and as it was what we call a "stock piece" (*i.e.*, a piece in which the company were accustomed to act frequently) his absence neither occasioned inconvenience nor apprehension.

At about two o'clock in the day, I received a elegram from Blackburn, stating that he was taken suddenly and dangerously ill, and was unable to act. Although concerned to hear this bad news, the difficulty was easily surmounted by my playing Macbeth myself.

Forty-eight hours later I was amazed to learn that he had acted Belphegor in Blackburn on the very night he was due in Hull!

Next day he telegraphed that he was better, and would act in Hull on Friday or Saturday; but my sympathy had changed to indignation, and in my anger I resolved that he should never act again in a theatre of mine.

Two years later, when I went to Manchester to fulfil an engagement at the Theatre Royal, I found that he was to close on the night before I opened. Charles Reade, who was staying with me at the Palatine, had never seen Dillon in "Belphegor," which was announced for that night, and as I had not seen him since his return to England, I persuaded Reade to accompany me to the play.

Two things struck us as we entered the theatre. There was an awful house, but there was yet a more awful sight upon the stage.

A worn, haggard man, in the dress of Paillasse,

stood before us. He was vainly trying to speak,
but failed to articulate a syllable. At last he shook
his head sadly, pointed to his throat, and motioned for
the prompter to ring down. As the curtain shut out
this sad picture, we rushed round behind the scenes.

When we reached the prompt entrance some men
were leading, partly supporting, Dillon off the stage ;
and thus it was that we two, who had once been
rivals, friends, enemies, after all these years, met
face to face.

For the moment I had only one feeling—" The
pity of it, the pity of it." The old time came back
to me, and I wanted to rush at him and hug him ;
but " the eye can be as vocal as the tongue," and
his eye said as plainly as his tongue could have
uttered the words, " To Hades with you and your
pity ! I'll none of it." So some proud blood which
I inherit instinctively caused me to draw back.

I remember this critical moment only to regret it.
At that time I was proprietor of a number of large
and important theatres which I might have opened
to him, and so perhaps have changed the whole
current of his life.

I can truly say that I have never forgiven myself,
and never shall to my dying day, for not following
the dictates of my heart, and availing myself of an
opportunity for reconciliation which, alas ! never
came again.

It was in 1868 that he reappeared at Sadler's
Wells as Lear, a part which he had never acted in

London. This performance was unquestionably his masterpiece, but neither the play nor the player attracted much attention.

The following year he acted a round of Shakespearian characters at Drury Lane, where he also enacted the part of Valjean in Bayle Bernard's unsuccessful play, " The Man of Two Lives," founded on Victor Hugo's great work, " Les Misérables."

At this time he complained, and I fear with justice, of the indignities to which he was now continually subjected by certain presslings, who had neither the capacity nor the culture to comprehend his mature and virile art.

After this engagement he remained in the country, acting here, there, and everywhere for upwards of four years. He returned to town once more in 1878, and opened at the Princess's in the revival of " Manfred," after which another interval of five years occurred prior to his next and last appearance in London.

On Saturday, September 26th, 1878, he reappeared at Drury Lane in the part of Leontes in " The Winter's Tale," and I regret to relate that on that occasion he met with even worse treatment than ever at the hands of his detractors.

At the maturity of his powers, his Othello and Iago, his Lear and Macbeth, his Coriolanus, Virginius, and Beverley (I shall never forget his exclamation, " My God ! my head turns round !") might challenge comparison with the achievements of any contemporaneous actor; while his first and second acts of "Belphegor," his Black Doctor, his Maurice ("La Dame de St. Tropez"), for fervour and grace, for passion and pathos, were equal to the best efforts of Frederick himself.

Of parts of society the only one in which he ever distinguished himself was Reuben Holt, in Westland Marston's delightful little play called "A Hard Struggle," which I saw on the first night of its performance. I remember well, how, overcome by emotion, he was about to collapse and sink into a chair; how he "missed his tip" and fell; how he baffled ridicule, and converted defeat into victory, by the marvellously graceful pose into which he instinctively threw himself, as he reached the ground.

Mrs. Dillon, too (who was doubtless frequently overweighted in the parts she played with him), was charming in "Medora" and "Lalla Rookh," and more than delightful in "Lilian." She gave a little burst of hysterical emotion in one situation of this play equal to anything I have ever seen.

This work, essentially modern, was altogether admirably acted—be it remembered, too, that it was produced years before the Robertsonian epoch. Paddy Barrett, as the male Malaprop (I forget his name), was capital, Shore was stylish and manly as the young doctor, and a youthful member of the Conquest family was charmingly sympathetic as the girl Amy.

Dillon's Evelyn was detestable—almost as bad as ——; but I must not become personal.

I did not subscribe to the popular appreciation of many of his most admired impersonations, notably his Hamlet, Richelieu, Melnotte, Don Felix, Benedict, Charles Surface, D'Artagnan, and Don César. Both of the latter were, to my thinking, more like "swaggering Bob" than the Gascon scion of a noble house, or the blue-blooded Hidalgo who claimed the privilege of remaining covered before the King of Spain.

Up to thirty years of age Dillon was a conventional actor. After that period, although he could never quite overcome his tendency to "strut," he set conventionalities at defiance, and although at no time did he ever descend from the colloquial to the commonplace, he became one of the most distinguished precursors of the modern school of acting.

In his interesting monograph of "The Jeffersons," Mr. William Winter (himself an eminent critical authority!) states (page 15) that "Garrick was exceedingly sensitive to those expressions of opinion, almost always idle, superficial, ignorant, and worthless, which mankind denominates criticism."

This ultra-sensitiveness was not confined to the great little Davy. On this subject the majority of actors are weak as children, and Dillon was weaker than most actors; he absolutely writhed, when, during the very period he was drawing tears from all eyes as Belphegor, certain airy young gentlemen, fresh from school, stigmatized him as a "melodramatic actor."

This easy and impertinent form of depreciating an artist who aspires to eminence in the exposition of the poetic drama has been fashionable ever since the word "melodramatic" came into vogue.

Small scribblers, ignorant of even the meaning of the word, have persistently availed themselves of this shibboleth for the purpose of decrying the excellence they are incapable of understanding.

When Macready thrilled all hearts in "**Gambia,**" "Rob Roy," and "William Tell," when Charles Kean took the town by storm in "Pauline" and "The Corsican Brothers," when Fechter electrified the *blasé* stalls in "**Ruy** Blas," they were all denounced as "melodramatic actors."

Now, in point of fact, even the great John Kemble himself was glad to learn the graces of melodrama from the eminent pantomimist Bologna.

Charles Kemble had reached fifty years of age before he made headway with the public, and his first stride was after he had played Karfa in "**Three-Fingered Jack**" at the Haymarket.

When this distinguished actor was superintending the rehearsals at the Olympic for the *début* of his *protégée*, Miss Glyn, he remarked publicly, apropos of some amenities of the press of the period: "What I admire most is the prescience of these sagacious gentlemen. It took them forty years to enable them to form an opinion about me. At length, when I was approaching my sixtieth year, they magnanimously admitted that I was a promising actor; and when, alas! I was past the time—getting

old and deaf—they proclaimed on the house-tops
that I was the greatest actor in the universe!"

Edmund Kean was really, from the sole of his
foot to the crown of his head, a melodramatic actor.
Of this school were James Wallack, Charles Dillon,
and Frederick Lemaitre, incomparably the greatest
genius of the French stage of our time.

Au contraire, Macready was never a melodramatic
actor, hence he remained *gauche* and angular to the
last.   Great as he unquestionably was, he would
have been a still greater actor had he learnt the art
of melodrame; yet he himself told me that to the
end of his career certain criticasters were continually
throwing it in his teeth that he was pre-eminent in
"Gambia" and "Rob Roy," but that he couldn't
speak a line of Shakespeare.   He! the greatest
Shakespearian actor of the age!

Edmund Kean, in his struggling days, was treated
yet more scurvily.

I once saw in a small country paper (the very
name of which I forget) the deliberately recorded
opinion of some "Triton among the minnows," that
"Mr. Kean might be tolerated in 'The Young
Hussar,' the speechless vagaries of Harlequin, the
gymnastic contortions of Kanko (the monkey in
'Perouse'), but that his attempts in the Shakespearian drama were simply preposterous."

I am more fortunate in being enabled by a strange
accident to quote the precise words of a Staffordshire
journal on the 'prentice efforts of the little great
man.

Many years ago, while acting in Lichfield, one of the members of our company found a screw of tobacco, which he had purchased in a chandler's shop, wrapped up in a fragment of the *Staffordshire Advertiser* of April 7th, 1809. Being "a diligent snapper-up of unconsidered trifles," I secured this scrap of paper. After all this time I exhume it.

Speaking of the performances at the Lichfield Theatre, the learned pundit of the *Advertiser* thus portentously formulates his *ipse dixit:*

" Mr. Kean, who has been figuring here as the tragic hero, is another instance of the blundering folly of misplacing actors, of which we see so many " (*sic*) "in country theatres. We do not recollect to see " (*sic*) "a man less gifted for a tragedian than this gentleman.

" Without energy, dignity, or the advantages of voice, he drags through the heroic scenes with a dull monotony, oppressive to himself, and doubly so to the audience.

" He appears to understand his author, but the effects of a clear conception are totally lost in the natural defects of his voice and person.

" The performer's genius is, nevertheless, of an elevated caste " (*sic*) ; "he is a good Harlequin !"

Complimentary this to the Othello, the Richard, and the Shylock of the age.

The classic John Vandenhoff informed me that when he made his first appearance in London, Mr. John Forster stated in his criticism that he (Vandenhoff) " had neither voice, face, figure, nor one single requisite, natural or acquired, for the adequate illustration of dramatic art."

Charles Kean also assured me that while acting at the Modern Athens in his youth, he was stigmatized as " an impostor whose very presence upon the stage was an insult to the intelligence of an Edinburgh audience !"

Similarly, up to this hour, wherever one goes, in society or out of it, for that matter, some yah-yah booby or other airs his opinion that tragedy is defunct upon the English stage; that Salvini and Rossi (the most melodramatic artists in the world!) are the only tragedians in existence; and that all English actors are merely " melodramatic."

The blockheads who use this phrase as a form of depreciation are not aware that their intended censure —if it were worth while to take it seriously—is really a compliment.

As an absolute matter of fact, the highest development of so-called melodrama is the most perfect type of histrionic art.

No one was more thoroughly imbued with the knowledge of this fact than Wagner, all of whose works are pure melodrame, and who actually derived his first melodramatic inspiration from poor Fitz-ball's forgotten but excellent drama of " The Flying Dutchman."

Any tyro with a taste for music and a knowledge of the mystery of rhythm, if he is careful to avoid those barbarous falling inflexions of the motive word which torture the educated ear, may ladle out blank

verse by the yard with propriety ; but **put him on**
the stage to play James Wallack's Massaroni, **Dillon's**
Black Doctor, Fechter's Obenreitzer, Irving's trial
scene in " The Bells," Barrett's third scene of Wilfrid
Denver, or Vezin's mad scene in " The **Man o'**
Airlie," where would he **be ?**

Of course there are degrees in everything.

Just as there are painters who, like honest Dick
Tinto, paint " La Belle Sauvage " for a signboard ;
and painters who, **like** Leighton, **paint** Helen of
Troy—

> " Fairer than the evening air
> Clad in the beauty of a thousand stars !"

so there are actors **who** writhe **and** wriggle, **and**
squirm to a tremulando, or who leap **into the corner**
at a chord in G ; but there are also actors who—

> " Suit the action to the word, and the word to the action."

who blend the music and the verse **in** one intellectual and harmonious whole ; who please the eye,
satisfy the ear, delight the heart, and enchant the
mind at one and the same moment.

These, and these only, are worthy of being called,
in the highest sense, " *melodramatic actors.*"

Unquestionably among these great artists Dillon
occupied a foremost, if not the foremost, place.

No actor of our time ever had so **many** chances,
and no actor (except Fechter !), ever so stupidly neglected them. **It** must, however, be urged in excuse,
that Dillon **was a** born Bohemian—his childhood

had been passed in poverty and in constant struggles to earn a precarious subsistence. His education, such as it was, was picked up by himself in highways and byways, and yet how thoroughly informed, and, indeed, saturated, his mind was with dramatic literature from the time of Æschylus to our own day! His powers as a talker were brilliant—indeed, he practically monopolized the conversation wherever he went---but whatever the theme of his argument, it always harked back to the one engrossing topic of Charles Dillon. His vanity was so frank, so *naïf*, so openly ostentatious, as to be amusing, though when it ceased to be amusing, it became trying and even intolerable. Yet, while subject to his personal influence, he was so engaging, so agreeable, and so ingratiating, that it was impossible to take him seriously, or to be angry with him.

He could often be generous, but he frequently failed to be just. From the very commencement of his managerial career to the end he was always in debt and difficulties. Borrowing money at one hundred per cent., and frequently paying two, may be pleasant as long as it lasts, but the issue cannot be doubtful.

Speaking to him once of a recent bankruptcy, he reminded me of the story of the drunken nigger, whose master reproached him with being "drunk again."

"No, not drunk again, massa," said Sambo; "him same old drunk."

After his last appearance at Drury Lane, as

WILSON BARRETT AS CLAUDIAN.

Leontes, Dillon was practically banished from London to the day of his death.

When I recall the last time I ever saw him, it seems, in connection with our early associations, almost like a page from a romance.

It will be remembered that Sheffield was the battlefield where, through his jealousy, and (I may as well admit it!) through my boyish folly, we had alternately ruined each other.

The fickle, ungrateful public had at length forgotten their former idol, and his last engagement had been a direful failure.

Goodness knows, I had suffered sufficient reverses of fortune in that locality, but on this occasion the wheel had turned, and we were playing " Henry V." to great houses.

I had been very unwell, and was only just recovering from a great commercial disaster, in which I had lost every shilling I possessed.

Richard Younge (my Iago during my first visit) was the manager, and he accompanied me to the railway-station to arrange about conveying our luggage to the next town. The station-master had been very obliging, and we invited him to take a glass of wine with us in the refreshment-room.

As we were in the act of pledging each other, a train glided slowly past the open doorway.

At that instant, I caught sight of a way-worn, but well-known, face leaning forward from a third-class carriage, and eagerly looking at me. As our eyes met, the face vanished as if by magic.

For the moment, I really thought that, carried away by old associations and a morbid imagination, " mine eyes were made the fools of the other senses," but the station-master assured me that I was under no hallucination.   It was Charles Dillon himself I had seen.

Of what was he thinking while the iron-horse ploughed his way to Chesterfield, I wonder ?

Was he stirred by the memory of some ancient kindness ? or was he recalling our foolish rivalries, our futile contests—perchance wishing, as I did, that we had the game to play over again ; the game we two, man and boy, had in our own hands once, had we only known how to play it ?

Perhaps !   We shall never know now.

I only know that we never met again, and that he acted his everlasting Belphegor that night in the little town with the crooked spire, while I remained to play Harry of Agincourt in the very theatre in which we had both encountered such strange vicissitudes of fortune.   *Telle est la vie !*

From that moment I lost all trace of him, and can only piece out the remainder of his career as I have heard it from those who were with him during its close.

The year of the great snow-storm which ventilated the London theatres, and ruined so many managers in town and country, found him acting with a " fit-up " in the wilds and fastnesses of Wales.   He was supported by a compact little band of staunch comrades, all ladies and gentlemen of more or less repute, who stood faithfully by their chief to the last.

Their efforts were in vain. The Celestial Host itself would not have tempted the good people of the Cwmry (small blame to them) from their comfortable firesides during that inclement weather.

He had been for years a martyr to rheumatic gout, and that incursion to Wales, telling upon an already enfeebled constitution, accelerated his end.

After this unfortunate campaign, he acted in Manchester, Liverpool, and other of the larger cities, and then resumed the direction of his loyal little company, with whom he went to a number of small towns in Scotland.

As there were no theatres in these places he travelled with his own scenery, and the rooms in which he acted were fitted up from week to week, or night to night—an operation involving incessant labour, trouble, and anxiety.

It was hard that it should come to this!

There can be no doubt that the mortification and the humiliation attendant upon these squalid and ignoble experiences preyed upon his mind.

The iron had entered his soul, and in moments of despondency and despair he was wont to say, in the bitterness of his heart, that, in the future, he saw before him the vision of a grim and grizzled man at a prompter's desk!

In other and more defiant moods he would exclaim :

'Never! while an arch of Waterloo Bridge remains standing!'

'Quick death is easy. He who dies slowly dies a thousand times.'

When death came to him, fortunately it came quickly, and found him erect and smiling.

It was at a small Border town, called Hawick, that the summons came.

On the opening night he played Othello, and although there was a wretched house, amounting to barely a few pounds, it was generally remarked that ne acted with all the old grace and fervour.

After the play, when he had finished dressing, he came and sat upon the stage, waiting for the acting-manager to bring him the miserable pittance which constituted his share of the receipts.

The primitive orchestra consisted of a piano, on which *entr'actes* were played behind the scenes by a member of the company.

Evidently the " chief " was in a despondent mood, for he remained silent and saturnine. Noting this, one of the young fellows of the troupe sat down to the piano and began to play some lively airs.

When he had finished, Dillon muttered :

" You have a light heart—a light heart, sir ; how I envy you !"

With that he sighed and turned away.

Could he have had a presentiment that the end was so near ?

Next morning he went down to the theatre to inquire if there were any letters. Although the

house had been **so bad on the** preceding night, **the**
impression created upon **the** scanty audience **was so**
favourable that a capital **week's** business **was** anticipated.   Hence, **he** was now elate and confident.

After his usual custom—and **a very** bad **one it**
was—he took the company to the adjacent tavern, and
stood drinks of humble malt all round, and told them
some piquant story **of his adventures in America and**
Australia; then they sallied **forth together** to explore
the town.

As they reached **the** middle **of the** High Street,
laughing **and** talking, **he** paused suddenly, put his
hand **to** his head, **just as** he **was wont** to do **in**
Beverley, and exclaimed, "God, **can** this be death!"

As the words left his **lips, he** fell **dead without a**
groan !

His muscles had been so trained to **harmonious**
motion, that habit had **become** second nature, and
one **of** those who stood beside him in that supreme
moment assured me that **in** the very *rigor mortis*
he instinctively **fell in an** attitude of classic grace,
even as Cæsar might **have** fallen beneath the steel
of Brutus at the base **of** Pompey's statue.

It **was** best that the **end** came as **it** did, for the
aspirations **which** had been more than fulfilled in the
summer **of his** existence died out in its dreary
autumn, and the future was **a** hopeless blank.

I was in Hastings when I heard that my poor lost
comrade was to **be** buried at Brompton the following
day.

An hour after the news reached me I was on my way to town. On the morrow, with a few staunch friends, I followed him to his last resting-place.

Although there had been no public notice of the funeral, a prodigious crowd—amidst which were many women—assembled to do honour to his memory.

This brief sketch of a brilliant but blighted career may well serve " to point a moral or adorn a tale."

As we sow, even so must we reap, and all the accomplishments of which the human mind is capable are but as " so much sounding brass and tinkling cymbals," where they are warped from the direct line of right by a defective moral sense.

As an actor, Charles Dillon was unquestionably one of the first of his epoch ; as a man, he had many genial and lovable qualities ; as for his faults, may they lie gently on him—as gently as the flowers those pale and weeping women cast that day upon his grave !

CHAPTER V.

"COME to town and see him at once. He is an actor after your own heart!"

Such was the burthen of a letter written me seven or eight and twenty years ago, by a near and dear friend, on whose judgment I could rely.

I came. I saw Ruy Blas.

There was a bad house, and not a particularly sympathetic audience.

The French actor came on in the livery of a lackey.

The loathsome garment clung to him "like the shirt of Nessus"—it seemed to burn into his flesh, to bite into his vitals. His cheek was pale—his eyes aflame.

I sat and shuddered with sudden and instinctive sympathy—in a white heat one moment, freezing the next.

He acted a scene without speaking. What need of speech with motion so eloquently expressive ?

At last he threw the thrice-accursed thing from him, and lo, the lackey was transformed into a prince —a prince, too, who stood beside a princely Hidalgo, for surely never before or since was seen a nobler impersonation than Walter Lacy's Don Salluste.

Augustus Harris the elder was wont to tell me that Fechter had taught Bon Gualtier. Bosh! If Lacy had not had it in him, all the teaching in the world could never have brought it out.

But to return to my peerless lackey. Imagine, if you please, a man of middle height; figure more sturdy than elegant; features distinctly Hebraic, vivacious, expressive, powerful, changeful as the colour of a chameleon's skin; olive-comp'exioned; piercing but penetrating eyes, now melting with the languor of love, now ablaze with the lurid light of hell; firm well-cut mouth, which opened and shut like the jaws of a bull-dog; massive head, with a thatch of dark brown hair; bull neck, splendidly poised, but a little too short. Such was Charles Albert Fechter when first I beheld him.

He was then a man of forty. Had I not known it, I should have guessed him five-and-twenty at the outside.

I had known much handsomer men among our own people—James Anderson, Leigh Murray and Henry Howe, at their prime; Mr. Butler Wentworth, a lay figure, though a magnificent one—but I have never seen a man with so much magnetic glamour as Fechter.

At first the voice seemed guttural, the French

accent unendurable, **but it was only at first. After
a** few moments the voice **made** music, and **I** forgot
all about the accent.

How the story of **his** unhappy love thrilled **me ;**
how it **stirred every** pulse of my heart ! **Methinks I**
can **hear him now** exclaiming :

> "I love her—I love her—that is all !"

And it was all ; **it was**

> " Love that hath the name
> **And** fury and force of swift bright shuddering **flame !"**

What **a** picture **he made**—a Titian or a Velasquez
(a Velasquez just stepped **down** from the frame)—
when he descended, like an eagle **on** a dove-cote,
upon the corrupt **and venal** council.

With what noble **ardour he** bullied **the blue-**
blooded scoundrels ! With what fascinating **and**
resistless force he made love **to** the charming Isabella
de Neuburgh, the lovely Caroline Heath !

Then that scene of " **The** Lion and **the** Tiger,"
between Don Salluste and **his** *ci-devant* valet—how
it set my blood on fire !

And the last **scene of all !—can I** ever forget it ?
—can anyone who **ever** saw **it** forget ?

> "I am not a lackey, but an executioner !"

The master himself has left it on record that in
" Ruy Blas " the great Frederick was " not a transformation, but a transfiguration." Fechter was both.

As for me, that night was a revelation to me, and
I was entranced—delighted.

Four-and-twenty years later I saw Madame Bernhardt and her company attempt "**Ruy Blas**" at the
Gaiety.

The great actress herself was slovenly, untidy,
badly dressed, and gabbled through her part like a
parrot; while, as for the Ruy Blas and the Don
Salluste, well—I will not pursue the comparison.

I, who, as a matter of conscience, rarely or ever
leave a theatre until the play is over, could not stand
this performance, and left before the last act (the
greatest act that ever was written except the last act
of "Othello") commenced.

As I recall that last act at the Princess's, and the
divine emotion I experienced, I protest I grow hot
and cold even now.

The triumphs of the art are so ephemeral that it
is fitting it should have these moments of supreme
exaltation.

To us who have witnessed, who have sometimes
been permitted to feel them, they leave pleasures of
memory which can never die so long as life endures.

"Ruy Blas" was what we call, in the argot of
the theatre, a *succès d'estime*, which means, in
homelier English, that it is a success which enables
the artist to air his reputation at the expense of
the manager's pocket.

Harris thoroughly believed in Fechter, and was
determined that he should succeed.

Our successes and our failures in the life of the
theatre are alike exaggerated, and the truth is never

known until the inevitable end comes, but too frequently, in the Court of Bankruptcy.

Who could have believed, had not my unfortunate
friend Mapleson attested it in open court the other
day, that he had paid a **certain** prima **donna**
£300,000 (latterly at the rate of £650 a night), **and**
that this generous creature absolutely "burst **him**
up," because **of some** difficulty about **one** night's
salary, and that, too, payable in advance—payable
before she had even earned it ?

It was not until after the ultimate rupture between
Harris and **Fechter** that I learnt from the former's
own lips that, **at** the very period **when** London was
ringing with the Frenchman's fame, "**Ruy** Blas"
was nightly involving the management in a ruinous
loss; and Fechter himself afterwards told me that
his engagement was to share with the management
after the expenses, that the expenses were **never**
taken except upon *one* night, and that all **he ever**
took for his services during the run of "Ruy Blas"
was some sixteen shillings and eightpence !

His next appearance was in "Don Cæsar," that
spurious offspring of Victor Hugo's superb ragged
cavalier, which was, if anything, a more decided
failure than "Ruy Blas."

And now for a small matter personal to myself.

Certain writers have said or insinuated that I made
myself conspicuous among English actors for my
hostility to Fechter.

On the contrary, I was ever foremost amongst his

friends and partizans, and believed in his genius from first to last—believe in it now.

What I did do, was to stand by my craft when his success was made the stalking-horse for the depreciation of English art and English actors.

No man more thoroughly despised this ostentatious adulation of himself at the expense of his brothers in art than Fechter.

One night at St. John's Wood, when he had had a little more wine than usual, he burst out with :

" Bah ! I wonder what the beggars would say if they knew I was a cockney, born in Hanway Yard, Oxford Street ?"

As a matter-of-fact, his dramatic inspiration and his early knowledge of the drama had been derived from constant visits to the gallery of Drury Lane or Covent Garden, to which elevated posts of observation he made his way every night he could beg, borrow or steal a shilling.

Thirty years later, when he opened at the Adelphi, he encountered an old actor (Mr. C. J. Smith) whom he had seen take a musical part in the pantomime of " Guy Faux " at Drury Lane.   To the astonishment of everybody in general, and of the old gentleman in particular, Fechter danced up to the old boy, and, taking him by both hands, spun him around like a teetotum to the music of " Guy Faux."

It is a remarkable thing in the annals of the theatre that the play of " Hamlet," after a reasonable interval of rest, is always a certain attraction.

Here is an illustration :

In my juvenalia I was acting in B——, and selected the noble Dane for my opening part. The house was crowded from floor to ceiling, and the audience singularly demonstrative.

In the innocence of my heart, I ventured to re- mark to the manager that I had no idea I was so well-known at B——, etc., to which that august potentate replied : " Young gentleman, if I could only find fifty-two Hamlets, I could play ' Ham- let' every Monday night in the year to overflowing houses."

Harris, who not only detested the Bard but openly avowed his detestation, finding " Ruy Blas " and " Don Cæsar " failures, reluctantly consented to fall back on Shakespeare and the " Prince of Den- mark."

Although there can be no reasonable doubt that Charles Dickens was right when he stated that " No innovation in art was ever accepted with so much favour by so many intellectual persons, pre-com- mitted to and pre-occupied by another system, as Fechter's Hamlet," there also can be no reason- able doubt that hostility to English art and actors gave point to the pens which attested the supremacy of the French actor's genius over his British com- peers.

Whatever doubts existed as to the orthodoxy or heterodoxy of Fechter's treatment, there could be no doubt of its success, and from that time he was the idol of the hour.

Money flowed in, and manager and actor divided between them something like five or six thousand pounds, after all expenses upon the run of this play.

As no two intelligent men (at any rate, none within the scope of my acquaintance) ever agreed about "Hamlet," no two actors are ever likely to do so ; for all that, I saw much to admire and delight me in the new "Hamlet," and was not slow to express my admiration.

It was at this time that we became personally acquainted.

The very night on which he first played "Hamlet" we met at the Café de l'Europe, then an intellectual and artistic centre.

Herman Vezin and I had gone there to sup when Fechter came in. Herman introduced us to each other ; we fraternized there and then, and made a night of it; indeed, day was dawning when we strolled off towards St. John's Wood together.

For the next six or seven years we remained on terms of friendly intimacy.

It is Wilkie Collins who says :

"There is a little villa in the north-western suburb of London, close to the eastward extremity of St. John's Wood Road, which I can never pass now without a feeling of sadness."

Nor I either.

I passed by it a few months ago "in the dead vast and middle of the night," and so potent is the force of fancy or the fumes of wine, or perhaps both combined, that I actually thought Fechter's ghost

came out and looked at **me** from the open **gate.**
Alas! as I drew nearer, " he made himself air, into
which he vanished."

But **I must** get **back from St.** John's Wood to
Oxford Street.

After Hamlet came Othello, which Fechter had
better have left alone. Despite its singularly prosaic
character, it was, however, by no means destitute of
thought, while **much of** the stage management was
admirable.

Charles Mathews, who shared my views about the
Othello, assured me that Fechter's Iago (which I
had the misfortune not to see) was an admirable and
picturesque performance, distinguished by vigour,
variety, and many-minded devilry.

Fechter or Bellew, or both, published a book of
their acting edition **of** " Othello "—a book which
is both unique and amusing.

They talked largely about publishing a series of
the Shakespearian plays with their emendations, but
" Othello " was enough and to spare.

Apropos of Shakespeare, Fechter told me that he
had acted Shylock and Macbeth in Paris, but I find
no trace of these performances in the records of the
Parisian theatres.

When the rupture with Harris came, which has
been already described in the Kean paper, Fechter
took the Lyceum.

A short time prior to the commencement of the
season, we were both acting in Liverpool. At that

time he had an idea of opening with "La Belle
Gabrielle," in which he offered me the opposite part,
which for reasons before stated I found it expedient
to decline.

Abandoning "La Belle Gabrielle," he succeeded
in engaging Phelps and the ill-fated Walter Montgomery for the purpose of opening with a
Shakespearian play, in which the whole of the
company were to appear.

During a visit to Paris, he saw Sardou's clever
adaptation of Paul Feval's wild and improbable story,
"Le Bossu," was struck with it, and produced it for
his opening piece on January 10th, 1863.

"The Duke's Motto" (so the English version by
John Brougham was called) "struck ile" immediately, and was played to crowded houses for the
entire season.

For a considerable period Phelps' name was conspicuously underlined in the Lyceum playbills.

Of course, no manager could be expected to withdraw a piece which was filling his coffers nightly ;
the position was, nevertheless, so mortifying to the
English tragedian's *amour propre*, and so injurious
to his reputation, that he desired to be released
from his engagement. Fechter was, however,
master of the situation, and, as he paid Phelps'
salary regularly, he held him to his bond.

Montgomery was similarly situated, and chafed at
the chain which bound him.

Fechter had an unfortunate knack of scratching
everybody the wrong way. No man made friends

CHARLES FECHTER.

with greater ease, or lost them with greater facility.
One of the first fruits of his uncertain temper was a
row with George Vining, his stage-manager, who
left him and went into management on his own
account at the Princess's, where he became a most
dangerous rival. Montgomery, impatient at being
debarred an appearance, also threw up his engagement, and joined Vining, whereupon Fechter sought
to obtain an injunction to restrain the former from
appearing elsewhere than at the Lyceum, when, lo
and behold, it oozed out that the salary of Walter
Montgomery, the most accomplished *jeune premier*
of his time, amounted to the munificent sum of £6
per week !

At present, the veriest tyro of a walking gentleman
demands and obtains much better terms.

The relations between Fechter and Phelps now
became somewhat strained, and things approached
a climax during an interview in which the former,
after intimating that the next production would be
" Hamlet," blandly inquired what part Phelps would
play in the piece.

" Why, Hamlet, of course," he replied.

" Oh ! but I play Hamlet myself," responded the
Frenchman.

" The d——l you do !" growled Phelps.

" Yes ! So I thought, perhaps, you would play
the Ghost !"

" You thought that I would play the Ghost to your
Hamlet—yours ! Well, d——n your impudence !"

With this the interview terminated, and Phelps'

engagement terminated soon after, amidst a blaze of legal fireworks.

Prosperity, which had turned Fechter's brain, parted company with him after his first season, and the remainder of his term was marked either by quasi successes, or a dreary monotony of failure.

"Bel Demonio" (which had been previously done by Boucicault, during the Farren management, at the Olympic, under the title of "Sixtus V.") did not eclipse the memory of Leigh Murray, though the recollection of Miss Kate Terry as the heroine stirs a tender spot in my heart.

John Brougham, the adapter of the play—a genial, jovial, delightful fellow, and a dear friend of the writer's—was the Cardinal Montalto, and a fine, graphic performance it was ; while Sam Emery made a great mark in a brusque soldier of fortune.

The play was magnificently mounted, and admirably stage-managed.

It ran for nearly a hundred and seventy nights, when, as ill-luck would have it, one of Fechter's attacks of spleen came upon him like a cyclone. Poor fellow, he was a martyr to this terrible disease ! Just as he was about to step through the window for the love scene in the fourth act, this diabolical disease rushed upon him, distending his stomach like a drum. Every button on his dress burst, and his spur caught on the pediment ; with the impetus he plunged heavily forward, falling upon his face, while the hook from the pommel of his sword was driven through the palm of his hand.

Despite the agony he suffered, **his will was in-**domitable, and he managed **to** finish the play.

For some time his life was in danger from lockjaw, but at length he recovered, and commenced his next season with the **" King's** Butterfly," a splendid **but** unsuccessful phantasy, which gave **place to " Bel-**phegor," in which **it was** expected **that Fechter** would make **a great hit.**

Although **this play had** achieved **a great** vogue through **the** inimitable **performance** of Charles Dillon, **as** yet it had **never been put** into decent English. When, therefore, it **was** rumoured that the author **of "** Great Expectations " had rewritten the drama, " great expectations " **were** aroused, **only to be** woefully disappointed.

" Belphegor !" But words **are** feeble **to express** how bitterly bad Fechter **was** in the **part in which** Dillon had made so great **a** mark **years before in** that **very** theatre.

On the night I witnessed **this** performance **I** heard quite as much of the prompter **as of "** Belphegor."

Fechter's son, Paul, played Henri on this occasion. His father **was** wont to relate with great glee that this airy young gentleman was accustomed to say to the members **of** the company, " My papa has talent, but *I* am a genius."

By-the-bye, what **has** become of this handsome clever youth ?*

---

* The ink was scarcely dry with which the above inquiry was written when I **read** in the evening paper the following tragic answer :

"The Roadside Inn" enabled Fechter and Harry Widdicomb to distinguish themselves highly as Robert Macaire and Jacques Strop. But, to my thinking, the Macaire of the former did not approach within measurable distance of Frederick, or even of James Browne, or Sidney Davis, two famous English actors.

"The Archer of the Guard" is chiefly remembered by Fechter's exclamation, "Archer of the guard, wash!" and the lawsuit for libel, which enabled Sam Emery to extinguish "The Glowworm," an extinction which kindled fires of undying hatred against him amongst certain minor members of the fourth estate—hatred which endured to the day of his death.

"Paul Fechter, son of the well-known actor, who was once lessee of the Lyceum Theatre, has just met with his death under exceptionally lamentable circumstances. He was fencing with his brother-in-law, when the latter, unfortunately, pierced the eye of M. Fechter, and the foil, although there was a button on its point, penetrated to the brain. The ill-fated young fellow fell to the ground bleeding profusely, cerebral paralysis ensued, and he never recovered consciousness. The brother-in-law has been in such a state of anguish since the tragic accident that he can hardly give a coherent account of the affair. The deceased died much regretted by all who knew him, and an enormous crowd of sorrowing friends followed his remains to the grave. Hardly less tragic than this young man's fate was that of Madame Amélie Villetard, who played most successfully on Wednesday last at the Théâtre Libre, and who died early on Friday morning from sheer shock to the system upon hearing of his death. Madame Villetard had been intimately acquainted with the Fechter family for many years, and she may be truly said to have died of grief."

Alas! the widowed mother of poor young Paul still survives. Poor lady! she has suffered more than most women, and now she has lost, not only the light of her life, but the prop of her declining years.

" The Master of Ravenswood " was an admirable and artistic production.

In some parts of the play Fechter was at his best, and the Lucy of Miss Carlotta Leclercq, then in the florescence of youthful beauty, was both touching and pathetic.

Of other works, he gave " The Corsican Brothers " (which neither for acting nor mounting could stand comparison with Kean's production), " Rouge et Noir," and the " Lady of Lyons," which I had not the good fortune to see.

Thinking it desirable to recall the memory of his former triumph, so as " to make a swan-like end fading in music," he decided to terminate his management with a revival of " Hamlet." Alas ! the fickle fashionable public had deserted their whilom idol, the glory had departed, and on the first night there was a wretched house, and an unsympathetic audience.

Fechter had feminine proclivities, and was as hysterical as a woman ; hence, he was taken suddenly ill with another attack of the mysterious malady, which caused the epigastrium to swell out into abnormal dimensions ; he collapsed at the end of the second act, and Ryder, who had played the Ghost in the first act, had to come to life again to play the three last acts of " Hamlet." He played the part for three nights more, during which he roared himself so hoarse that after the third performance he was scarcely audible ; hence he, too, found it expedient to throw up the sponge.

It was the last week of the season, and he had taken the theatre for a short time to introduce a German-American actress, one Madame or Mademoiselle Vestvali. Being this lady's manager, all the responsibilities of the enterprise rested on his shoulders, and he therefore found it necessary to preserve his strength in order to devote his energies to his fair client.

Subsequently he told me that, in grateful acknowledgment of his services on this occasion, Fechter presented him (Ryder) with his Hamlet dress.

Some time afterwards, when they were at loggerheads, and Fechter was stigmatizing Ryder as a robber and a ruffian, and I don't know what else, I reminded him (Fechter) of the above incident.

"Yes, my boy," rejoined he triumphantly, "I certainly did give the hook-nosed, herring-gutted villain my old Hamlet dress; but I gave it him because it would no longer fit me!"

It was in vain that Barnett—Fechter's actingmanager — urged Ryder to act for only another night.

"No," rejoined "honest Jack," in the vigorous vernacular of which he had always a copious supply on hand; "I've shouted myself hoarse. Let the purpureal Frenchman try a little shouting on his own hook."

Finding Ryder still obstinate, Fechter said to Barnett:

" Well, as this *voleur* will not act, and I cannot, you must go and get a Hamlet."

Away went Barnett to the agents to see if there were any Hamlets " knocking about."

On his return, after an hour or two's absence, Fechter eagerly inquired :

" Well, well, have you got one ?"

" No," replied Barnett ; " I've been to all the shops where the article is sold, but they haven't got one in stock."

Finding it impossible to provide a substitute, the theatre was closed on the Friday, and Fechter had to wind up the season himself, on the following night, which he did with a very bad grace.

On this occasion I presented myself at the box-office for admittance ; but Barnett persistently, though politely, alleged that I had seen " Hamlet " often enough to serve for the rest of my life, and insisted on escorting me to the club opposite.

This opposition excited my curiosity ; so, taking the earliest opportunity for bidding him good-night, I went round to the gallery, deposited my modest shilling, and found myself one amongst a gallery audience of (ill-omened number) thirteen ! The other parts of the house were proportionately empty Fechter walked through the part in a sullen, listless manner ; the whole performance was melancholy and depressing in the extreme ; and when at length the curtain descended in solemn silence, an Irishman of the proletariate, who sat just before me, roared out :

" Phelps for ever! Fechter be blanked! Hurroo!"

And thus ended Fechter's unfortunate management at the Lyceum.

A year or two afterwards I induced Phelps and Fechter to meet at Charles Reade's house, in Naboth's Vineyard, to " bury the hatchet and smoke the pipe of peace."

When they met, the old lion was grim and taciturn, and the young tiger nervous and embarrassed ; but before the dinner was half over they thawed, and by the time they got to their cigars (which Reade, despite his detestation of tobacco, stood like a martyr) they were sworn friends.

Their experiences were rare and unique, and Reade drew them out with wonderful facility ; for upon occasion he could be as good a listener as a talker.   Altogether this was a delightful evening. When we broke up, Fechter confided to our host :

" Ah, Mistare Reade! he is a grand old man, and I loafe him like a brother ; but, *entre nous*, he cannot play Hamlet !"

On the other hand, as I saw Phelps into his cab, he growled :

" After all, John, he's not a bad fellow for—for— a Frenchman ; but, by ——! he can't act Shakespeare !"

I was present on the first night of " No Thoroughfare," and went round to see Fechter before and after the play. Before the curtain rose, I found him in a terrible state of collapse, actually going on

the stage with his dresser following him with a basin
—for the same purpose that Mr. Steward is re-
quisitioned aboard ship with the indispensable and
prevalent pannikin ! When the curtain fell, he was
radiant—triumphant ; and well he might be, for he
had scored one of the successes of his life.

A capitally-acted play this, from stem to stern.

I saw it afterwards in Paris as " L'Abîme."
Berton was excellent in Obenreitzer (thanks, he
himself said, to Fechter) ; but the other people were
not " in it " with our English players. The beautiful Leonide le Blanc was not fit to hold a candle to
Carlotta Leclercq ; nor was the gentleman who
played Vendale to be compared with Neville, nor
the Joey Ladle to be named in the same century
with Ben Webster.

The *dénouement* was, however, altered by the
French adapter with great advantage to the play.

Apropos of the stage business of this drama :
Fechter was wont to maintain that nothing on earth
ever runs to waste.

He was himself accustomed to give unconscious
illustrations of the veracity of his theory.

Par exemple, in the original " business " of " Ruy
Blas," when the Princess refuses to forgive the love-
lorn lackey, he poisons himself. In " Othello,"
when the Moor wounds Iago, the Ancient, according to established custom, stanches the wound with
his kerchief, and gasps in derision, " I bleed, sir, but
—not killed !"

Now mark what Fechter did.

In "Ruy Blas" he did not poison himself, but was wounded in the conflict with Don Salluste, so that, literally, he died from loss of blood.

When the Princess demanded, "What ails thee ?" he boldly appropriated Iago's business—handker-chief, blood, etc., included — as, stanching the death-wound, he replied, with a smile of anguish, 'Oh! nothing. You curse me, I bless you—that is all."

Having thus anticipated Iago, when he came to the subsequent production of Othello, he suppressed Iago's business altogether, and when ultimately he came to Obenreitzer, he appropriated Ruy Blas' original business, and very beautifully he did it, too.*

I told him an expedient I had invented to re-juvenate Robert Landry—the hero of my poor friend Watts Phillips's noble play of " The Dead Heart," of which I had a monopoly in the pro-vinces.

Landry emerges from the Bastile a broken-down old man ; but the peril of the woman whom he loves quickens the " dead heart " into newer and diviner life. Hence I devised a "make-up " based upon

---

* His original vocation was that of a sculptor. He utilized that accomplishment by modelling a statuette during the representation of a play, whereupon Melangue (another sculptor-actor) took the wind out of his sails by modelling a huge figure in Benvenuto Cellini.

"Never mind," said Fechter to me. "I'll give him a twister in my next part. I'll make a pair of shoes on the stage ! I wonder how the beggar will get over that ?"

I am under the impression that that pair of shoes has not been made yet.

the idea of Maximilian, the sea-green and incorruptible, and wore a wig of beautiful white hair.

" A capital idea **for** Monte Cristo, **my boy,** when *he* emerges from the Château **D'If!"** said Fechter.

" Not a bit like the author," said **I.**

" Confound the author ! What has he to do **with** my make-up, I should like to know ?" **he replied.**

I really thought he **was** joking, but **he was quite** in sober earnest, **as I** saw when, instead **of the dark** *jeune France* beard, black crop, and evening dress, he " made **up " for** Monte Cristo in a beautiful white wig and **black** silk pantaloons. Despite the pronounced failure of this play **at the** Adelphi, it **was a** great success **in** America, **and remains so to this** day.

After this production, he came into the **country to** star, but alas ! he came too late.

I went over to Manchester and **saw** him act " Black and White," one of his most inimitable performances, upon **a** Saturday—the great popular night there—to the worst house ever known in the annals **of** the Theatre Royal, Manchester.

From thence he came to fulfil engagements with **me at Leeds, York,** and Bradford.

In the two first towns we cleared our expenses and had pleasant times, but in Bradford the houses were simply awful.

The manager of the Bradford Theatre refused to accede to Fechter's terms, and I was therefore constrained to take the St. George's Hall, the rental of which was £20 a night—an amount we never reached!

A most amusing *contretemps* occurred on the night of his benefit.

To enhance the attraction, we put up the three first acts of " Hamlet," and " Black and White."

He merely travelled with a handful of people, and it therefore became necessary for him to engage one or two persons to make up the cast of " Hamlet "— notably, a gentleman was required for the Ghost. Now, it will be remembered, the Ghost makes his last appearance in the third act of the play.

There was a wicked house—something under £15!

On the representative of the Ghost applying to Fechter's treasurer for the reward of merit—which had been put down at the modest sum of a rural guinea—that worthy said :

" Oh, Mr. X., look at the house! We really must cry quits for half a guinea. Remember, Mr. Fechter has only played *half* of ' Hamlet !' "

" Yes," replied the inexorable X., " but I've played *all* the Ghost !"

Mr. X. got that guinea.

It was here, alas ! that the rupture came which always came to Fechter's friendships.

In this case I thought it was not entirely his fault. I was away in town, when his representative offered my secretary an insult of the grossest

character—an insult, too, which reflected on me, and
was compromising to my commercial reputation.

On my return Fechter was on his way to Bristol.

I wrote him, as I thought, a temperate letter on
the subject, and received a reply thus worded :

" You are too much of a Grand Sultan for me.
When you deign to ' descend from your pedestal,' I
shall be willing to meet you as of old.

" Yes! my man did what he did, not by my
orders, certainly, but he has, nevertheless, my entire
approval."

Anger is nothing less than a short-lived madness,
and in view of what has since occurred, I can scarce
forgive myself for my ill-conditioned reply, which
ran to this effect :

" The next time I descend from my pedestal, if
you have any regard for your health, keep out of
my way."

So there was the end of an intimacy of seven or
eight years—an end which I have never ceased to
deplore.

In 1870 Fechter went to America, where Charles
Dickens had been the *avant coureur* of his fame.

New York received him with open arms. The
Hub of the universe proclaimed him the greatest
actor living, and he was as great a social as he was
an artistic success.

A little stability of character, a little command of

temper, would have assured him an unassailable position; but, alas! it was the besetting sin of a nature femininely effusive, yet profoundly egotistical and intellectually arrogant, always to make friends to-day and to lose them to-morrow.

A friend (Mr. Arthur Cheney) built a new theatre in Boston expressly for Fechter.

His theory of management was superb, and, indeed, his productions were admirable and artistic; but his management of men and women was detestably autocratic, so much so that no man of spirit could submit to it.

During a short reign of twelve months he succeeded in embroiling himself with everybody whose friendship was worth having; then he threw up the reins, and disappeared without beat of drum.

He came back to England and acted a short engagement, but the glory had departed, and he played to "a beggarly account of empty benches!"

Returning to America, he wrecked his own fortunes and those of others in attempting to build a model theatre in New York—a theatre which was never completed; at least, not under his management.

In 1873 his star began to wane, and after acting a few nights at the Lyceum, in New York, to almost empty houses, the theatre closed at a moment's notice.

A few months afterwards he played a new part for a few nights at the Park Theatre.

The result was another fiasco.

That was the beginning of the end.

The genius which had dazzled and delighted both hemispheres now rushed headlong on a downward course.

It was at this time that a near and dear friend said to him :   .

"Charles, you are always kicking the ball away from your feet."

"Well," he replied, "it always comes back to me. It is my own ball, and, as you English say, I suppose I can do what I like with my own."

"Certainly ; but you will kick it away once too often, and then it will not come back."

His friend was right.

He did kick it away once too often, and, alas ! it never came back.

In 1876, while skating, he fell upon the ice and broke his leg.

When the news reached England I wrote him, and received in reply a letter, too sad and too sacred to be published here ; suffice it, that it foreshadowed not only the end of his artistic career, but the end of his life.

During the entire period of our intimacy I had never once noticed the slightest tendency towards that which ultimately proved his downfall.

This pernicious habit combined with physical infirmity, ill-health and increasing obesity to shorten his artistic career.

It is said that during his last visit to New York, to consult a physician as to his malady, he saw a

once popular actor, who had fallen into flesh, essaying Romeo.

"Poor fellow!" said Fechter, "he little knows
how his huge paunch renders him ridiculous. They
shall never say that of me. No; I have played my
last part!"

From that time forth he never appeared on the
stage.

Possibly he had been wiser to have arrived at
that conclusion earlier, for, like the Roman knight
whom Nero condemned to the degradation of the
circus, he had lived a day too long for his fame.

He had always said his crowning ambition was
"to keep a farm and carters."

If so, his ambition was realized.

Mr. Cowper, a well-known English actor recently
deceased, told me that, while acting in Philadelphia,
a somewhat obese agriculturist in a long coat of
homespun and a broad-brimmed hat drove up with
his team to the theatre.

To Cowper's astonishment and delight he discovered that the farmer was Fechter, who came to
seize and bear away his old friend to his farm of
fifty-seven acres at Rockland Centre, in Bucks
County.

The Englishman met with a hearty welcome.
Dogs and guns and fishing-rods abounded, but the
great actor's heart was far away.

His spasmodic fits of gaiety were varied by
intervals of sadness and silence.

The mere mention of his meteoric career in Eng-

LAURA KEENE AS PORTIA.

land came **back upon and stabbed him, even** as 'tis said the memories **of Holyrood** and Culloden came back and tortured **the** wretched Charles **Edward** during his declining years.

The world **had** been **at his feet ;** he **had been** satiated with praise, surfeited **with** adulation **;** he had been idolized **by women, envied** by men **; his** friends and intimates **had** been **"the** choice **and** master spirits of the age," **and now——**

"After all," growled **he** savagely, **"Charles V. retired to die in** a monastery ; why shouldn't Charles Fechter **die in a farmhouse ?"** Then with a sudden transition **to tearful tenderness, he** continued : **"When** you **get back to England, if you see** anyone who cares for poor **Charley—man or woman—** give my love to 'em **; and now** good-bye, old **fellow."**

As Cowper drove away, Fechter stood at the **farm** gate gazing with great hungry yearning **eyes, as** it seemed, through space **to** the other **side the** sea ; and **thus** he, who had once been **the *beau-iddal*** of Ruy **Blas,** Hamlet, and **the** rest of that noble brotherhood, faded away into the gray mists **of** evening.

Soon after **that** memorable visit he faded further away **still, and on** August 5th, 1879, he passed into the great **and** generous silence which lies beyond the land of shadows.

Since his death, Rumour with her thousand lying tongues has been busy with his fame.

It is well to speak of a man as you find him.

I always found him a charming companion, and the most hospitable of hosts.

He was delightful so long as you let him have his own way, and his own way of having it ; cross him, and you caught a Tartar ; scratch him, and you discovered a temper so unreasoning and so impatient of contradiction, so arrogant, so overbearing and insulting, that it remains to this day a mystery how he escaped being killed long before his time.

It is said that in Dickens's household the master was called " Mr. Always Right," while Fechter was christened " Mr. Never Wrong."

One thing is quite certain : he was but too wont to believe that everyone was wrong but himself.

Per contra, he had many large and generous impulses ; above and beyond all, he was neither a tuft-hunter nor a snob.

When Swelldom rushed rampant after him, he was wont to say to his comrades : " Come away, boys, let's get to ourselves ; I hate fools."

He was a great actor, a great stage-manager, an accomplished artist, an admirable sculptor ; in a word, he was a genius.

In the cemetery at Philadelphia there stands a monument which was raised to his memory by another unfortunate actor, lately and prematurely deceased, named John McCulloch.

It is a bust of Fechter, crowned with a wreath of laurel. On the base thereof these words are inscribed :

" Genius has taken its flight to God !"

CHAPTER VI.

" A GREAT man's memory may outlive his life half a year, but by 'r Lady he must build churches then."

Frederick Balsir Chatterton was not a great man, and, as instead of building churches he merely managed theatres, there is little probability that his memory has outlived his life half a year ; and yet the record of a career which commenced on the lowest round of the theatrical ladder, and which culminated at thirty years of age in the sole management of our great National Theatre, is sufficiently romantic and remarkable to deserve commemoration.

It seems as if it were but yesterday that I first met him, alert, active, and obliging, as he pursued his humble calling in a subordinate position in the front of Drury Lane Theatre.

It was during the management of the renowned E. T. Smith that I (then a hot-blooded youth) went with a couple of friends to see a wonderful Egyptian drama called " Nitocris," written by the once famous Fitzball, whose admirable drama of " The Flying

42—2

Dutchman" first inspired Wagner's muse of fire : Fitzball, who wrote a greater number of successful dramas than all the dramatists of the present decade put together, and yet during all his life never received for all his work half the amount which has been paid certain popular authors nowadays for a single piece.

The seats for which I had paid were claimed by three fast young men, who alleged we had taken their places. Hot words ensued, which ultimately led to blows, with the result that in five minutes' time we found ourselves at Bow Street.

Smith actively interfered to prevent scandal, but I remained obdurate, and our assailants were locked up for the night, and fined forty shillings the next morning, our testimony being corroborated by Chatterton, who had witnessed the assault. I little thought then that the next time I met that young man in Drury Lane Theatre he would be the manager thereof.

Ultimately we became on terms of friendly intimacy, an intimacy which subsisted until my management of the Queen's, when an event occurred which helped to wreck his fortunes and ruin mine, and led to our total estrangement for a considerable period.

It was only when I found that he had "fallen from his high estate" and that fair-weather friends had deserted him, that we became reconciled.

. Latterly, during the few months which immediately preceded his untimely death, he was wont to drop in upon me of an evening, and over a glass of grog and a cigar he would beguile the time by "acting his young encounters o'er again."

During these moments of confidence he revealed certain traits of character — certain subtle depths of emotion, of which I had hitherto believed him incapable, and of which he had certainly displayed no trace during our previous intimacy.

Those who only knew the outward husk of this man would doubtless have been astonished to find the kernel so sweet and sound ; yet those who knew him most intimately, while constrained to admit that he was strong-headed and wrong-headed, frequently ill-tempered (much of this might justly be attributed to a tendency to spinal disease), and but too often arbitrary and overbearing, knew also that he was capable of the most generous actions, and that he had a heart as impressionable as that of a child, as tender as that of a woman.

The truth was, and an ever-present bitter truth it was to him, he knew but too well that his breeding "lacked the repose which marks the caste of Vere de Vere."

At the period when other members of his family were put to school, he was fighting the battle of life ; hence his education had been cruelly neglected ; and although he had stored his mind with everything he could pick up on the way, he was so morbidly sensitive upon the subject of his shortcomings, that he was ever ready to construe the most innocent remark into a reflection upon his early misfortune.

Besides this, he was a martyr to *mauvaise honte,* and was continually tilting at windmills which existed only in his own imagination.

If this super-sensitive nonsense had been thrashed out of him in his youth, it would have cured him of many of the faults which in after-life made him so many enemies.

Extremes are ever neighbours, and he was in a state of perpetual oscillation between the excess of *brusquerie* and the extreme of sentiment.

His dominant ideas, however, were love of family, and (incredible as it may appear to those who only knew him superficially) an absolute reverence for the highest form of dramatic art.

His first ambition was to restore the fallen fortunes of his family; his next, to make the National Theatre worthy of its great traditions. How far he failed or succeeded in both undertakings, the following story will show. Anyhow, he did his best, and the best can do no more than that.

I can scarce do better than quote his own words, of which I made notes at the time, and which I compared and collated with him afterwards.

The figures of speech are sometimes quaint and forcible, but they are his own, and eminently characteristic, so I let them stand to give colour to the narrative:

" I was born in London in September, 1834; my people hailed from Portsmouth, where my grandfather had been a professor of music. He was the son of a gentleman of property in Leicestershire,

who left an entailed estate, which my noble grand-
sire proceeded in due course to disentail, and to
'waste the inheritance.' **To the** day of his death it
was a sore point with my poor old uncle John, **as**
the eldest born, that **he** had been thus defrauded **of**
his birthright; **my father, being a** younger **son,** did
not view it in **the** same light, **but he still felt**
aggrieved; and he might well be **so,** for he had
continual cause to complain **of the** poverty which
my grandfather's profligacy **and** extravagance entailed upon his descendants.

" This airy old gentleman **was left** a widower **with**
a young family, including **three** boys, of whom the
eldest was John Balsir Chatterton, the celebrated
harpist; the second, **Edward, was** my father; the
youngest, Frederick, was **also a** harpist, **and is still**
living. My grandfather resolved that his sons
should become great as harpists, and he proceeded
accordingly to dragoon them in a very rough and
ready way into a knowledge of the instrument. **He**
succeeded in thoroughly licking into shape John and
Frederick; but my father, being rather a dare-devil
and a ne'er-do-weel, was ultimately given over as
hopeless, and left to carve out a career for himself.
Both my uncles came to London at an early age,
and, notwithstanding some sore struggles with fortune, soon succeeded in making a position for themselves in the musical world.

" My dear old dad remained, however, for many
years a ' Jack of all trades.' For some time he tried
'to get **a** living as a music-publisher and vendor of

musical instruments, which frequently brought him into contact with his brothers, the harpists, who by this time had become rivals and irreconcilable foes, to the great regret of my father, who continually urged me to take warning by their example as to the fatal consequences of disunion in families. He was never weary of instilling into my mind the truth of the old fable of the Bundle of Sticks.

"At the same time he would endeavour to stimulate my ambition in order that, notwithstanding his own want of means, I, and my brothers and sisters, might not hereafter be compelled to take an inferior social position to that of my cousins, three of whom became officers in the army, while the fourth entered the Indian Civil Service.

"While I was still quite a child, dad became box book-keeper at Sadler's Wells Theatre with Tom Greenwood, whose wife and my mother, to the time of their death, were most intimate and bosom friends. My earliest recollections date from that period; I was never happy when out of the theatre, and was continually worrying Greenwood to let me 'go on' in the pantomime. This, however, went very much against the grain of both father and mother, who had made up their minds that I should become a professor of music. Accordingly I was placed under William Aspull, brother of the celebrated George Aspull, the musical prodigy, who died at an early age from the effects of too good living at the Court of George IV.

"Poor old Aspull! How good he was to me!

Not content with drumming into me the principles of music, he even endeavoured to repair my defective education (for I must tell you I was continually being taken from school owing to my father's pecuniary difficulties) by persuading me to attend as often as I possibly could at the library of the British Museum, where I picked up a certain amount of desultory information. My favourite work, however, was Shakespeare, which was then being published in penny numbers.

" I used to invest in a ' penn'orth ' every week, and carry it about in my jacket pocket, morning, noon, and night, reading it in the streets, or anywhere I could get the chance, till I had learnt the ' bard ' almost by heart. I flatter myself I know more about him than you tragedy Jacks or the erudite penny-a-liners ever gave me credit for!

" There was a continual conflict raging in my mind between filial duty and music on the one hand, and natural inclination and Shakespeare on the other.

" Ultimately I succeeded in melting the heart of old Greenwood, and persuaded him to allow me to ' go on ' in the pantomime for the modest stipend of sixpence a night, which made me the happiest lad in London. My happiness, however, was of short duration, for when my uncles, who were rapidly coming to the fore, found their hopeful nephew being kicked and cuffed about by the clown, they immediately rounded on my poor dad for disgracing the blood of the Chattertons by permitting his eldest

born to become a super! The result was that
my dramatic career was nipped in the bud, and I
was henceforth forced to devote myself to music
alone, until I had mastered the principles of the
art, from 'Pop goes the Weasel' to Beethoven's
concertos.

"Thus some years passed away. At length,
when I was about seventeen, I got to know two or
three amateurs connected with the Rawston Street
Theatre, Clerkenwell, where Phelps made his first
appearance; Pym's, in Gooch Street; and last and
least, the Cabinet at King's Cross. Here I became
acquainted with a young fellow named Jennings,
who is now a solicitor in a big way in Lincoln's Inn
Fields.* He was then a solicitor's clerk at eighteen
shillings a week, and found it necessary to eke out
his slender income by speculating in sundry amateur
performances. Hitherto I had wondered how these
affairs came off at all—*i.e.*, who 'paid the piper'—
but I soon became initiated into the mysteries of
management.

"At this time G. V. Brooke was taking the town
by storm at the Olympic. He had recently acted
in a new drama by the then lessee (Captain Spicer),
called the 'Lords of Ellingham.' I went with
Jennings to see it. We were both struck with the
piece, and he resolved to have a night with 'The
Lords,' and with such 'Commons' as he could
attract to the Cabinet.

* Strange to say this gentleman died exactly three days after
Chatterton.

" Upon the understanding that I was to induce some stage-struck aspirants, more verdant than ourselves, to pay liberally for the privilege of making fools of themselves, I was allotted the part of young Farningham in the play, and Higgins in the farce of ' Boots at the Swan.'

" On payment (in advance) of the sum of three shillings, I received twelve shillings' worth of tickets, every one of which I sold to my friends, so that you see I got my parts for nothing and made nine shillings by the transaction. It was a dear nine shillings though, for it ultimately cost me £1,500, as you will see by-and-by !

" From that moment, however, I made up my mind to be a manager, and in the pursuit of that vocation I resolved to restore my family to the position from which it had fallen by the improvidence of my grandfather. After assisting in several of Jennings's performances with more or less (generally less) success, I concluded to try to ' paddle my own canoe.' My ambition now urged me to a higher flight than I had hitherto attempted, so I resolved to try conclusions with Othello. This brought me into collision with Jennings, who thought he was privileged to play Iago for nothing. A Mr. Watts, an ironmonger in the Edgware Road, however, very promptly paid thirty shillings for ' mine ancient,' and, what was better still, paid the money down, so Jennings took offence, and retired in a huff. A Mr. Bellamy paid seven and sixpence for Roderigo ; Brabantio, Montano, and Lodovico paid three and

sixpence each ; and a Mr. Hayman (a clerk in the
railway clearing-house) paid two pounds for Cassio.
By-the-bye, Hayman afterwards became a great pro-
moter of companies in the City, cleared upwards of
£60,000 by various speculations, and ultimately, it
is said, lost his head from some reverse of fortune.
The ladies, of course, paid nothing ; in fact, we were
only too glad to get them.   Desdemona was a Miss
Henderson, a charming little creature with a beautiful figure, fair hair, bright eyes, and a musical voice.
Emilia was a Miss Blanchard, who, I observe, has
been recently acting with Mrs. Langtry at the
Prince of Wales's, under the nom de theatre of Miss
Adelaide Bowring.   My programme included ' Box
and Cox,' then a popular farce amongst amateurs,
and two fellows named Pybrow and Tom Briggs
paid three and sixpence each for the honour of
exhibiting themselves as the hatter and the printer.

" My expenses were : Theatre and gas, £1 ; costumes, £1 ; band, comprising harp, viola, and cornet,
7s. 6d. ; printing, 7s. 6d. ; hire of wigs, 6d. each
(these we paid for ourselves)—in all, £2 15s. So
that you see, as the receipts from the sale of parts
amounted to £4 8s. 6d., I had actually cleared
£1 13s. 6d. before we opened the doors.

" Jennings turned up at the commencement of the
performance, and demanded free admission. As we
were under the impression that he meant to kick up
a row, we refused to let him in, whereupon he retired
vowing vengeance, and he kept his vow, for, meeting
my ' Box and Cox ' (Pybrow and Briggs), he took

them into an adjacent tavern, where he made them
as 'tight as a drum.'

" He was himself 'powerfully refreshed' when he
made his way behind the scenes after Othello.
He triumphantly demanded, ' Now, Mr. Clever,
what are you going to do without your " Box and
Cox ?"'

" ' I will show you,' said I. With that I bolted
out then and there, exactly as I was, with the black
on my face, to the Argyll Tavern opposite, where I
knew I should find Johnny Clarke (afterwards of
the Strand) and his chum, young Massey, who was
brother of the proprietor of the theatre. They had
played ' Box and Cox ' scores of times, and jumped
at the idea of having a go in at their favourite
parts without paying for them, so that difficulty was
easily got over.

" I fear I did not distinguish myself much in
Othello, but, in addition to the £1 13s. 6d. I had
cleared by the sale of the parts, I disposed of
upwards of £3 worth of tickets, so that you see
I actually paid myself from £4 to £5 for the
privilege of murdering the Moor as well as Desdemona !

" After this I acted a good deal at the Soho, playing
Macbeth and Claude Melnotte, and I suppose playing the deuce with them.

" All this time, however, I was getting my living by
teaching music, in which I had become fairly proficient. To add to my income, I went every night
to help my father at the Marylebone, where he had

joined Mrs. Warner in the management of the front of the house.

" The continual sight of the performances of that great actress, and the admirable company by which she was surrounded, fired my dormant ambition, and I resolved to cut the amateur business and go in for the real thing.

" Every morning found me at the agent's offices in Bow Street, where I always got the same answer, 'We want actors, not amateurs.' Ultimately, however, I got a berth with E. T. Smith at the Lane, where I first met you on the night of the row. I thought you were a young military swell, and was rather surprised to find you an actor.

" At the end of my first season with Smith, I had saved a few pounds, and, finding that no one would have me as an actor, I made up my mind to take a theatre and act all the big parts myself. Accordingly I went into management at Rochester. The business was so bad that I went out of it again as soon as I could, and, sorely disheartened, made the best of my way back to town on 'Shanks's mare' with Harry Sinclair, who was afterwards with me so long at Drury Lane.

" Then came a spell of misery and privation.

" My father was incensed at my idiocy, as he called it, in leaving the musical profession in the vain idea of becoming an actor. My dear mother, bless her heart! did all she could to help me, but that was not much.

" At last, when I had reached the very back of

God-speed, Charles Dillon engaged me as acting manager at the Lyceum, and from that time I never looked back.

" Although he made a great mark himself and had a splendid company, poor Dillon began in debt and difficulty, and remained so to the end. As I had a little *nous* in financing, I got him over many of his troubles ; but they were too strong for him, or he was too weak to grapple with them.

" If he had had a little more ballast he would have been the biggest man of his time. Poor Charley !

" It was during this engagement that I became acquainted with Edmund O'Rourke, better known as Edmund Falconer, whom Dillon brought up to town with Marie Wilton, Toole, Calhaem, MacNeil, Shore, and other country actors. At the end of the second season Dillon came to grief, and went back to the country. Falconer, who had already made a mark with a piece called ' The Cagot,' had written a comedy called ' Extremes,' which was actually in rehearsal when Dillon collapsed.

" Falconer now proposed that we should take the Lyceum for the summer season, for the production of this play. We did so, and although the piece was produced under adverse circumstances, it was a success. Leigh Murray was engaged for Frank Hawthorne, the leading part, but he disappointed us at the last moment, and Falconer had to do Frank himself on the first night. Subsequently, however, Murray played the part, and scored in it.

" At the end of the summer season we went to Manchester with the play, where Leigh, who had now become very erratic, again disappointed us ; but fortunately we found an adequate substitute in Harry Vandenhoff, then a capital light comedian, and one of the handsomest men on the stage. We made a little money by this experiment, and returned to the Lyceum for the autumn, beginning our season with a revival of ' Extremes,' which again ' struck oil.' Unfortunately, however, we were not ' all over ' money, and a difficulty arose about the rent. My father had now arrived at the conclusion that, after all, I was not such an absolute idiot as he had imagined. My brothers and sisters had always, I may say, worshipped me, looking up to me as a big brother who was going (they did not quite know how) to do something wonderful, and I fully made up my mind I would not disappoint them. Anyhow, I took precious good care they should not suffer from the lack of education from which I had suffered in consequence of the straitened circumstances of my family. I resolved, therefore, that my two younger brothers should be brought up for the liberal professions, and I made one of them a doctor and the other a solicitor. My youngest brother, who was fifteen years my junior, had always been a great pet of mine. I nursed him through a long and dangerous illness of four months' duration when he was only four years old, and the affection thus cemented has never cooled from that time to this.

CHARLOTTE CUSHMAN.

"Apropos of him, it has often been suggested that in the speeches I have made and the letters I have written to the papers, I had a 'ghost'; now, if the truth must be known, that ghost was no other than this boy. Before he was old enough to do this I sometimes had recourse to poor Charles Kenney, but in every case the ideas put forth were my own. I always found the nuggets, though Horace and Charles Kenney may have polished them up a bit.

"To return, however, to the rent. My father, I am bound to say now, did everything in his power to make atonement for his negligence in the past; hence, he it was who, in this emergency, came to the rescue and accepted my bills for £500.

"Mr. Arnold, the proprietor of the Lyceum, took them as security; so, thanks to dear old dad, that difficulty was tided over.

"We had now to prepare for our Christmas novelty, and William Brough came to propose a burlesque on the Iliad called the 'Siege of Troy.'

"Falconer was favourably impressed with the subject, and alleged that he could produce the piece on as splendid a scale as 'Lalla Rookh' (which had been a great success with Dillon) for £500. We had a little money in hand, my father lent me a little more, and we went ahead with our preparations. But instead of costing only £500, the infernal thing cost £1,500. Only imagine! There were upwards of sixty-three speaking parts, thirty

of which we cut out after the third performance!
Though supported by the strongest company in
London, it was the most dismal failure I ever witnessed. Had it been worth looking at, people were
prepared to jump at it. We took £200 by our
first performance at the matinée on Boxing Day,
and £215 at night; but they found us out at once,
and on the second night down we dropped to £50.
We continued to drop and drop, until we were at
length compelled to drop the dreary abortion altogether. Then came the question of ways and
means, and I had to get my father to back a bill
for £300 to meet the salaries; while, on his part,
Falconer proposed to bring in a Mr. L. and a Miss
F., who undertook to provide capital to carry on
with.

"When the acceptance for £300 became due, I
was compelled to appropriate the whole week's
receipts to meet it. I lost all heart, and proposed
that if Falconer's friends would guarantee the
Saturday's treasury, I would retire altogether. This
proposal was accepted, and I was really glad to
wash my hands of the whole affair. At this juncture Madame Celeste came to the rescue, and
offered Falconer £500 to go out. He jumped at
the proposal, which enabled him to settle with his
creditors and retire, leaving her mistress at the
Lyceum for the next two years.

"For my part, after a time I became restless and
dissatisfied. I had tasted blood, and could not keep
out of speculation, so I persuaded my father to

take the St. James's, which was going begging at a nominal rent.

"I went into the management ostensibly on my own account, although the governor, who prudently kept in the background, was really the responsible party. It was just as well that he did so, as I came a cropper, mainly owing to an unfortunate lawsuit with Sam Emery. This was my first experience in litigation. I have had plenty of it since, and in nearly every case have been successful, thanks to the skill and ability of my brother Horace, who, as soon as he was old enough to be admitted to practise on his own account, became my legal adviser.

"The old man remained in possession of the St. James's, and ultimately made a very good thing of it by transferring the remainder of his lease to Alfred Wigan.

"At or about this time, the 'Colleen Bawn' was produced at the Adelphi, and Falconer was engaged for Danny Mann. Though anything but a good actor in other parts, he was 'all there' in this, and made his mark. After a time, however, he had a row with Boucicault (everyone has a row with him; that is, if they only know him long enough!), and got the sack. Falconer and I had come to loggerheads before we parted; but one afternoon we met in the Strand; he said something civil, I responded, and we agreed to bury the hatchet.

"By this time Celeste had had enough of the Lyceum, and it was once more in the market. Falconer had employed his leisure by writing a comedy called 'Woman,' founded on the Yelverton case, which was then in everybody's mouth. He had also revised an old drama he had produced in Liverpool years before. This work was taken from the 'Tales of the O'Hara Family,' and afterwards became famous as 'The Peep o' Day.'

"The question was how to get the theatre. Next day, at my suggestion, he interviewed Arnold, who was very gracious, and offered it for a month at £60 per week, payable weekly, in advance, with the refusal of a fortnight longer. Falconer had no coin, but the governor lent me £100.

"Next day we paid our first week's rent, and we boldly commenced operations with a borrowed capital of £40, and a debt of £60!

"We opened with 'Woman,' and, by Jove! I thought we were going to shut with it, business was so awfully bad. We had the utmost difficulty in meeting our first treasury; however, we did meet it somehow. I remember we were chaffed by the critic of a certain popular journal, who instituted a comparison between us and Celeste, politely and charitably remarking, 'when respectable managers close, adventurers rush into the breach.' Modest this in a paper owned by a firm which only a few months before had been jobbing printers in a very small way!

"Falconer was dreadfully cut up by this doubtful compliment, but it did not trouble me in the slightest degree. I had something more important on my mind. The year following was the year of the

second great Exhibition, and I could think of nothing
else, especially as Arnold had already advertised
that the theatre was to let for that period.

"Our second Monday night was worse than our
first, and Falconer was awfully down on his luck
about the trade treasury, which was due at two
o'clock the following day. When the play was over
that night we stood in the portico at the theatre,
looking down Exeter Change, which shone out clear
and bright in the moonlight.

"'Fred,' said Falconer, 'I fear it's all u.p. with
us. I'm just afther thinking hwat the divil we're to
do for to-morrow's threasury.'

"'I'm not thinking of anything of the kind,' said
I; 'I'm thinking how the deuce we are to collar this
theatre for the season of the Exhibition.'

"'Ah, g'long; you might just as well think of
collaring the moon yondher, and shutting her up
in a lanthern, like a farthing rushlight.'

"'Perhaps not. Anyhow, don't you fret about
the treasury, I'll get my old man to see after that.
You go first thing to-morrow to Arnold, and offer
him my acceptance for £1,000 to secure the theatre
for next year.'

"My father helped us over the treasury, while
Falconer went to Arnold, who seemed rather
dubious about the proposal.

"At last he replied, 'No, no, I can't do that; but
I'll tell you what I will do. Bring me £500 in a
fortnight, and I'll withdraw the advertisement, and
take Chatterton's acceptance for the other £500.'

" Falconer came back to me more down on his luck
than ever, and was surprised when I told him to return immediately and accept the proposal.   Notwithstanding, back he went, and closed with Arnold.

" Then came the tug of war.   I arranged for two
benefits the week after, which realized £200 ; £100
I borrowed from my father ; £200 more I got on
his acceptance from Seale, Low and Co., the bankers.
The £500 was paid to the moment, Arnold took
my acceptance for the remaining £500, and the
theatre was secured for the Exhibition.   That was
the turning-point of our fortunes.   We kept our
heads above water by a succession of wonderful and
desperate expedients, until the production of ' Peep
o' Day' enabled us to clear £16,000 after paying
all outstanding liabilities !

" Of this £16,000, a third belonged to me according to agreement ; but Falconer only paid me some
£1,400 or £1,500, and gave me his I.O.U.'s for the
balance of £3,500.   At this time he had become so
elated with success that he took a large house at
Fulham, started a carriage and pair, etc. ; besides
which he, who had hitherto been the most temperate, and, indeed, most abstemious of men, became
suddenly afflicted with an insatiable thirst, which for
some years acted like a poison on his blood and
brains, and was the cause of all our subsequent misunderstandings and his ultimate ruin.

" Just as I thought our troubles were over, unfortunately for us, Fechter quarrelled with Harris, and
left the Princess's.

"As it was now an open secret to the initiated that nearly all Fechter's wonderful triumphs had been direful financial failures, London was closed to him unless he could ' set up a tambourine of his own.'

" In this juncture his fashionable friends rallied round him, provided him with ' the sinews of war ' which enabled him to take the theatre over our heads for a term of years at a considerably increased rental, and we were bowled out without ceremony.

" At this very time, E. T. Smith had secured a new lease of Drury Lane, by the conditions of which he was bound to entirely redecorate the theatre at considerable expense, in accordance with specifications prepared for that purpose by the architect to the proprietors. Smith had dabbled in so many speculations at Her Majesty's, at Cremorne, and elsewhere, that he was unable to carry out his contract ; hence he made advances to Falconer, and the result was that he took the theatre, paying Smith £5,000 for his lease, and covenanting to expend over £7,000 upon decorations.

" In order to enable Falconer to make these payments, I lent him, or, to be more precise, consented that the £3,500 he owed me should stand over.

" Although my name did not appear ostentatiously in the management, a formal agreement was entered into between Falconer and myself in September, 1867, by which it was stipulated that, in consideration of the advance of £3,500, I was to have a nominal salary of £300 a year, and a clear third of the profits.

" By the time the requisite payments—amounting

to £12,000—had been paid, we had not a shilling left at the commencement of the season.

"We opened at Christmas, 1862, with a pantomime, which did not make so big a hit as we had anticipated.

"After the pantomime came 'Bonny Dundee,' one of the most pronounced of Falconer's many failures. Bad as it was, the splendour of the get-up might have saved the piece, had it not been for an unlucky accident. Although the audience had been much exercised by the 'Massacre of Glencoe,' the killing and slaughtering were over; and they had endured it with silence, if not with equanimity, when, unfortunately, an effeminate young man appeared upon an eminence overlooking the scene of the massacre. As he gazed down on the murdered Macdonalds, he lisped, in the most ladylike manner, 'Oh, how dreadful!' whereupon some wag in the pit responded, 'Right you are, old man; it *is* dreadful!' This evolved a yell which sealed the fate of the piece. From that moment 'Bonny Dundee' was doomed, and the curtain fell amidst roars of derision.

"This was a healthy look-out, for, besides the loss involved in the production, Falconer from that moment continued to go more and more to the bad. He would insist upon playing his own pieces, and we produced 'Next of Kin'—another fiasco—and a dreary 'Tale of the Terror,' which was near shutting us up altogether.

"By this time my patience had become exhausted, and I insisted upon our reverting at once to the legitimate and classic drama. Circumstances enabled me to carry out my views sooner than I anticipated.

" My earliest experiences had been at Sadler's Wells, where Phelps was a demi-god. I thoroughly believed in him; hence, when he returned to the West, and quarrelled with Fechter, I persuaded Falconer to engage 'the grand old man,' who proved the greatest and cheapest feature we ever had. His reception on the first night of 'Manfred' was as if a field of artillery were fired about our ears. I never heard such a thing before, and never shall again. The people went mad. The play was produced on a scale of almost unparalleled splendour. Telbin's Alpine scenery in particular was simply perfection. I was now enabled to realize the dream of my life— to restore Old Drury to its position as the home of the poetic drama, from which it had been deposed by E. T. Smith.

" For sixteen long years I persevered in this endeavour, with varying success, I admit. I am bold, however, to say that the reputation of the National Theatre never suffered in my hands. I preferred to borrow money at usurious interest, rather than have recourse to the dubious means, which have been, and, I fear, are still, resorted to by some people who do not disdain to extract coin from the pockets of any idiot at the price of allowing incompetent demireps to air their ignorance and incapacity, and to pollute by their presence an atmosphere which should be consecrated to nobler uses.

"As Sir Giles says, 'I name no parties;' but, to prevent misunderstanding, I wish to state emphatically that I'm not referring to 'Gus,' who is a right-down good fellow, though he has bowled me out, and stepped into my shoes.

"Poor Falconer about this time had got into a state verging upon imbecility, owing to his unfortunate infirmity; and in March, 1864, there was a heavy amount of arrears due for rent, and for other pressing liabilities. The whole of the responsibility now devolving upon my shoulders, I insisted upon a fresh agreement being drawn up, providing for my open admission into the partnership, on the usual terms of an equal share of profits and losses; and that my name should appear as joint-manager in all bills and advertisements.

"Although Falconer was nominally bound to find half the capital, as a matter of fact, from this time forth he never found another shilling.

"Smith, who, as you know, was a very astute person, had taken care to keep a foothold in the theatre by retaining the manager's room and his own box.

"These became veritable thorns in our flesh; and he took good care to make it as hot as he could for us, and I had to devise the means for checkmating him.

"His agreement with the proprietors was, that he was to pay the annual rental for a term of two hundred nights, and so much more per night for every extra performance. Now, although we were responsible to him, we were not responsible to the proprietors.

"We soon brought matters 'to Hecuba' by dividing the rent into fifty-two parts; that is to say, we only paid so much per week on account of the fifty-two weeks of the year, and by the time we had reached the 200th night of the season, £1,800 was due from Smith to the proprietors. They looked to him for payment, and he looked to us to get him out of the hole.

"At this stage of affairs, he invited me to dine with him one day at Ashburnham House.

"After dinner, without circumlocution, he proposed that I should go in with him and throw Falconer over altogether. Of course I refused point-blank. Finding I was not to be had, he then offered to retire if we would pay the arrears due to the proprietors, and give him a bonus of £250.

"He gave us forty-eight hours to make the requisite arrangements. If not completed by that time, he swore that he would throw the affair into Chancery.

"After a hasty consultation with Falconer, during a lucid interval, I found that with my father's help I could scrape together £1,000; but where to get the second thousand I did not know.

"All at once it dawned upon me that John Knowles, of Manchester, the 'theatrical pawnbroker,' as poor Byron christened him, had advanced

Charles Mathews, Dillon, Buckstone, etc., large
sums. He was reputed to be very rich, and to be
desirous of having a finger in every pie ; so, arming
myself with two bill-stamps for £500 each, I took
the first train to Manchester.

"When I reached the theatre he was not there,
but Chambers, his manager, told me I should find
him at home. So up I went to Trafford Park, and,
sure enough, there he was, just sitting down to
dinner alone in his snuggery. You know what a
rough diamond he was.

"'Well, Chatterton,' said he, 'have summat to
eat. We've got nowt but beer and hashed mutton ;
but beer's Bass, and mutton's Southdown. There
you are, lad ; fall to.'

"When I had done justice to the mutton, he
resumed :

"'Weel, and what on earth brings you to Trafford
Park ?'

"With that I told him that we wanted to borrow
£1,000.

"'Eh, man ! a thousand pounds is a lot o' brass !
Why, you had a heap on't t'other day. Oh, weel, a
fool and his money is soon parted ! What reet had
yon Irish idiot to go and set up carriages, and
horses, and flunkies, and that sort of muck ?—and
to buy picturs too ? It takes a man o' taste to buy
picturs. Did you ever see mine ? Coom here, lad,
and I'll show you.'

"With that, he took me into the drawing-room,
and showed me his collection, of which he was not

a little proud—and well he might be, for it was
unique.

" ' Sit down,' he continued, ' and have a glass o'
whisky-and-water, and a cigar. Now coom to cues.
How about security ?'

" ' Well,' said I, ' you shall have the right to act
" Peep o' Day " up to Christmas. After you have
taken your working expenses, the profit shall go
towards repaying you, thus : One-third for interest,
and the remainder to be devoted to the repayment
of the principal.'

" ' 'Tain't good enough, lad,' said he ; ' try again.'

" ' Well, then,' said I, ' look here. I'll throw you
Telbin's panorama of the Lakes of Killarney into
the bargain.'

" This was, as you may remember, a magnificent
work. Anything in the shape of a picture 'fetched'
Knowles, so he rose to the bait.

" ' I have got no coin,' said he, ' but I'll accept
bills. Go you back to town and send 'em me.'

" ' No occasion for that,' I replied, ' here they
are '—and I produced the two slips of blue paper.

" ' I see you've left nowt to accident,' he said as,
with a grin, he accepted the bills.

" Then he wrote a hasty note to G., the famous
art publisher of Pall Mall.

" ' Tak' 'em to him,' he said ; ' and now cut your
stick, and mind you let me have the Panorama here
as soon as possible."

" I travelled all night, and, after a tub and a shave,
was with G. at half-past ten next morning.

" The note was to this effect :

" ' DEAR G.,—Do these ; they are all right.

" ' J. K.'

" G. hummed and ha'd, and then said, in his cautious way :

" ' It is very easy for Mr. Knowles to say they are all right, but suppose he should die before they are due ?'

" I exerted my powers of persuasion, and ultimately induced Mr. G. to give me a cheque for £500 (less bank-rate of interest) for one bill. He declined, however, to cash the other, so I went there and then to S., in Covent Garden, and got him to discount it at 20 per cent.—and very cheap I thought it. I have been glad to pay 100 per cent. since.

" Before night the £1,800 was paid to the proprietors, Smith was paid his bonus of £250, and we remained sole monarchs of Drury Lane.

" Big as old Drury is, unfortunately, through perpetually recurring misunderstandings, it soon became too little to hold Falconer and myself.

" In the autumn of 1865 we were heavily in debt, and things got from bad to worse between us, until at length he filed a bill in Chancery against me for a dissolution of partnership, in which he repudiated all responsibility for the £3,500, and other moneys which I had advanced.

" To make a long story short, after a deal of litigation, our creditors, who were pressing, came to the conclusion that their only chance of getting paid was by sticking to me. The result was, that they **forced** Falconer into bankruptcy. As a natural **conse-quence**, our partnership came to an end, and with it the lease of Drury **Lane!**

" My position was anything but an **enviable one.** The partnership owed about £10,000, for **which, as** I had not become bankrupt, I, of course, was solely **responsible.** However, I tendered **for a new** lease, and **got it;** and **in** due course **I paid off every** shilling **of** these liabilities !

" Falconer (who I have always thought was a victim to his surroundings) went to Her Majesty's, where he produced a play called 'Oonah,' founded on one of Carleton's stories, called '**Fardaroosha the** Miser.' The curtain did not drop upon this unfor-tunate drama until between one and two o'clock **on** Sunday morning. By this time the audience, which had got very sparse, became impatient.

" Falconer acted an old miser, **who, in** the last scene, is placed on his trial for murder. There was the usual burlesque paraphernalia of **a** court of justice—judge, jury, witnesses, etc. Counsel for the prosecution and defence had been heard, when, amidst continually increasing irritation **on** the part of **the** auditors, Old Neville, who was the judge, began to sum up the case. 'Gentlemen of the jury,' said he, ' you have heard my learned brothers for the prosecution and the defence ; you have also heard the evidence, in which I must say there

appears to be a slight discrepancy. In order, however, to remove any doubt which may exist in your
minds, I will read my notes.'

"At this moment an indignant pittite roared
out : ' No, no ; don't. Hang the old duffer at
once !'

" This was a settler for ' Oonah,' and for poor Falconer, who next day took his departure without beat
of drum for America.

" In the autumn of 1866 I found myself sole
manager of Drury Lane. I determined to play a
high game, and to start with a flourish of trumpets.
Accordingly I put forth a programme, setting out
that I intended to produce the works of the great
English dramatists, and that I had engaged Miss
Helen Faucit, Mrs. Hermann Vezin, Phelps, James
Anderson, Barry Sullivan, Walter Montgomery,
Walter Lacy, and a host of other well-known artists.
I sent a copy of the prospectus to Mr. Macready,
and received from him an autograph letter in the
following words :

6, Wellington Square,

" ' Cheltenham,

" ' October 23, 1866.

" ' Dear Sir,

" ' In acknowledging the very handsome
tribute you offer to my humble endeavours to maintain the dignity of my late profession, I can only
wish you, as I most cordially do, every possible

TYRONE POWER AS CONNOR O'GORMAN.

success in the honourable and arduous task you have undertaken, and remain,

> " 'With esteem and respect,
>> " ' Yours very sincerely,
>>> " '(Signed) W. C. MACREADY.

" 'F. B. Chatterton, Esq.'

" This letter I have treasured as one of the proudest possessions of my life, and, in every vicissitude of fortune, I have always endeavoured to deserve the good wishes which Mr. Macready so generously accorded me.

" Let me, however, return to poor Falconer for a moment. On his arrival in America he found our noble cousins coining money out of ' Peep o' Day,' not a shilling of which ever found its way into his pockets.

" A cruel scandalous anomaly, this American copyright business. While he was almost starving out there, thieves and pirates were making fortunes out of this drama.

" After staying in the States for a year or two, he came home under a greater cloud than that under which he went out. On his return he tried his luck again at the Lyceum with a new piece called ' Innisfallen ; or, The Man in the Gap,' but this also was a ' frost.' Poor chap, it was all downhill with him from this time. Subsequently we became friends again, and I did my best to help him until his death.*

---

* On the morning of the funeral, the widow of Edmund Falconer sent a magnificent wreath of flowers to be cast upon Chatterton's grave. This touching tribute speaks volumes for this poor lady's appreciation of his relations with her dead husband.

" I have already described to you, for your Phelps book, the series of Shakespearian revivals which I produced with his aid ; but I don't think I ever told you of the row in connection with ' Formosa,' or of the dispute with Sims Reeves. I had engaged the great tenor to act in 'Guy Mannering' at a salary of £50 a night. At the last moment he wrote to say that he could not sing on the night advertised for the opening. I accordingly sent for William Harrison to take the part of Henry Bertram. Reeves was offended at this, and wrote to say that as I had chosen to put someone else in his part, he should decline to fulfil his contract at all. Ultimately I brought an action against him, and received £1,500 damages. I should have preferred, however, that he had fulfilled his engagement, for the £1,500 was only a fractional part of what I might have fairly expected to realize had he carried out his contract.

" Despite this unfortunate misunderstanding, let me say that, to my thinking, Reeves is not only the greatest English singer of our time, but I believe the very greatest that ever lived, not even barring Braham !

" To come to the ' Formosa ' dispute. For some time we took over £1,600 a week, but about Christmas we dropped down to £600. Boucicault wanted to reproduce the piece after the pantomime, but, seeing the signs of the times, I declined. The Irish Question was hot in men's minds, and the country was in a state of ferment over Gladstone's

Irish Church Disestablishment Bill. There was a row
at Weston's Music-Hall, and a poor Life Guardsman
was assassinated in Bloomsbury ; in point of fact,
the **time was ripe** for the revival of ' Peep **o' Day,'**
the proprietorship **of** which had **now** reverted **to me,**
in consequence of Falconer's bankruptcy.

" I engaged him, however, on liberal terms for his
original part. **We** produced the play in Lent, and
absolutely cleared £2,000 by it—think of that! A
profit **of** £3,000 in Lent! This was wormwood to
Boucicault, **who** had already brought a hornet's-
nest about my **ears in** the correspondence concern-
ing ' Formosa,' **where,** yielding to pressure, at his
instigation **I** had indiscreetly permitted myself **to**
be made the mouthpiece of his **now** historical platitude, that ' Shakespeare spelt ruin and **Byron bank-**
ruptcy !' Notwithstanding the tempest which has
for years raged round these words, **I can only say**
that, so far as my own **personal** experience goes,
they **are,** unhappily, but **too true ;** for, during the
many years in which I endeavoured season after
season **to** uphold the legitimate drama at Drury
Lane, **it was** never a calculation as **to** how much I
was going **to gain** before Christmas, but how little I
could afford **to lose** out of the prospective profits of
the pantomime.

" In 1870, however, the whole complexion of
things changed. Andrew Halliday (whom **I** had
known for years), with all the shrewdness of a canny
Scot, suggested to me that it might **be** possible to
steer a middle course between Shakespeare and

pieces of the 'Formosa' class; a course which, while producing plays not unworthy of the reputation of the National Theatre, would still be sufficiently modern and interesting to attract the general public. Accordingly he proposed the dramatization of the 'Waverley' novels, and the production of them on a magnificent scale, with the aid of the best actors that could be secured.

"At this period Phelps and I had, unfortunately, through this infernal 'Formosa' business, got to loggerheads. We brought cross-actions against each other for breach of contract, which were referred to Mr., now Mr. Justice Wills, who curiously enough decided that we were both right and both wrong, and gave us each a verdict in our own actions, so that in the result we had each to pay our own legal expenses, which was all the satisfaction we ever got out of it. Having found that we had both made fools of ourselves, the next thing was to make friends; so, acting on Halliday's suggestion, I decided to produce a dramatized version of the 'Fortunes of Nigel,' and engaged Phelps to play the part of the Scotch king and Trapbois the miser, both of which he did to perfection. The result was that, for the first time in my experience at Drury Lane, the play produced in the autumn did not entail a loss; on the contrary, there was a small margin of gain. Now this meant that the profit of the pantomime, instead of being anticipated by the loss in the previous production, as hitherto, remained intact!

" Needless to say, we decided to continue the experiment, and during the next three years we produced 'Amy Robsart,' 'Rebecca,' and 'The Lady of the Lake,' all three of which were successes. By the first and second I cleared about £6,000, and by the last £4,000.

" Halliday was, without exception, the least vain and egotistical dramatist I ever came across. Not only would he accept suggestions while the drama was still in manuscript, but even after its production. It was our invariable practice to sit in the front of the house watching the play scene by scene, and making such excisions and alterations as we thought would conduce to its more perfect success.

" I am happy to say I was enabled to pay him some thousands of pounds for author's fees.

" Poor Andrew! He died prematurely, and his loss was a severe blow to me. Outside my own family, I don't think I ever deplored any man's death more than I did his.

" It was while flushed with this temporary success that I took that fatal step which led slowly but surely to my irretrievable ruin.

" After the 'Formosa' episode, Boucicault and I drifted apart, and the next I heard of him was that, having entered into some arrangement with Mr. Benjamin Webster, the result was that the latter was on the point of being made bankrupt by pressure brought to bear upon his bankers.

"A mutual friend pointed out that it would be a kindly act to rescue the poor old gentleman, who had

been so many years before the public, and that if I
could do so, and associate myself in the management
of the Adelphi and the Princess's, I should not only
have the satisfaction of defeating Boucicault and
rescuing Webster, but should emancipate myself
from the exactions of the Drury Lane proprietors,
and the incessant persecutions to which I had been
subjected for a series of years by their architect, who
was continually worrying me by giving me notices of
repairs and decorations which almost drove me to
distraction.   Unfortunately I did not stop to calculate
the consequences of such a step, as undoubtedly I
ought to have done.

"You see, I was at this time making about fifteen
or sixteen thousand a year, beside which I had a
large balance at my bankers', and my credit was at
its zenith.   Accordingly, after having been informed
that, in addition to the £6,000 due by Webster to
the bank, there were a few outstanding liabilities,
I consented to join him.   The first thing I did
was to go to his bankers, and tell them to at once
debit me with the £6,000 for which they were
pressing him ; the next was to clear Boucicault
out, bag and baggage.   This done, I proceeded to
manage the Adelphi and the Princess's, as well as
Drury Lane.   I might as well have attempted to
drive the horses of the sun.   My poor old dad tried
to dissuade me from this suicidal act, but it was in
vain that he pointed out that three theatres were
more than one man's work, however energetic he
might be.   I answered 'that if a sailor knew his

work, it was as easy to navigate a fleet as a ship !'

"I learnt afterwards, to my sorrow, that a manager of theatres, unlike the admiral of a fleet, has not under his orders captains as competent, or possibly more competent even than himself. As it was impossible to be in more than one place at a time, the inevitable result followed, that what I made in one theatre I lost in the others.

" Had I stuck to the Lane alone, or rather, I should say, had I not been harassed by the proprietors, through their architect, I should be there now, but I could not withstand the temptation to have it in my power to tell these gentlemen when next they threatened me with their contracts and their covenants, that I would take myself elsewhere if they did not cease from their persecutions.

" For a year or two after I joined Webster, the large profits I made at the Lane enabled me to bear the continual drain in the two other theatres ; but when, in 1873, at Halliday's suggestion, I inaugurated the fresh lease with Shakespeare's 'Antony and Cleopatra,' alas ! it only served to provide another proof of the truth of the unfortunate saying which has since become proverbial.

" To make matters worse, Webster's liabilities turned out to be much heavier than I had anticipated, and as he was unable to find a shilling towards the continually-increasing deficit at the Adelphi and the Princess's, he consented to give me a lease of both theatres, at rentals of £3,500 and £2,500 per annum, whereupon I released him from his liability for the £6,000 I had advanced him. On the security of these leases I was enabled to raise a few thousands from time to time, so I continued to struggle on as well as I could.

" In 1876, however, there was a momentary gleam of sunshine. I made £20,000 net profit in six months !

" ' The Shaughraun ' at Drury Lane with Boucicault, and ' Rip Van Winkle,' with Jefferson at the Princess's, filled these houses nightly. The Adelphi held its own with ' Notre Dame ' until we transferred ' The Shaughraun ' there, upon the production of the Pantomime at the Lane.

" For the brief space of a few weeks I enjoyed the supreme felicity of being the manager of the three most successful theatres in London. The money literally poured in, but Boucicault had his usual facility for making things pleasant.

" Was ' The Shaughraun ' a success ?

" ' Well, yes, comparatively so ; but not sufficiently successful to pay for the continual anxieties and irritations it entailed.'

" During our rehearsals, the lady who was to play Moya ' dried up ' at the last moment. We had to induce Mrs. Boucicault to play the part, and as there were domestic dissensions going on, which ripened into an open rupture soon afterwards, the operation required a good deal of delicate diplomacy.

" There was a capital house the first night, and on the second, Saturday, we went up to £360.

"You remember how admirably Boucicault played Conn, and how handsome the fellow looked. Well, one night Falconer came round after the play to see me, and while discussing some matter of business, Boucicault came into my room.

"He was denuded of his hyacinthine locks (of course you know that his head is as bald as a billiard-ball), and he had an atrabilious look, as if he had just ate something which didn't agree with him. The rival dramatists accosted each other with more courtesy than cordiality; indeed, if they were cordial in anything, it was in their dislike to each other. The success of ' The Shaughraun ' was worm-wood to the author of ' Peep o' Day;' so, taking stock of Boucicault's cadaverous mug, Falconer said :

"'Ah, Dion, how well *you* look *on* the stage !'

"'Yes,' replied the other ; ' and how well *you* look *off* it !'

"As long as the business kept up, Boucicault was very pleasant ; but as soon as it fell off, he showed his teeth. He endeavoured to persuade me to run ' The Shaughraun ' through the Pantomime season. When he found that I did not seem to see it, he said to Edward Stirling :

"'Tell Chatterton that I can't have my baby strangled by his beastly Pantomime ; and unless he can take "The Shaughraun" to the Adelphi at Christmas, I shall take the Queen's, and transfer the piece there.'

"Of course this was something like putting a loaded pistol to my head; but 'needs must when' Dion drives, that is, if he has the whip-hand. So it was arranged for him to go to the Adelphi for six months, beginning on Boxing-night.

"I was engrossed up to my ears with the Pantomime at the Lane, but every day, and almost every hour, brought me news of wars, and rumours of wars, from the Adelphi. Boucicault had the stage entirely to himself, and after his fashion made it hot for everybody. Beverley's scenery was not good enough. Imagine Beverley not good enough for Boucicault! He insisted on new scenery, and got it too. Then Rose Leclerq, who had played Claire Ffolliot at the Lane, was too mature and majestic for the Adelphi, and Fanny Josephs was engaged instead, and Sam Emery (the best character actor on the stage) was not good enough for that jackeen, Mr. Corry Kinchela!

"On Boxing-night Boucicault said 'he thought that he was going to be supported by artistes, not by barn-stormers.' Needless to say that this and other complimentary references to the company and the management were repeated to me, doubtless with additions.

"That night a modest American, whom he employed to represent him, came round behind the scenes at the Lane, and actually while I was engaged in superintending the transformation scene, said in the most airy manner, 'I wish to speak to you, Mr. Chatterton.'

" ' When the transformation scene is over I am at your service, sir,' I replied.

" ' Guess I must wait, then,' said the Yankee.

" ' I guess you must !' said I.

" When the scene was over, I led the way to my room, and desired the gentleman from America to fire away.

" 'Well, sir,' said he, ' Mr. Boucicault is very dissatisfied with the arrangements, both before and behind the scenes, at the Adelphi, and he desires to cancel the engagement at once. I hope you perceive, Mr. Chatterton, that I have a disagreeable duty to perform !'

" ' I do perceive it, sir,' said I, ' and I must do you the justice to say that you perform it as disagreeably as it can be performed. Go to Mr. Boucicault, and tell him I am even more dissatisfied than he is, and I shall be very glad to cancel the engagement in a month from this date.'

" Next day Dion wrote, acceding to this proposal.

" During the whole month we never exchanged one word, good, bad, or indifferent, with each other.

" The country was in a state of commotion about the Fenian business, and Boucicault, to improve the occasion, wrote a letter to Dizzy (who was then Prime Minister) demanding, in the name of the Irish nation, and in that of the author of ' The Shraughraun,' the release of the prisoners then under sentence for treason-felony.

" He did not, however, make much out of the Asian mystery-man, who neither noticed Boucicault nor his letter.

" Charley Kenney certainly said that one evening, at Lady Waldegrave's, Boucicault's name was mentioned, and Dizzy, turning round to Monty Corry, his secretary, said : ' Boucicault ! Strange name ; I think I've heard it before. Is it someone in the conjuring business ?'

" I think, however, this is too good to be true, and was one of those sweet things that Kenney was always improvising for the good of his friends. Be that as it may, this miserable business, which commenced in farce, ended in tragedy, and tragedy of the most terrible kind.

" Boucicault inserted sensational advertisements in the newspapers on his own hook, and to checkmate him, I inserted others ; so our quarrel was a good thing for the papers.

" At the beginning of the last week he said to my acting manager :

" ' Saturday is my last night, and I should like a little demonstration, merely such a demonstration as an artiste has a right to expect on such an occasion. I therefore request that the pit, gallery, and upper circle, may not be overcrowded. Issue fifty tickets less than the usual number in each part of the house, and debit me with the deficit !'

" Of course my man immediately communicated with me on the subject. I smelt a rat, and, having ascertained that the greater portion of the boxes and stalls had been taken by Boucicault's friends, I reserved the remainder for my own.

" In point of fact, I anticipated a scene, a seditious speech, and an organized demonstration against the Government, to enable Dion to make his exit to America amidst a blaze of fireworks. Being fore-warned, I resolved to be forearmed, and took my measures accordingly.

" Sending for Jack, my 'packer,' I desired him to get me a hundred of his 'bull-dogs' for Saturday night. Next, I sent for my friend P., the builder, and arranged with him to let me have a hundred of his men. Then I got another friend, upon whom I could rely, to bring fifty Lillie Bridge athletes. It was arranged that each contingent was to be at the doors at three o'clock on Saturday afternoon. Every man was to be provided with a ticket, and to be paid eighteenpence each besides. They had explicit in-structions not to interfere with the play or the players, but if a cry arose for 'a speech,' they were to shout it down ; and if the Boucicault faction proved obstreperous at the last extremity, heads were to be punched, as gently as possible ; but still they were to be punched ; 'not too much punching, but just punching enough.'

" When the curtain rose, the house was crowded, the audience fervid and demonstrative.

" At the end of the first act there was a double call, and a laurel wreath, with green ribbons, was cast at Boucicault's feet.

" At the end of the second act, he was called

for again and again, and pelted with sham-rocks.

"At nine o'clock I arrived. I had barely got inside the theatre when an inspector of police came up. The man was pale and livid, and could scarcely gasp out his awful intelligence.

"There had been an accident on the Great Northern Railway, near Huntingdon, in which poor Willie, Boucicault's eldest son, had been killed. The news knocked the breath out of my body.

"'Good God!' I exclaimed, 'how is the father to know it?'

"'Don't trouble about that, sir,' said the inspector; 'I'll go and tell him.' And the man was actually bolting round to the stage-door to blurt out the fatal news there and then, had I not seized and muzzled him. One thing was quite certain, the tidings must be kept back from Dion and his wife till they got home. So, giving imperative orders that no stranger was to be permitted behind the scenes, I made my way on to the stage, where, the very moment I entered, I encountered Boucicault face to face.

"He accosted me somewhat defiantly with:

"'So you've turned up at last!'

"'Yes; I've come to do honour to the occasion,' I replied.

"I had a bad time of it for the next hour, for I had to keep up a smiling face, and try to talk upon indifferent subjects, thinking all the while of how the news was to be broken.

"Willie was the apple of his father's eye. If

there was one human being Dion Boucicault loved in the world besides himself, it was that poor boy.

"At last, with the end of the play, and the customary calls and recalls, came a roar from Boucicault's partizans : 'Boucicault! Speech! Speech!'

"This was responded to by a counter-roar from my myrmidons of 'No! No! Chatterton!'

"I remained in the prompt entrance, prepared for all emergencies. At last the uproar in front culminated in a tumult, during which it seemed as if the house was coming down about our ears.

"Boucicault, who had gone to his dressing-room, came down, and meeting my stage-manager, remarked in the most ingenuous manner :

"'Dear, dear! This is dreadful! Where is Chatterton?'

"'There,' replied the stage-manager, pointing me out ; whereupon Dion came up and inquired :

"'Don't you think I'd better go on?'

"'No,' said I sturdily ; 'I don't think anything of the kind!'

"'I really must!' said he.

"'You really mustn't,' said I.

"'But they'll tear the house down!'

"'It's my house, not yours ; so that's my lookout!'

"'By G——! I will go on!' snarled Boucicault savagely.

"'Then you'll have to walk over my body first ; and when you've done that my carpenters have their orders to prevent your going on. Now look here'

said I, 'let's talk common-sense; you've had your
little innings; you've had all the compliments, all
the honours any actor or author can desire, but your
engagement is over; you're out of it, and I'm boss
of the show; so it's "no good kicking against the
pricks!"'

"With that we glared at each other. Then there
was a lull in the storm in front. After a minute's
reflection he simmered down, and said in his pleasantest manner:

"'Very well; come to my room, have a glass of
wine, and let us shake hands, anyhow.'

"So that difficulty was tided over, but 'the
greatest was behind.'

"Dion was now at his best, and was as jolly as
he could be; and when he is jolly, he is one of the
pleasantest fellows breathing. Mrs. Boucicault was,
as she always is, charming. The difficulty was how
to tell them of their bereavement.

"I was unequal to the task, and so I left them.
When I got on the stage, my man told me that our
family physician, Dr. R., and Boucicault's brother
William were both in front of the house.

"I went round and told them what had occurred
as well as I could. We then arranged for William
Boucicault to get Dion home, and the doctor kindly
undertook to be in waiting at Langham Place to
break the sad intelligence.

"Ill news spreads apace, and I found, on returning
to the stage, Miss Foote and Mrs. Edmund Phelps
crying bitterly, and waiting to descend with their

JOHN BROUGHAM.

condolences on the poor mother when she came out
of her dressing-room ; but I bundled both the ladies
out of the theatre, for which, of course, I was put
down as an unsympathetic brute !

" I had a cab waiting at the royal entrance in
Maiden Lane, and when Mrs. Boucicault came
downstairs, I packed her into it, saying that Dion
had gone home and wished to see her immediately.
She turned pale, and looked dubiously at me.
' There's nothing wrong, Mr. Chatterton—nothing
about W— Willie ?' she inquired.

" I hadn't the heart to tell her, so I said, ' Nothing
particular, only Dion has a friend or two to supper,
and he wants you at once.'

" With that she drove off.

" She would know the news soon enough—too
soon.

" Poor little woman ! it was a sad thing for her,
sadder for her than anyone.

" How futile and puerile seemed all our miserable
quarrels in the presence of this calamity !

" God knows how the father and mother passed
that night ! I only know I never closed my eyes
till morning, for thinking of the poor lad that lay
dead at Huntingdon.

" After the brief spell of good-luck, during which
I netted £20,000, things took a turn for the bad,
and from bad they got to worse.

" The three theatres were too much for me. It
had taken me years to crawl up the hill at snail's

pace ; I came down with a rush in half the time. Day and night were passed in cabs oscillating 'twixt the Lane, the Strand, and Oxford Street. However badly I did at the Adelphi or the Princess's, I generally contrived to make both ends meet at the Lane, but at last even old Drury began to fail me.

"My first false step was another quarrel with Phelps, who always had a large and certain popular following. My next was to engage Rossi and Co. to oppose Salvini, when you had him at the Queen's. The result was most disastrous ; we played down to £14 and even £12 a night, with stalls at a guinea. My third big blunder was a great get-up of 'Richard III.' to oppose your 'Henry V.'; with this we played down to £18, and there was a loss of nearly £6,000 on the production.

"To make matters better, Mapleson, who had for some years taken the theatre during my vacation for the Italian Opera, threw me over, and went to Covent Garden.

"The pantomime was not so successful as usual, so with the view of recouping myself, I produced on Easter Monday a new play by Mr. Henry Spicer (author of 'The Lords of Ellingham '), called 'Haska.'

"A manager has no right to indulge in either sentiment or superstition ; but the truth is, I was a little influenced by both feelings when I undertook to produce ' Haska.'

"You recollect my telling you of my boyish experience at the Cabinet, when I cleared nine shillings by playing young Farningham, and how this

fluke first directed my thoughts towards management. **Well, when Mr. Spicer** proposed in the most
liberal manner to put down £1,000 towards **the**
production of his new drama, I jumped at the proposal, being impressed with the idea **that it** would
retrieve my fortunes.

" This **play** was **the** subject **of** the shortest and
quickest Chancery suit on record.

" A few days before its production, it transpired
that before arranging with me, Spicer had authorized
Ryder and Greenwood to negotiate with **a** third
party. **They had the** MS. in their custody for some
time, and as they **made** no sign, **he** naturally concluded the matter had fallen through, whereas, when
we made our announcements, they intimated that
they had entered into a previous arrangement for **its**
production by a Persian lady of remarkable beauty,
calling herself Madame Zuleika, and said to **be** the
daughter of our Ambassador **at the** Court **of**
Teheran.

" The play was to be produced upon a certain
Saturday. On the Wednesday before, this lady
issued **a writ** against Spicer and myself, and served
me with notice of motion to be heard on Thursday,
for an injunction restraining me from producing the
play. The injunction was granted by Vice-Chancellor
Bacon. Next morning, Friday, I went to the Court
of Appeal, and obtained permission to appeal the
following day. On Saturday morning the Vice-
Chancellor's decision was reversed by the Lords
Justices, so you see there was a Chancery suit begun

and ended in four days, and 'Haska' was actually acted that night!

"Unfortunately my presages of success were not fulfilled, and Spicer, who had parted with his £1,000 like a man, seeing a succession of wretched houses, suggested the withdrawal of the piece at the end of the first fortnight.

"I replied, 'No, sir; you have behaved like a prince, and the piece shall go for the month, whatever be the result. Besides, you are not aware that it is in some measure through you that I am now manager of this theatre.'

"With that I told him the history of the performance of 'The Lords of Ellingham' at the Cabinet Theatre six-and-twenty years before.

"'Haska' was a disastrous speculation for both of us, for besides Mr. Spicer's £1,000, I lost £1,500 more on the month's run.

"Finding it impossible to get on with the three theatres, I got rid of the Princess's upon equitable terms to Mr. Walter Gooch, and I disposed of the lease of the Adelphi Theatre for the sum of £12,000 to the Messrs. Gatti.

"Webster in the meantime, however, instituted an action to set aside the leases, alleging that he did not know the contents of the deed under which I released him from payment of the £6,000 he owed me. His case, however, entirely broke down, and judgment was entered for me without my counsel having been even called upon!

"This was the last of my serious lawsuits.

Apropos of which, it has been alleged that this law
business was in great measure the cause of my
coming to grief. This was simple nonsense. In
nearly every instance I gained my causes; besides
which I had my brother to look after my interests,
and to keep me out of litigation if it were possible to
avoid it.

" The real cause of my downfall was having three
theatres when I ought to have been content with
one, that one, too, the first, the finest, and the
cheapest in the world.

" In '77 we opened with an adaptation of
' Peveril of the Peak,' by Wills, which was a direful
failure.

" I have often been accused, and with justice, I
admit (it is easy to be wise after the event!), of being
irascible, and with making use of strong language.

" There are things, however, which might make
even a saint forget himself, and here is a case or two
in point :

" When we were about to produce this precious
' Peveril of the Peak,' a lady belonging to a distinguished histrionic family, the name of which she
inherited, without a scintillation of its ability, wrote
for an engagement. Upon telegraphing for her
terms, her husband (one of those noble youths who
live on their wives' earnings) wired back, naming
£200 a week as her modest stipend.

" Considering that I only paid the first of living
actors £60 a week, this was more than I could
stomach ; and I replied to the gallant son of Nep-

tune, 'Make it shillings, and consider the matter settled.'

" Needless to say that I made a friend of that gentleman and his *cara sposa* for the rest of my life.

"At or about this very time, when I was in a 'sea of troubles,' a fellow like a groom stalked into my sanctum, announcing himself, after the fashion of the Claimant, as an officer and a gentleman, and a ' Bart. of G.B.'

" Upon inquiring his business, the gallant youth told me he wanted an engagement. Upon inquiring what parts he played, he replied, 'Charley Mathews' line;' but he continued with becoming modesty, 'Charley isn't in it with me, you know.'

" ' Very likely,' I replied, ' very ; but may I take the liberty to ask where you have acted ?'

" ' I have not acted yet in public ; but I have had considerable experience in regimental theatricals, amongst swell people, at country houses,' he ingenuously replied.

" ' How about terms ?'

" ' Well,' he said, ' I shouldn't require more than a guarantee of sixty pounds a night, and a share of the expenses.'

" ' Precisely—I see. You'll pay *me* sixty pounds a night, and guarantee *my* expenses !'

" The 'Bart. of G.B.' didn't see the joke, and retired, protesting that I was ' no gentleman.'

" These are two instances only out of thousands which are constantly occurring. It is scarcely to be

wondered at, that a man should occasionally lose his
temper, when pestered by gad-flies like these.

" In '78 I got a new lease of the theatre, and
arranged to open with a big get-up of ' The Winter's
Tale.' Phelps and I had once more buried the
hatchet. I was in hopes that he might have been
strong enough to play his farewell engagement,
which would have pulled us through triumphantly.
Our negotiations, however, came to nothing, and I
engaged Charles Dillon in his place.

" The newspaper folk came down upon him like a
load of bricks. When they do agree, the unanimity of
these gentlemen is wonderful. Why they ' went for '
Dillon, I don't know, for he was certainly the best
Leontes of this generation. The cast was a strong
one, including Mrs. Hermann Vezin, Miss Wallis,
Miss Fowler, Ryder, Cowper, Compton, Calhaem,
Edgar, Russell, etc. Then we had Beverly's
scenery ; but the piece was a failure, and we had
to get it out of the bills as soon as possible.

" Up to this time, I had been flattered to ' the top
of my bent.' Whatever I said or did was right.

"' To say ay, and no,' to everything I said. ' Ay, and no,' too, was
no good divinity,'

as I now found to my cost.

" The news of my losses had got buzzed abroad,
and my credit was seriously compromised. The
rats began to desert the sinking ship, and we were
drifting on the rocks.

" Hitherto my successful flukes had been pro-

nounced marvels of managerial sagacity.   My over-
flow of bile had been attributed to the eccentricities of
genius.   Now, my failures were due to my 'darned'
ignorance   and   my   'blarmed'   presumption—my
outbursts of temper to my ungovernable brutality !

   " I had been a rough diamond ; I was an untutored
savage !

   " These things had never been discovered during
my prosperity ; but now that adversity had set in,
instead of being the most liberal of managers and
the best of good fellows, I was the most rapacious
of hard task-masters, the most atrabilious of ruffians.

   " When I found these rumours in the air, I knew
that the end could not be doubtful.   My losses up
to Christmas were over £7,000.   Nothing but a
triumphantly successful pantomime could save me.
For the first time during my management of the Lane
the pantomime was a miserable failure.   The cause
was not far to seek.   There was a certain troupe of
pantomimists whom, for years, to the detriment of
everyone else, I had made the all-absorbing feature
of my Christmas fare.   For years I had kept them
on, at continually increasing salaries, until at length
they became paramount.   Their ability was unques-
tionable ; but the truth is, they were played out, and
their attraction was over.

   " When, for the first time in all my career, I was
unable to meet my salaries on Saturday, these
worthy people were the very first to strike ; and it
was principally through their action that the theatre
closed at a moment's notice, and hundreds of people

were thrown out of bread. After this, a meeting of the company was called, the result of which was thus described in a letter to the papers by my friend and faithful adherent—the great painter, William Beverly:

"'THE CLOSING OF DRURY LANE THEATRE.

"'TO THE EDITOR OF THE " DAILY NEWS."

"' SIR,

"' Having been connected with the Theatre Royal, Drury Lane, for a great number of years, you will perhaps permit me to say a few words on the sudden closing of the theatre. I have, I am sorry to say, suffered from the troubles of a theatre more than once, and therefore I certainly am a pretty good judge of what takes place under such circumstances. There is such a thing as a sailor's love for his ship, and I believe there is a good deal of the same sort of feeling with the actor for his theatre. I am quite sure, with the exception of three or four persons, at the large meeting held on the stage of Drury Lane, that everyone felt sorrow for the good ship Drury, and lamented that she had suddenly bumped on a rock. Her complement of men, women, and children would gladly have set to work with a will to get her off again; they all agreed to short commons and less grog for a week or two, with the exception of three or four grumblers. At the end of three weeks the programme would have been played out, and the public have had fair warning that the old ship must be laid up for repairs.

With one voice the large meeting agreed to stand by her. They required no time for consideration; their own credit and that of the ship was at stake. This was no matter of help to Mr. Chatterton; the captain was overboard, and too far away for help; but help to all the smaller dependents of the immense establishment; and what was it asked? A reduction of income for a week or two from Mr. —— and his sisters. I am a much greater sufferer than this family by my connection with Drury Lane. If we all acted on the principle of Shylock—his bond, and pound of flesh—what would become of the well-known sympathy and brotherly love shown by the theatrical profession for all cases of distress? If just before Christmas I had produced my bond, and pointed with my brush to the pound of flesh, and said, " I will have it ;" or, in the hateful word of the present day, "I strike!' there could have been no pantomime! I must be forgiven for this piece of egotism; I only speak of it to show there are some who look a little beyond self in this world. I finish these remarks by saying that this is the first time I have ever known an instance when a sudden disaster came upon a large establishment that any of the important people ever refused to help for a time, to prevent so large a number of dependent workers being thrown out of employment.

" ' I remain, with much respect,

" ' Your obedient servant,

" ' W. R. Beverly.

" ' 26, Russell Square,

" ' Feb. 15, 1879.'

"At this period my liabilities were great ; but so they had been before, and I had retrieved everything—as I might have done again, with time and opportunity ; but I could get neither. And so it came to pass **that the** management, during **which I** had through every vicissitude of fortune paid my way, and upheld the dignity of the National Theatre, was brought to an abrupt and ignominious termination.

" It doesn't bear to think of. ' That way madness lies !' Yet let me be just. There is a great deal of good knocking about of which the world knows nothing. Here is a case in point. When the crash came there was **a sum of** £200 due to the public who had booked their seats in advance at the box-office. Not to repay this would have been infamy. In desperation I went **to** my bankers, Ransom and Bouverie (to whom I was already heavily indebted for a very considerable over-draft), and told them exactly how I was situated. In the most gracious manner Mr. Pleydell Bouverie patted me on the shoulder, and said, ' You shall have the two hundred pounds, old fellow, and we hope to see you soon on your legs again !' As Mark Twain would say, ' I went away.' Yes, I went away without a word. My heart was too full for words just then ; but I know my eyes told what my tongue couldn't speak.

" And now for more goodness—from a quarter where I had the least right to expect it.

" Within eight-and-forty hours of the closing at

Drury Lane a meeting was called at Covent Garden
Theatre, where the utmost sympathy was expressed
for my misfortunes.   A subscription list was opened,
which Messrs. Gatti, the then proprietors of the
theatre, headed with fifty guineas—with the result
that a fund of £300 was there and then formed for
my family, besides which, the Gattis gave me the
gratuitous use of the theatre for a benefit, at which
all the leading actors in town appeared.

"A meeting of creditors was then called.   The
bulk of them proved most considerate—some more
than others.   I shall never forget one—Mr. Moses—
from whom I had frequently borrowed money.   I
had always repaid him with large interest until this
period, when, unfortunately, I owed him £1,000.
He came to the meeting, and with tears in his eyes
handed in his proof to my lawyer.

"'Take this—give it to Chatterton,' said he.
'Tell him, if I had it, he should have ten times as
much; but, anyhow, if ever he wants a fiver or a
tenner, he knows where to find Ike Moses.'

"The poor fellow died a few weeks after.   Just
my luck!

"Well, I received my order of discharge, and was
once more a free man, and was not altogether without hopes of getting a renewal of my lease at Drury
Lane.   At the time of my collapse the proprietors
had in hand a deposit of £1,500 to secure payment
of the rent, and although no rent was actually due
when we closed, they at once claimed the deposit as
forfeited.   Having taken the opinion of counsel, to

the effect that such a forfeiture was illegal, my trustee commenced proceedings to recover the £1,500.

"When I tendered for a new lease I was met with an intimation that it was impossible to entertain my proposal so long as this action was pending, but that if I could induce the trustee to withdraw it, the aspect of affairs would be entirely changed.

"Accordingly, I saw him, and by pointing out the uncertainties of litigation, and promising to make good the amount to the estate hereafter, I induced him to withdraw the action.

"No sooner, however, had he done so than the committee immediately let the theatre to the present lessee, of whom I may say, without disparaging either his enterprise or ability (both of which are indisputable), that at that time he was entirely unknown as a manager, and had no moral claim whatever on the proprietors, whereas I had been associated with the theatre for a space of sixteen years, during which I had paid for rent alone a sum of something like £80,000 : besides which, I had paid a considerably larger sum than that for repairs, decorations, scenery, properties, etc., yet, thanks to the magnanimity of this irresponsible proprietary body, after all my trials and struggles I was left high and dry without a shilling !

"What I should have done at this crisis of my fortunes—or rather my misfortunes—had it not been for the generosity of the Gattis, I don't know.

"I have already told you that they gave me

£12,000 for the lease of the Adelphi. This, of course, was a stroke of business, and I'm glad to find it has turned out a good stroke for them.

"It was not business, however, which induced them to lend—or rather to give—me £500 to enable me to struggle through the last season at the Lane, and it was sheer goodness of heart which prompted them to head my subscription list with fifty guineas, to proffer the gratuitous use of the theatre for my benefit, and finally to rehabilitate me by making me their manager, and putting me at the head of affairs at Covent Garden the next season !

"Our pantomime there made a great mark, and we should doubtless have done big business had it not been for the dreadful snow-storm, which ruined half the managers in town and country. Doubtless you remember ; half a dozen West End theatres were closed at a moment's notice in consequence of the streets being impassable.

"Circumstances in connection with my complimentary benefit at the end of this season led to a rupture with the Gattis which I have never ceased to deplore.

"It is a simple act of justice to them to say that a more liberal, large-hearted pair of men I have never met.

"Nor was I indebted to their generosity alone, for Irving gave me the Lyceum, and everything in it, for my benefit during this season ; and, as usual, all the actors of note acted, and amongst them they made me a present of upwards of £500.

"Of late it has been the fashion to institute injurious comparisons between my management and that of certain other managers ; but common honesty might have suggested to some of my detractors that it would have been only ordinarily decent to bear in mind the fact that all, or nearly all, of the celebrities of **to-day were** yesterday members of my company. There is scarcely a representative manager or actor in the highest department of art who has not served in the rank and file of my company. Look at the names! There were Helen Faucit, Lilian Neilson, Miss Wallis, Miss Caroline Heath, Mrs. Hermann Vezin, Madge Robertson (Mrs. Kendal), Miss Amy Sedgwick, Miss Atkinson, **Miss W**oolgar, Madame Celeste, Madame Ristori, Lydia Foote, Edith Stewart, Mrs. Frank Matthews, Miss Poole, Carlotta and Rose Leclercq, Fanny Josephs, Jenny Bauer, Miss Hudspeth, Mrs. Howard Paul, Mrs. Billington, Miss Edith Wynn, Miss Emily Cross, Rebecca Isaacs, Madame **Fanny** Huddart, Phelps, James Anderson, Walter Montgomery, Barry Sullivan, Creswick, T. C. King, the Boucicaults, Fechter, Jefferson, Ben Webster, Charles Dillon, Ryder, Walter Lacy, Sims Reeves, Salvini, Rossi, Swinbourne, William Beverly, Bob Roxby, Tom Powrie, the Webbs, Vezin, George Belmore, Henry Marston, Addison, Paddy Barrett, Wilson Barrett, James Fernandez, Cowper, Clayton, Howard Russell, Fitzjames, W. Terriss, William Harrison, Henry Drayton, Charles Harcourt, Charles Warner, David Fisher, Harry Sinclair, W. McIntyre, Calhaem,

Sam Emery, J. B. Howard, and last, not least, Henry Irving ; in point of fact, with the single exception of yourself, every actor of the poetic drama has served under my banner.

"My dead authors were Shakespeare, Milton, Byron, Göethe, Richard Brinsley Sheridan, Sheridan Knowles, Bulwer and George Colman. My living ones were Boucicault, Edmund Falconer, Bayle Bernard, Tom Taylor, H. Spicer, Andrew Halliday, W. G. Wills, E. L. Blanchard, Byron, and Victor Hugo. Now I should like to know any manager since Macready who has a better muster-roll to show !

"By an extraordinary coincidence, at or about the very period of my collapse at the Lane, Phelps collapsed at the Imperial.

"He had been connected with my first associations at the Wells—with almost my last at old Drury.

"Although his reputation was established before mine commenced, yet it was through my aid it reached its zenith.

"When his star was in the ascendant in the west, mine rose with it ; and when we parted, good fortune and I parted company.

"He is happy, for he is dead ; but his name and his work will live after him, but I fear mine will be forgotten. . . . . .

"You are very good to say so, but I can't deceive myself. I feel that I am almost forgotten already,

HENRY IRVING.

and the knowledge is hard to bear, for after all, for twenty years the record of my career, with all my faults, with all my errors of judgment (God knows they are only errors, for I always did the best according to my lights!), forms part and parcel of the history of the English drama in this century.

"Thanks! No more. Good-night."

So far Mr. Chatterton's story, which was here interrupted by his last fatal illness.

Before continuing the narrative, it appears desirable to point out what is the most remarkable fact in connection with his career.

Until his advent no lessee, since the time of Sheridan, has ever ruled over Drury Lane for a longer period than seven years.

The Committee held sway over the new theatre for six years; Elliston's management extended over seven years; Bunn's, six years; Macready's famous management lasted only two years; Anderson's two; and E. T. Smith's, six years; so that, in point of fact, the unfortunate Chatterton's tenure absolutely lasted as long as the entire term covered by the lesseeships of Bunn, Macready, Anderson, and E. T. Smith.

The year after he left Covent Garden, yielding to bad advice, Chatterton was unfortunately induced to tempt fortune again by embarking in management at Sadler's Wells Theatre. The result was most disastrous. The receipts at no period of the season ever approached half the expenses. Nor was this the worst.   As there was no capital to work upon, the productions were of such a character as to be absolutely ruinous to his reputation.

I well remember going down to Islington with Robert Buchanan to see the pantomime.   It was, I think, the saddest sight I have ever witnessed.   An empty house, and a shabby, tawdry show which would have discredited a respectable barn.

I could not help recalling the splendours of Drury Lane, and contrasting them with this " thing of shreds and patches."

We went round to see him, and found him profoundly depressed.   It was quite evident that he had reached the bottom of the hill.

A few days later the theatre closed abruptly.

It was here his career commenced, and here it virtually ended.

So much for the manager, now for the man.

De mortuis nil nisi bonum is a just as well as a generous axiom ; all, therefore, that befits a friend to say in this relation is that, wilful, irascible, and wrong-headed as Frederick Balsir Chatterton often was in the days of his prosperity, he was always large-hearted and benevolent.   Bad temper and false pride were his weak points ; kindness and generosity were his strong ones.

His bad qualities arose from defective early training ; his good ones from the natural promptings of a heart that

" Was open as day to melting charity."

He was not only a most affectionate father, but
a most lavish one, whilst throughout his career he
never personally indulged in any greater extravagance than was involved in the hire of a hansom
cab. He allowed his children to enjoy all the
luxuries which his station at that time justified. He
was, however, particularly careful to instil into their
minds that his position was a precarious one, and
that it behoved them to take advantage of the
educational facilities placed at their disposal, so that
in the event of any reverse of fortune they might
be enabled to hold their own in the world. Incredible as it may appear to those who only knew him
superficially, he had a deep sense of religion, and
for many years, while his children were yet quite
young, he not only accompanied them to church,
but upon occasions when the weather did not permit
of this, he read the Church service to them in his
own dining-room. In his home, which (until misfortune overtook him) was at the " Hawthorns,"
Clapham Road, it could be seen at a glance that
the owner was a man of taste and refinement.
There was no gaudy, ostentatious display of wealth,
but he had a great love for pictures and musical
instruments. For music he maintained his attach-
ment to the last, and would frequently sit for hours
beside his daughter, while she practised the harp,
and suggest the light and shade which his critical
ear told him would add to the effect. For many
years he possessed a vigorous constitution, which
unfortunately he abused from too much confidence

in his strength, which resulted ultimately in the break-up of his nervous system. Until this calamity occurred he was a man of indomitable energy.

His favourite maxim was, " Never hurt a man a little ;" and another, " The whole man to one thing at a time."

He had a contempt for shams, and a keen appreciation of whatever was either artistic or beautiful ; added to which he was of a sociable, lovable, though a wild, unconquerable nature, and though opinions may differ upon many traits of his character, none could deny that he was essentially a *man.*

I might cite a hundred instances of his impulsive generosity. Having observed on a certain occasion that a distinguished Hibernian member of the orchestra was " fou," Chatterton sent for him to the treasury, with the intention of dismissing him there and then. Before he could open fire with those verbal missiles which he was but too wont to scatter recklessly on the slightest provocation, the poor fellow intervened with :

" Howld hard, guv'nor ! Shure I know I desarve all I get and more, but whin I tell yez that my boy, my only one, is lying dying at home wid the fayver, while I'm thrying to tickle this infernal catgut, you'll not be too hard on a poor divil because he tuk the dhrop to drown the throuble of his heart."

" That'll do," roared Chatterton ; " not another word. Here ! take this to the missis," thrusting a five-pound note in his hand. " Be off and jump into the first hansom, and get home as fast as you can."

The great **tie of family was** always predominant with him.

Meeting me **one** day when **he was at** the height of his prosperity, he burst out :

" **My** father is dying ! You know how much he likes you, and he takes **to** few people ; for God's sake go and see him, **if only** for **five** minutes ; it will be a gleam **of** sunshine **to** the old **man."**

His devotion to his mother, too, was **very** touching **and beautiful.** Looking **over** the **old** lady's papers a few days after her death, her youngest son, Horace, discovered one which she had never trusted **out** of her **sight.** She preserved **it to** the last, as though **it were a** talisman. **It was** dated thirty years back and **ran thus** :

" MY DEAR MOTHER,

"The idea of your being without **money** makes me unhappy, so please accept the enclosed ten-pound note, with best love, **from**

" YOUR LITTLE BOY."

The reader will doubtless remember Chatterton's early preceptor and music-master, Mr. Aspull. This good **old** man fell into misfortune, was left alone in the world, **and** from some cause or other was unable to follow his profession as teacher of music.

Chatterton came **to** the rescue, and made him his private secretary (almost **a** sinecure, as all the actual work was done by **a** junior clerk) ; and when, at **a** later period, the poor musician became incapable of

fulfilling even these nominal duties, his quondam
pupil took him to his own home, where he tended
him as if he had been his father, till in the fulness
of time the old man died, with his last breath
invoking blessings on his benefactor.

Chatterton was wont to say that, in the moments
of his deepest adversity, the recollection of that
parting benediction was an ever-present consolation
to him.

For some time after the fiasco at Sadler's Wells,
he earned a precarious livelihood by giving readings
from Dickens with more or less success.

Apart from considerable dramatic aptitude and
power of individualizing character, these recitals were
feats of memory of a remarkable character.   He
recited the whole book of " The Christmas Carol "
without even a note to refer to.

Through all his life his memory had been phenomenal.   How he got at his facts and figures no
one ever knew, since he never kept a diary.   While
engaged in large financial operations (he rarely
turned over less than £100,000 per annum) he
never by any chance forgot the maturity of an
acceptance.   He was death on dates, and could tell
with infallible accuracy the exact period of every
notable occurrence from the time of the flood downward.

It was always his impression that he had mistaken his vocation, and that nature meant him to
have been a great actor ; so he avenged himself

upon the inappreciative public by teaching other
people to act.

Amongst his pupils he had **two or** three clergy-
men, and two **or** three members of Parliament.
His efforts in this direction were, however, **con-**
tinually impeded by the inroads of ill-health. He
was a martyr to rheumatism, from which every
nerve in his body suffered. Even his eyes were not
exempt.

My engagements having taken me into the pro-
vinces, I had lost sight of him **for** a considerable
time, when, about four years ago, **I** found him in
humble lodgings **in the** Strand. He was almost
totally blind from rheumatism **in** the eyes, was
racked with excruciating pains, **and** was thoroughly
disheartened; indeed, utterly broken down. Even
then his pride remained invulnerable. **He** might
have found **a** home with every comfort **at** his
brother's house, but he elected to stay where he was

Upon ascertaining the state of the land, I took
upon myself to consult with his friends as to the
propriety of his taking a benefit. The urgency of
the **case** admitted of **no** delay, and in less than
a week all the necessary arrangements were made.

Mr. Augustus Harris kindly conceded the use of
Drury Lane Theatre; nearly all the managers and
actors in town gave their services, and the public
responded with a rush. The receipts, at popular
prices, reached nearly £500; and I believe I am
not in **error** when I state that the pit and gallery

receipts were, upon that occasion, if not the largest, certainly amongst the largest, recorded in the annals of Drury Lane.

This genial recognition on the part of the public impressed him with the sense that he was not wholly forgotten, and it had a wonderful effect upon his health and spirits.

I really thought that he had taken a new lease of life ; but the fillip was only temporary, for he was soon again prostrated by illness.

After an interval of nearly twelve months, he began to make arrangements for the annual benefit on which he was now compelled to rely for actual subsistence for himself and family.

It is bootless to enlarge upon the succession of disappointments, mortifications, and humiliations which attended his efforts on this occasion ; it is enough to say that, preying upon an enfeebled con-stitution, they accelerated the end.

To many of his brothers in art he was indebted for much sympathy, and he was never weary of dilating on their kindness ; but all were not alike, and he was keenly, too keenly, alive to the semblance of an indignity.

Previous to the final breakdown, he wrote me on January 28th, 1886, thus :

" I have been confined to the house since Monday with bronchitis. . . . . Enclosed is a list of some of the free benefits given under my management at Drury Lane."

This list was as follows :

Paul Bedford (2).	Horace Wigan.'	Edmund Falconer.
Webb Children.	Benjamin Webster.	Hospital Saturday.
Theatrical **Fund (2).**	J. B. Buckstone.	Mrs. A. Mellon.
Surrey Fire.	W. H. Compton.	Belmore Children.
Mrs. Liston (2).	J. Fitzjames.	H.M.S. *Captain.*
Dramatic College (3).	Pavilion Fire.	Chicago Fire.
Alfred Wigan.	Leigh **Murray.**	American Relief Fund.

After this attack he rallied a little, and on Saturday, February 6th, was well enough to come and dine at my house.

He was then suffering from an alarming attack of laryngitis, the distressing effects of which were but too painfully apparent.

At the beginning of the evening he was very much depressed and out of sorts, but while actually engaged over a hand of whist, I received a letter from our mutual friend, Toole, with a kind communication to him which stirred him up a little. He then began, as usual, to bubble over with anecdotes of our old comrades.

A bitter east wind had set in, and just before he took his departure, he remarked jocosely : " If I get a dose of this going home, it will be a settler. It was just such a pleasant, balmy, gentle, zephyr-like breeze as this that cooked poor Halliday's goose. A short time before his death, Charles Millward (who combines the manufacture of pantomimes with the manufacture of mortuary mementos) had paid Halliday a friendly visit. A delicious nor'-easter had begun to blow great guns, and I was complaining bitterly of the cold, which almost froze the marrow in my bones.

"'Ah, well!' remarked Andrew ruefully; 'I suppose I had better make my will at once, for if this infernal gale keeps going for four-and-twenty hours longer, it will be a case of "exit Andrew Halliday, and another job for Charley Millward."'

"And so it was, for poor Andrew reached the end of his journey the very next day."

I don't think that at that moment Chatterton had the faintest idea that he himself was travelling at railroad-speed in the same direction. Someone else in the company had though, for a lady who was present said, the moment he left the room, "We shall never see Mr. Chatterton alive again!" Her words were but too prophetic.

Two days later I had a letter from him to this effect :

"MY DEAR C.,

"Please thank T. for me. It will be thirty years come next September since poor Dillon opened the Lyceum, where I first met T. . . . As to the present benefit, I am so ill that I am unable to look after it myself, and I feel I dare not trespass any farther on your valuable time. All things considered, I had better postpone it till the autumn, when, perhaps, I may be more successful. . . . This weather is giving me 'fits,' and my cold, or laryngitis as the doctor calls it, is now worse than ever. Thanks

for all your good offices. If you are passing **by**
give me a look in.

" **F. B. C.**"

A week later he wrote as follows :

" Feb. 13.

" I have been awfully bad since I last wrote, and
on Wednesday I thought I was going the long, last
journey. On Thursday I received the tidings **of
my mother's death.** Her burial **takes place** to-day,
and I am forbidden to leave the house, so cannot
pay my last respects to the best of mothers.

" **Please** tell Irving and Toole I am obliged by
their generous solicitude ; **I hope** to see you on
Tuesday."

Alas ! he never saw **me** again.

Truly, " in **the** midst of life **we** are in death."
On the following Thursday, **on** the occasion of the
première **of** " The Lord Harry," at the very moment
that the present manager of Drury Lane and **I**
were patiently waiting shoulder to shoulder amongst
the crowd for our overcoats at the cloak-room of
the Princess's, his predecessor was breathing his last
breath.

When he left my house on that fatal Saturday, he
went home to die. From the very first the doctors
pronounced the case hopeless. It was found that **in**
addition to bronchitis of the most virulent character
he was suffering from an enlargement of the thyroid
gland. For this **there** was but one remedy—trache-
otomy. Even if this operation had been successfully

performed, the probability was that his life would only have been prolonged a few days—perhaps only a few hours ; it was therefore wisely, and I may add mercifully, abandoned.

All that care and kindness, however, could do to alleviate his sufferings was done.

On Wednesday, February 17th, when the end drew nigh, his brothers, Percy and Horace (to whom he was devotedly attached, and who, indeed, were devotedly attached to him), were sent for. A slight change supervened, it was hoped for the better ; but on the following morning he said, with the utmost composure :

"Good-bye ; God bless you ; I'm dying !"

From that moment the dreadful stertorous breathing ceased ; the respiration became calm and gentle, until at length he fell asleep and never woke again.

Death came to him as a merciful release.

When I saw him in his coffin, three days afterwards, the metamorphosis was astounding. He looked as young as when I first knew him. The "pale magician" had given a dignity and a distinction to his features, and with his potent wand had mercifully obliterated all traces of the sordid cares and troubles of the past.

Poor Chatterton ! Although only fifty years of age, he was prematurely old and broken.

He might truly say with the Master :

> " I have lived long enough ; my way of life
> Is fall'n into the sear, the yellow leaf."

He was the *doyen* of London managers, yet not one member of the craft followed him to his grave. He had given employment to thousands of actors actresses, musicians, and operatives, yet of all those who had eaten his bread and served under his banners when he was the Napoleon of the theatrical world, barely half a dozen came to do honour to his memory.

A few old friends and comrades, however, who had held faithfully by him through every vicissitude of fortune, followed him, with his brothers and myself, to his last resting-place at Brompton Cemetery, where, "after life's fitful fever, he sleeps" beside the mother whom living he had loved so well.

L'ENVOI.

Singularly enough, the last sheet of this book awaits me here upon my return from Old Drury, full of the glories of the first night of "The Armada," surely one of the most magnificent pageants ever witnessed, even in the theatre over which poor Chatterton presided so long.

> " My bell I ring, I pull the string,"

and down falls the curtain upon both the Victors and the Vanquished.

As it shuts them out, other well-known faces arise around me ; other well-remembered voices ring in my ears, startling the stillness of the night with the cry : " Are we then forgotten ?"

Not so, dear friends ; if I live long enough there will be time left to tell your story and mine.

Till then rest in peace.

Sept. 22, 1888.

THE END.

BILLING AND SONS, PRINTERS, GUILDFORD.